CHINESE

This book is written for those who desire to acquaint themselves with the elements of the spoken and written language of the Chinese people.

There are about 1,200 different characters in the book. These, if thoroughly learned, will enable the student to converse freely on matters of everyday importance. I urge the student to *write* the Chinese characters as the best means of memorising them, as the book is designed to enable the student to read and write Basic Chinese as well as to speak it.

The Author

TEACH YOURSELF BOOKS

CHINESE

H. R. Williamson
M.A., B.D., D.Lit.

TEACH YOURSELF BOOKS
Hodder and Stoughton

First printed 1947
Eighth impression 1980

This volume is published in the U.S.A. by
David McKay Company Inc., 750 Third Avenue,
New York, N.Y. 10017

ISBN 0 340 05773 4

Printed in Great Britain for Hodder and Stoughton Paperbacks,
a division of Hodder and Stoughton Ltd,
Mill Road, Dunton Green, Sevenoaks, Kent
(Editorial Office: 47 Bedford Square,
London, WC1 3DP)
by Fletcher & Son Ltd, Norwich

PREFACE

Much of the world's progress in mutual under-standing and co-operation depends on our being able to understand one another's speech, and on our acquaintance with each other's literature. With the idea of contributing a little towards these worthy objectives, I have prepared this short introduction to the language of the Chinese people, many of whom I have learned to respect, and whose culture I greatly admire.

I am conscious of many imperfections in the work, which has been prepared mainly in the course of long journeys.

I am greatly indebted to many friends who have co-operated with me in preparing the book for publication. Such include Mr. and Mrs. Su Cheng of the Chinese section of the B.B.C. who, with other Chinese co-workers there, have helped with the Chinese translation of the dialogues. In addition Mr. Su has written the whole of the Chinese characters at the end of the book. Professor Edwards of the School of Oriental Studies has given me many helpful suggestions, and I have found Professor Simon's book on the Study and Writing of Chinese Characters most useful. The Rev. A. J. Garnier, formerly General Secretary of the Christian Literature Society for China, has rendered generous help in the reading of the proofs. He has also prepared the valuable Dictionary and Character

Index at the end of the volume. I owe much also to my wife and daughter Evelyn for work on the manuscript itself.

Finally I should like to express my thanks to my publishers for their patience in waiting for the manuscript and for many courtesies attendant upon the preparation of the work for publication.

H. R. Williamson.

CONTENTS

vii

INTRODUCTION

THIS book is issued in the hope that it will be useful to many who desire to acquaint themselves with the elements of the spoken and written language of the Chinese people. As a student of the language for nearly forty years I am well acquainted with the difficulties which confront the student who may have to work without the aid of a Chinese teacher. But I can assure the student at the outset, that if he or she will persevere for a period of six months, concentrating for two hours daily, genuine and satisfying progress will be made.

I recommend strongly that two friends should if possible study together. The main section of the book consists of forty dialogues. These should be recited aloud. If you can form a small group for study, the dialogues might be recited by couples in turn for the benefit and criticism of the rest. If you are working alone, by all means read the dialogues aloud, and endeavour to memorise them. As they are arranged in the main as connected discourses, memorising should be quite feasible.

If there should be a Chinese who knows the National Language (kuo yü) in your neighbourhood, avail yourself of his help. Your main difficulty will lie in acquiring the correct intonation of the words, and the right rhythm of the phrases and sentences. The best progress in this connection will be achieved by reading or conversing with a Chinese.

There are about 1,200 different characters in the book. These, if thoroughly learned, will enable the student to converse freely on matters of everyday importance. I urge the student to *write* the Chinese characters as the best means of memorising them, as the book is designed

1

to enable the student to read and write Basic Chinese as well as to speak it.

Don't let the difficulty of intonation unduly discourage you. For your comfort let me say that intonation varies considerably in different parts of China, and that the Chinese themselves experience difficulty in this respect as they move about the country.

PLAN AND SCOPE OF THE BOOK

1. *Sound Tables, Spelling Chart, Romanisation, Tone marks.*

After reading this Introductory Chapter, the student should make himself thoroughly acquainted with the Table of Sounds and the Spelling Chart. From these it will be seen that there are 409 different sounds in the language, and that these are built up from sixty-two basic syllables, either independently or in combination.

No system of Romanisation has as yet been devised which reproduces the sounds of the Chinese language with perfect accuracy. But the divergencies between the sounds as actually spoken, and as reproduced by the system of Romanisation adopted in this book, are so slight that no discouragement need be felt on that account.

The system of Romanisation adopted is that of the late Sir Thomas Wade. The writer has found that system extremely helpful himself, and many of the better known writers of Chinese text-books and dictionaries, both British and American, like Hillier, Goodrich, Soothill, Giles, Wells-Williams and MacGillivray, adopted it. Dictionaries and text-books by these noted sinologues are likely to be on the market for many years to come. The Chinese Government has recently promulgated a new system of Romanisation which aims at showing the tone as well as the actual pronunciation of the word without extraneous aids. But as yet there are no dictionaries published in that particular system, and that is a serious obstacle to those who want to study Chinese now.

The tones are marked by numbers, 1, 2, 3 and 4, both in the vocabularies which accompany the dialogues, and in connection with the Chinese character index which is included at the end of the book. This also is in line with the method adopted by the aforementioned scholars.

2. The Dialogues.

There are forty dialogues on various topics designed to make the student familiar with the terminology of everyday affairs, domestic, social, travel, personal, political and the like. The selection of the themes of these dialogues has been guided by a desire to meet the need of a student making his first contacts with the Chinese people.

Chinese is a living language, and is constantly changing in form and terminology. I have sought with expert Chinese assistance to select phrases and sentences as they are spoken by Chinese of average intelligence to-day. A few phrases of modern newspaper Chinese are introduced here and there, and I have not ignored altogether the older and picturesque language of Chinese etiquette. But the aim of the writer is to make the student feel at home with the ordinary folk in China to-day. The language is rich in proverbial expressions, and so I have devoted one lesson to that particular aspect of the colloquial.

3. The Vocabularies.

Each dialogue is accompanied by a vocabulary, which includes the new characters as they appear in Romanised and Chinese form, with their meaning and intonation. Most Chinese characters have many meanings. The vocabularies do not give exhaustive definitions of the characters. But the particular meaning of the character as found in the lesson under review is given, together with the other more important meanings as found in the popular dictionaries.

4. *The Notes.*

Each dialogue also is followed by a few short notes, consisting chiefly of idiomatical and grammatical comments, designed to introduce the student gradually to the chief idioms and rules.

5. *The Chinese Text of the Dialogues.*

This section follows the dialogues in the Romanised form. Some students will perhaps choose to confine themselves to the Romanised section, and the writer knows many good speakers of Chinese who scarcely recognise a single Chinese character. But it is hoped that the student will include this section in his studies, as it will not only add to his interest in the spoken language, but will also prepare him for reading a Chinese newspaper, most of which are now printed in the colloquial style.

The two sections are separated in the book so that the student can test himself by trying to reproduce the Chinese from the English and Romanised section, and *vice versa*. That is one of the most profitable ways of learning the language. The student will note that the lessons in the Chinese section read from right to left and from top to bottom of the page. That is the way that Chinese is printed.

6. *The Grammar Section.*

The writer has endeavoured to introduce the student to the main rules of grammar gradually and piecemeal in the dialogues. But it seemed advisable to gather up the basic rules in this special section, which has been kept as compact as possible. The student can refer to this section at any time in the course of his study. The main purpose, however, in the mind of the student should e to memorise the dialogues, sentence by sentence, phrase by phrase. If that is done the rules of grammar will be unconsciously acquired. Do not be too analytic n your approach to Chinese. Remember that a sentence n Chinese is the equivalent of a sentence in English. In other words, acquaint yourself with ideas and thoughts as they are expressed, rather than with individual words.

. *The Writing of Chinese Characters.*

All the characters found in the dialogues have been reproduced as a Chinese writes them, and collated at the end of the book in the order in which they appear n the body of the book. The short introduction to his section gives the student the main rules of writing Chinese. He will be well advised to copy these characters, not only for the artistic interest which this will impart, but also for the aid it will afford to the memory. May repeat that the best way to memorise the Chinese characters is to write them.

This section also forms a dictionary of the book, and s followed by a few paragraphs to guide the student n the use of a Chinese dictionary by means of the 214 Radicals.

In conclusion let me say that anyone of average intelligence and perseverance can gain a working knowledge of Chinese. So in the words of one of the Chinese proverbs which you will find in the book: " Don't mind going slow, as long as you keep going."

GUIDE TO PRONUNCIATION

This Chart or Guide represents an attempt to reproduce in the letters of the English alphabet the sounds of Chinese words as they are pronounced in the National or Official language. Admittedly any attempt of this kind is open to criticism, as the pronunciation of certain Chinese words cannot be exactly reproduced by the letters of the English alphabet. But the following table, comprising 409 different sounds, will be found to approximate sufficiently closely to the generally accepted Chinese pronunciation.

The system of " orthography " adopted is that of the late Sir Thomas Wade, which is found in the popular dictionaries and text-books produced by British and American scholars, like Wells-Williams, Giles, MacGillivray, Hillier, Soothill, etc.

The famous dictionary of K'ang-Hsi contains over 40,000 different Chinese characters. Giles' dictionary contains 10,859. But the actual number of different sounds (if we exclude for the moment the device of " intonation ", which multiplies the sounds by anything from four to eight times this number, according to the district in which the language is spoken), is just over four hundred, accepting the limitation referred to in the first paragraph above.

The multiplication of basic sounds arrived at by " intonation " will be referred to separately.

Here then are the 409 different sounds found in Chinese

No.	Written form.	Approximate sound in English spelling.

1. **A.** Ah!
2. **Ai** *or* **Ngai.** I as in bind, *or* ngai, the -ng being the final sound of -ing.
3. **An** *or* **Ngan.** As in man.

4. Ang or Ngang. Ahng.
5. Ao or Ngao. Ow as in how, owl, etc.
6. Cha. Jah as in jar.
7. Ch'a. Chah as in Charge, Charlie.
8. Chai. Ji, the -j sound being the equivalent of the soft g in gibe.
9. Ch'ai. Chi as in China.
10. Chan. Jan as in January.
11. Ch'an. Chann as in channel.
12. Chang. Jahng.
13. Ch'ang. Chahng.
14. Chao. Jou as in joust.
15. Ch'ao. Chow, the Peking dog, or chow as in chowder.
16. Chê. Jer as in Jeremiah, the -ch being the equivalent of the soft g in germ.
17. Ch'ê. Cher as in cherish.
18. Chên. Jun as in junk.
19. Ch'ên. Chun as in chunk.
20. Chêng. Jung as in junction.
21. Ch'êng. Chung, the " ung " as in bung.
22. Chi. Jee as in jeep.
23. Ch'i. Chee as in cheese.
24. Chia. Jyah, the " y " being as short -i in bin, the whole being something like the -jia in Fujiama.
25. Ch'ia. Chyah, the medial " y " being like short -i as in chin.
26. Ch'iai or K'ai. Chi-eye, the -i being short as in chin, the -kai as in kite.
27. Chiang. Jiahng, the -i being short.
28. Ch'iang. Chiahng, the -i being short.
29. Chiao. Jiow, the -i being short and " ow " as in how.
30. Ch'iao. Chiow, the -i being short and " ow " as in how.

31. **Chieh.** Jyeh, the -yeh being equivalent of -ye in yes, preceded by a short -i, *e.g.*, jiye, the whole sound being like -gia in colle*gia*n.

32. **Ch'ieh.** Chyeh, the yeh being equivalent of ye in yes, preceded by a short -i.

33. **Chien.** Jyen, the en sounding like the en in enter, and the -y like a short -i as in bin.

34. **Ch'ien.** Chyen, the en sounding like the en in enter, and the -y like a short -i as in bin.

35. **Chih.** Jirr, like the initial sound in giraffe.

36. **Ch'ih.** Chirr, the nearest being the chir in chiropodist.

37. **Chin.** Jin, the -j being like soft -g in ginger.

38. **Ch'in.** Chin as in English or as in chink.

39. **Ching.** Jing as in jingle.

40. **Ch'ing.** Ching as heard in chink, without the final " k ".

41. **Chio.** Jeo *or* as -gio in prodi*gio*us.

42. **Ch'io.** Cheo, the -eo as in geology.

43. **Chiu.** Ju *or* Jew *or* Jioo, but the short -i sound must be pronounced between the -j and the -oo.

44. **Ch'iu.** Chu *or* chioo, the -i being short as in bin and the -oo sounding like -oo in ooze (cf. chew). For the above two sounds, parallels may be found in deuce, the -eu coming fairly close to the -iu of the Chinese, *or* tune, where the -u approximates fairly closely to the -iu in the Chinese.

45. **Chiung.** Jyung, in which the -y is like a short -i as in bin, and the -ung is sounded like -ong in mongrel. In fact it is practically the Lancashire hung as in hunger, hungry and the like.

46. **Ch'iung.** Chyung. And see the last.

No. Written form.   Approximate sound in English spelling.

47. Cho. Joh as in John, but drawled slightly like jorn, horn.

48. Ch'o. Ch'oh, the -oh as in *cho*res.

49. Chou. Joe as in Jones.

50. Ch'ou. Choe as in an*cho*vy.

51. Chu. Ju, the -u as -oo in moon. (*N.B.*—There is no suggestion of a short -i after the J as suggested for chiu above.)

52. Ch'u. Choo as in choose.

53. Chua. Jwah.

54. Ch'ua. Chwah.

55. Chuai. Jwi, the -i being long as in wine.

56. Ch'uai. Chwi, the -i being long as in wine.

57. Chuan. Jwan, the -an as in man.

58. Ch'uan. Chwan, the -an as in man.

59. Chuang. Jwahng.

60. Ch'uang. Chwahng.

61. Chui. Jway.

62. Ch'ui. Chway.

63. Chun. Jun, the -un being like the -on in motion (the Lancashire -un).

64. Ch'un. Chun, the -un being like the -on in motion (the Lancashire -un).

65. Chung. Jung, the -un being like the -on in motion (the Lancashire -un).

66. Ch'ung. Chung, the -un being like the -on in motion (the Lancashire -un).

67. Ch'uo. Chwo, the -o being short as in lock.

68. Chü. Jü, the -ü being as in French. Say -oo with pursed lips, the tip of the tongue being close to the front teeth.

69. Ch'ü. Chü, the -ü being French as in the last.

70. Chüan. Jüan, the -ü being French and -an as in man.

71. Ch'üan. Chüan, the -ü being French and -an as in man.

No.	Written form.	Approximate sound in English spelling.

72. Chüeh. Jüe, the -ü being French and -e as in yes.
73. Ch'üeh. Chüe, the -ü being French and -e as in yes.
74. Chün. Jüin, the -ü being French and -i very short.
75. Ch'ün. Chüin, the -ü being French and -i very short.
76. Ê or Ngê. Er as in hesitant speech, or as -er in herd.
77. Ên or Ngên. Un as in under.
78. Êrh. Er as in her, tip of tongue pointing to roof of the mouth and mouth slightly open.
79. Fa. Fah as in father.
80. Fan. As in fancy.
81. Fang. Fahng.
82. Fei. Fay as in faint.
83. Fên. Fun as in funny.
84. Fêng. Fung, the fun as in English.
85. Fo. For as in fortune, or the -o as -oa in hoary.
86. Fou. Foe, the -oe sounded as the -o in photo.
87. Fu. Foo as in fool.
88. Ha. Hah as the har in harness, with the -r scarcely sounded.
89. Hai. Hi as in high.
90. Han. Han as in handy.
91. Hang. Hahng.
92. Hao. As in how.
93. Hê. Hu as in huddle.
94. Hei. As in hay.
95. Hên. As in hun.
96. Hêng. As in hung.
97. Ho. Hoar as in hoary.
98. Hou. As hoe.
99. Hsi. She, although the -h is a little lighter than in the English, with the upper teeth protruding slightly.
100. Hsia. Shya, the -h being light, the -y being like -i in bin, and the -a being short as in sham.
101. Hsiang. Shyahng, the -h being light, the -y being like -i in bin, and the -a being long as in father.

No. Written form.   Approximate sound in English spelling.

102. Hsiao. Shyow, the -h being light, the -y being like -i in bin, and the -ow as in how.

103. Hsieh. Shye, the -h being light, the -y being like -i in bin, and the -ye as in yes.

104. Hsien. Shyen, the -h being light, the -y being like -i in bin, and yen like the Japanese coin.

105. Hsin. Shin, the -h being light.

106. Hsing. Shing, the -h being light.

107. Hsio. Sheo, the -h being light, almost as in sheol, with -e like short -i.

108. Hsiu. Shyou, the -h being light and you as in English.

109. Hsiung. Shyung, the -h being light, the -y being like short -in in bin, and the -un in -ung being like the -on in motion.

110. Hsü. Shü, the -ü being the French -ü.

111. Hsüan. Shüan, the -ü being the French -ü and the -an as in man.

112. Hsüeh. Shüe, the -ü being the French -ü and the -e as in yes.

113. Hsün. Shüin, the -ü being the French -ü and the -i short as in pin.

114. Hu. Hoo as in hoot.

115. Hua. Hwah.

116. Huai. Why as in English.

117. Huan. Hwan, with the -an as in can.

118. Huang. Hwahng.

119. Hui. Hway, the -way as in sway.

120. Hun. 'Hun, the -un being like the -on in motion.

121. Hung. Hung, the -un being like the -on in motion.

122. Huo. Hwo, the -wo being like the -wo in wonder, or the whole like -hoa in hoary.

123. I. Ee as in weed.

124. Jan. Ran, the J being practically the English R.

125. Jang. Rahng, the J being practically the English R.

No.	Written form.	Approximate sound in English spelling.

126. **Jao.** Row, the J being practically the English R and -ow as in how.

127. **Jê.** Ru as in rubble.

128. **Jên.** Run as in English.

129. **Jêng.** Rung as in English.

130. **Jih.** Rirr, the -irr being like the -hir in chiropodist, with the lightest possible emphasis on the -r.

131. **Jo.** Ro as in roster, robin, etc.

132. **Jou.** Roe as in English.

133. **Ju.** Rue as in English.

134. **Juan.** Ruan, the -u being neither short nor long and the -an short as in man.

135. **Jui.** Ruay, the -u being neither short nor long and the -ay as in hay.

136. **Jun.** Run, but with the -un sounding like the -on in motion.

137. **Jung.** Rung, but with the -un sounding like the -on in motion.

138. **Ka.** Gah as in garden.

139. **K'a.** Kah as in card.

140. **Kai.** Gi as the first syllable of gynecology.

141. **K'ai.** Ki as in kind.

142. **Kan.** Gan as in began.

143. **K'an.** Kan as the English can.

144. **Kang.** Gahng, the -g being hard as in garden and the -ah as the long -a in father.

145. **K'ang.** Kahng, the -ah being like long -a in father.

146. **Kao.** Gow, the -g being hard as in garden and the -ow as in cow.

147. **K'ao.** Cow as in English.

148. **Kei.** Gay as in English.

149. **Kên.** Gun as in English.

150. **K'ên.** Kun sounded as the first syllable in country.

151. **Kêng.** Gung, the gun being as in English.

152. **K'êng.** Kung, the -un as in English gun.

153. **Ko.** Go as in gore, with -o modified by -r.

No.	Written form.	Approximate sound in English spelling.

154. **K'o.** Ko as in cord, with the -o modified by the -r.

155. **Kou.** Go as in English.

156. **K'ou.** As coa in coat.

157. **Ku.** Goo, the -g being hard as in gum and the -oo as in moon.

158. **K'u.** Coo as in English.

159. **Kua.** Gwah, the -g being hard as in gun and the -ah long as in father.

160. **K'ua.** Kwah as in quarrel.

161. **Kuai.** Gwi, the -g being hard as in guy and the -i as in wine.

162. **K'uai.** Kwi, the -i being long as in wine, the whole as -qui in quite.

163. **Kuan.** Gwan, the -g being hard as in gun and -an as in man.

164. **K'uan.** Kwan, the -an as in man.

165. **Kuang.** Gwahng, the -g being hard as in gun and the -ah like long -a in father.

166. **K'uang.** Kwahng, the -ah like long -a in father.

167. **Kuei.** Gway, hard -g.

168. **K'uei.** Kway, as the -qua in equator.

169. **Kun.** Gun, -g being hard and -un as the -on in motion.

170. **K'un.** Kun, the -un as the -on in motion.

171. **Kung.** Gung, the -g being hard and the -un as -on in motion.

172. **K'ung.** Kung, the -un as the -on in motion.

173. **Kuo.** Gwo, hard -g and the -wo like the carter's whoa!

174. **K'uo.** Kwo. See 173; like the -qua in equal.

175. **La.** As la in pentatonic scale.

176. **Lai.** Lie as in English.

177. **Lan.** As in languor.

178. **Lang.** Lahng.

179. **Lao.** Low, the -ow as in cow.

180. **Lê.** Lo as in gallon.

181. Lei.   Lay as in English.
182. Lêng.   Lung as in English.
183. Li.   Lee as in leeward.
184. Lia.   Liah, the -i short as in gin, the -ah long as in yard.
185. Liang.   Liahng.   See 184.
186. Liao.   Liow, the -i short and the -ow as in cow.
187. Lieh.   Lieh, the -i short and the -eh as the -u in butt.
188. Lien.   Lien, the -i short as in bin and the -en as in hen.
189. Lin.   As in linen.
190. Ling.   As in filling.
191. Liu.   Lioo, the -i being short as in bin and the -oo as in ooze.
192. Lo.   Like the -lo in lord.
193. Lou.   Low as in below.
194. Lu.   Like the -loo in balloon.
195. Luan.   Lu-an, the -lu as the -loo in look and -an as in man.
196. Lun.   The -un as the -on in motion.
197. Lung.   The -un as the -on in motion.
198. Lü.   The French -ü.
199. Lüan.   The French -ü and -an as in man.
200. Lüeh.   The French -ü and the -eh as the -u in butt.
201. Ma.   As in English.   Ma, nearly mar.
202. Mai.   My as in English.
203. Man.   As in English.
204. Mang.   Mahng.
205. Mao.   Mow, the -ow as in how.
206. Mei.   As in English may.
207. Mên.   As Mon in Monday.
208. Mêng.   The -en as -on in Monday.
209. Mi.   As English me.
210. Miao.   Miow, the -i being short as in bin and the -ow as in cow.

No.	Written form.	Approximate sound in English spelling.

211. Mieh. Mieh, the -i being short as in bin and the -eh as -u in butt.

212. Mien. Mi-en, the -i being short as in bin and the -en as in hen.

213. Min. As in English mint.

214. Ming. As in English looming.

215. Miu. As in English mew.

216. Mo. More.

217. Mou. Mow a meadow.

218. Mu. Moo as cows do.

219. Na. As in English nasty.

220. Nai. Nigh.

221. Nan. As in English Nancy.

222. Nang. Nahng.

223. Nao. Now, meaning at present.

224. Nei. Nay.

225. Nen. Nun, as in English.

226. Neng. Nung, the -ung as in lung.

227. Ni. Knee.

228. Niang. Ni-ahng, the -i being short as in bin and the -ah long as in father.

229. Niao. Ni-ow, the -i short and the -ow as in cow.

230. Nich. Ni-eh, the -i short and the -eh as the -u in butt. An alternative would be the -ia in brilliant.

231. Nien. Ni-en, the -i short and the -en as in hen.

232. Nin. As in nincompoop.

233. Ning. Ning as in beginning.

234. Nio. Nio as in quaternion.

235. Niu. New as in English.

236. No. Noah of the Ark.

237. Nou. No as in English.

238. Nu. Noo as in noon.

239. Nuan. Nüan, the -ü as in French and the -an as in man.

No.	Written form.	Approximate sound in English spelling.

240. Nung. Nung, the -un as -on in motion.
241. Nü. Nü, the French -ü.
242. O *or* Ngo. Oar as in English, *or* Ngoar.
243. Ou *or* Ngou. Owe as in English, *or* Ngowe.
244. Pa. Bah ! as in English.
245. P'a. Pa as in English.
246. Pai. Buy.
247. P'ai. Pie as in piebald.
248. Pan. Ban as in band.
249. P'an. Pan as in English.
250. Pang. Bahng, the -ah being as the long -a in father.
251. P'ang. Pahng, the -ah being as the long -a in father.
252. Pao. Bow, the -ow as in how.
253. P'ao. Pow as in powder.
254. Pei. Bay as in English.
255. P'ei. Pay as in English.
256. Pên. Bun as in bundle.
257. P'ên. Pun as in pundit.
258. Pêng. Bung as in English.
259. P'êng. Pung, the -ung as in the last.
260. Pi. Bee.
261. P'i. Pea.
262. Piao. Bi-ow, the -i being short as in bin and -ow as in how.
263. P'iao. Pi-ow, the -i being short as in pin and -ow as in how.
264. Pieh. Bi-eh, the -ieh being like the -ia in brilliant.
265. P'ieh. Pi-eh, the -ieh being like the -ia in brilliant.
266. Pien. Bi-en, the -ien being like -ien in Oriental.
267. P'ien. Pi-en, the -ien being like -ien in Oriental.
268. Pin. Bin as in English.
269. P'in. Pin as in English.
270. Ping. Bing as in scrubbing.
271. P'ing. Ping as in shopping.
272. Po. Boa as in feather-boa.

| No. | Written form. | Approximate sound in English spelling. |

273. P'o. Por as in port but the -r only lightly sounded.
274. Pou. Bow, rhyming with show.
275. P'ou. Poe, Edgar Allan, rhyming with toe.
276. Pu. Bu as in bush, or Boo as in boot.
277. P'u. Poo as in pool.
278. Sa. Sah, sounded as in sartorial, with light -r sound.
279. Sai. Sigh as in sight.
280. San. San as in sanatorium.
281. Sang. Sahng, the -ah long as the -a in father.
282. Sao. Sow, rhyming with now.
283. Sê. Su as in sun.
284. Sên. Sun as in English.
285. Sêng. Sung as in English.
286. Sha. Shah of Persia.
287. Shai. Shy as in English.
288. Shan. Shan as in shanty.
289. Shang. Shahng, the -ah like long -a in father.
290. Shao. Shou as in shout, rhyming with snout.
291. Shê. Like shir in shirt.
292. Shên. Shun as in English.
293. Shêng. Shung, the -un as in the last.
294. Shih. Shih, almost like the chi- in chivalry, but with the -i carrying a slight -r sound after it.
295. Shou. Show as in English.
296. Shu. Shoe as in English.
297. Shua. Shwah.
298. Shuai. Shwy, the -wy as in why.
299. Shuan. Shwan, the -an as in man.
300. Shuang. Shwahng.
301. Shui. Shway.
302. Shun. Sh-un, the -un as the -on in motion.
303. Shuo. Shwo, the -wo as in won.
304. So. Soa as in soar.
305. Sou. Sow, rhyming with mow.

306. **Ssu.** The sound when men are hissing, Ssss . . . ssss . . . followed by the -u lightly sounded. If you say bus as in omnibus, carry on the final -s with the sound of the preceding -u to follow: you will get somewhere near the correct pronunciation.

307. **Su.** Soo as in soothing.

308. **Suan.** Swan as in swank.

309. **Sui.** Sway.

310. **Sun.** S followed by -un with the sound of -on in motion.

311. **Sung.** S followed by -un as -on in motion and -g.

312. **Ta.** Dah as in dart, but with -r very lightly sounded.

313. **T'a.** Ta as the child says thank you.

314. **Tai.** Dye as in English.

315. **T'ai.** Tie as in English.

316. **Tan.** Dan as in Daniel.

317. **T'an.** Tan as in English.

318. **Tang.** Dahng.

319. **T'ang.** T'ahng.

320. **Tao.** Dow, rhyming with now as in down.

321. **T'ao.** Tow, rhyming with now as in town.

322. **Tê.** Der, almost as the -der in yonder, but with -r scarcely sounded.

323. **T'ê.** Ter, almost as the -ter in daughter, but with -r scarcely sounded.

324. **Tei.** Day.

325. **T'ei.** Tay, the river of that name.

326. **Têng.** Dung as in English.

327. **T'êng.** Tung as in tungsten.

328. **Ti.** Dee, the river of that name.

329. **T'i.** Tea as in English.

330. **Tiao.** Di-ow, short -i as in bin, with -ow as in how.

331. **T'iao.** Ti-ow, short -i as in bin, with -ow as in how.

332. **Tieh.** Di-eh, the -ieh being like the -ia in brilliant.

No.	Written form.	Approximate sound in English spelling.

333. T'ieh.   Ti-eh, the -ieh being like the -ia in brill*i*ant.

334. Tien.   Di-en, short -i as in bin, with -en as in hen.

335. T'ien.   Ti-en, short -i as in bin, with -en as in hen.

336. Ting.   Ding as in pudding.

337. T'ing.   Ting as in putting.

338. To.   Doa, almost like the -dore in adore, with -r lightly stressed.

339. T'o.   Toa, almost like tore, but -r scarcely stressed.

340. Tou.   Doe as in English.

341. T'ou.   Toe as in English.

342. Tsa.   Dzah, nearly like Tsar of Russia.

343. Ts'a.   Tsah.

344. Tsai.   Dzigh, rhyming with sigh.

345. Ts'ai.   Tsigh, rhyming with sigh.

346. Tsan.   Dzan, the -an as in man.

347. Ts'an.   Tsan, the -an as in man.

348. Tsang.   Dzahng.

349. Ts'ang. Tsahng.

350. Tsao.   Dzow, the -ow as in how.

351. Ts'ao.   Tsow, the -ow as in how.

352. Tsê.   Dzu, the -u sound as in sun.

353. Ts'ê.   Tsu, the -u sound as in sun.

354. Tsei.   Dzay, rhyming with hay.

355. Tsên.   Dzun, rhyming with run.

356. Ts'ên.   Tsun, rhyming with run.

357. Tsêng.   Dzung, rhyming with bung.

358. Ts'êng. Tsung, rhyming with bung.

359. Tso.   Dzoa, rhyming with boa.

360. Ts'o.   Tsoa, rhyming with boa.

361. Tsou.   Dzoe, rhyming with doe.

362. Ts'ou.   Tsoe, rhyming with toe.

363. Tsu.   Dzoo, rhyming with zoo.

364. Ts'u.   Ts'oo, rhyming with too.

365. Tsuan.   Dzwan, the -an as in man.

366. Ts'uan. Tswan, the -an as in man.

367. Tsui.   Dzway.

368. Ts'ui. Tsway.

369. Tsun. Dzun, the -un as the -on in motion.

370. Ts'un. Tsun, the -un as the -on in motion.

371. Tsung. Dzung, the -un as the -on in motion.

372. Ts'ung. Tsung, the -un as the -on in motion.

373. Tu. Do as in English.

374. T'u. Too as in English.

375. Tuan. Dwan, the -an as in man.

376. T'uan. Twan, the -an as in man.

377. Tui. Dway.

378. T'ui. Tway.

379. Tun. Dun, but with the -un as the -on in motion.

380. T'un. Tun, but with the -un as the -on in motion.

381. Tung. Dung, but with the -un as the -on in motion.

382. T'ung. Tung, but with the -un as the -on in motion.

383. Tzu. Dzuh, with teeth closed, lips open, tip of tongue pointing downwards and close against the lower front teeth.

384. Tz'u. Tsuh, with teeth closed, lips open, tip of tongue pointing downwards and close against the lower front teeth. Take guts, say the -ts and carry on some of the preceding -u.

385. Wa. Wah, the -ah as the -a in jar.

386. Wai. Wye as the river of that name.

387. Wan. Wan, the -an as in man.

388. Wang. Wahng.

389. Wei. Way.

390. Wên. Won as in English.

391. Wêng. Wung, to rhyme with lung as in English.

392. Wo. Whoa as the carter to his horse.

393. Wu. Woo as in English.

394. Ya. Yah, almost like -yar in yard, but with scarcely any -r sound.

395. Yai. Yigh, to rhyme with sigh.

396. Yang. Yahng.

397. Yao. Yow, to rhyme with cow.

No.	Written form.	Approximate sound in English spelling.

398. Yeh.   Ye as in yes.

399. Yen.   Yen, the Japanese coin.

400. Yi.   Yih, the -i short as in bin.

401. Yin.   Yin.

402. Ying.   Ying.

403. Yo.   Yoa, to rhyme with boa.

404. Yu.   You as in English.

405. Yung.   Yung, with the -un as the -on in motion.

406. Yü.   Y, with French -ü.

407. Yüan.   Yü-an, the -ü being French and the -an as in man.

408. Yüeh.   Yü-eh, the -ü being French and the -eh like -u in butt.

409. Yün.   Yüin, the -ü being French and the -i very short, almost unsounded.

SPELLING CHART OF CHINESE WORDS

The 409 different sounds, which are found in the Guide to Pronunciation, and which, within the limits of the Roman alphabet, represent all the sounds in the Chinese language as spoken to-day, are made up of sixty-two separate syllabic sounds, if we confine ourselves to what are usually termed Initials and Finals. Chinese has often been designated a monosyllabic language. That is true in the sense that all the separate characters, or words, in the language can be pronounced as one syllable. However, on close analysis, it is found that many of these so-called monosyllables can be more accurately regarded as di-syllables or even tri-syllables, allowing for a Medial between the Initial and Final sounds. Moreover, in the language as spoken to-day, very frequently two or even three separate characters are required to denote a single concept or term.

The student will find below a chart of the sixty-two sounds which, in various combinations, form the 409 different sounds of the language. These are divided primarily into two sections, called respectively Initials and Finals. There are twenty-four Initials and thirty-eight Finals. Of the Finals, however, eleven sounds are used independently to form separate words, although they also enter into combination with other sounds. These eleven sounds are listed in a separate Section III.

I. INITIALS

No. Written form.   English equivalent.

1. Ch.   J as in jeep.
2. Ch'.   Ch as in cheap.
3. F.   F as in fan.
4. H.   H, the aspirate, as in hand.

No. Written form.   English equivalent.

5. **Hs.** Sh, a sound varying in different parts of China between a real -sh as in shell, and a pure -s as in sell, varying according to the extent to which the upper teeth are advanced beyond the lower when the sound is made.

6. **J.** R as in run, ran, etc., varying again between -r and -y.

7. **K.** G hard as in gay, gum, etc.

8. **K'.** K as in kerb, and many initial hard c's like can, card.

9. **L.** L as in lane, long, etc.

10. **M.** M as in man, maze, etc.

11. **N.** N as in nap, near, nose, etc.

12. **P.** B as in bow, band, bin, etc.

13. **P'.** P as in pin, pool, pan, etc.

14. **S.** S as in sand, sum, sin, etc.

15. **Sh.** Sh as in shun, shot, etc., but also varying between this and -s, approximating especially to the latter when preceding -a, -ai, -an.

16. **Ss.** Ss, a hissing initial sound as in snake. To produce this sound say " bus " as in omnibus, then add the sound of the " -u " which precedes. Put " the b-us " in reverse !

17. **T.** D as in done, dab, etc.

18. **T'.** T as in time, tan, tin, etc.

19. **Ts.** Dz, the terminal sound of pods -ds, or the initial of Tsar.

20. **Ts'.** Ts, the terminal sound of pots -ts.

21. **Tz.** Z, the terminal sound of goods -ds, or as the -z in zebra. It is difficult to distinguish between 19 and 21. If possible make the sound in 19 a little lighter.

22. **Tz'.** Ts as you hear the terminal in blitz -tz.

23. **W.** W as in wand, win, won, etc.

24. **Y.** Y as in you, yellow, etc.

II. Finals

[*Note.*—Di-syllables with medial vowels -i, -ŭ or -ü are eighteen in number. They are 35–40, 44–46, 50–54, 57 and 59–61.]

No. Written form.   English equivalent.

25. A.   Ah, the long " a " in father, rather, etc.
26. Ai.   I as in wine, sigh, lime, etc.
27. An.   An, shortly sounded as in man, can, tan, etc.
28. Ang.   Ahng, with the " a " always long as in father, etc.
29. Ao.   Ow as in owl, how, etc.
30. E.   Er, like the -ea in earn, learn, etc., the -r scarcely being heard.
31. Ei.   Ay as in way, pay, say, etc.
32. En.   Un as in junk, hung, under, etc.
33. Eng.   Ung as in bung, lung, sung, etc.
34. I.   Ee as in peep, jeep, deep, etc.
35. Ia (medial -i).   Ya, the -a being short as in Yankee, yam, etc.
36. Iai (medial -i).   Yai, a short -i as in bin, followed by a long -i as in high. The sound is represented by the e-i- in b-e(h)-i(nd).
37. Iang (medial -i).   Yang, short -i as in 36, followed by -ahng as in 28.
38. Iao (medial -i).   Yao, short -i as in 36, followed by -ow as in 29.
39. Ieh (medial -i).   Yeh, short -i, followed by the -u sound in butt, or like the -ie in experience.
40. Ien (medial -i).   I-en like the -ien in experience, or short -i as in 36, followed by -en as in hen.
41. Ih.   Irr as -ir in chiropodist or in giraffe.
42. In.   In as in English, bin, gin, etc.
43. Ing.   Ing as in English, telling, willing, etc.
44. Io (medial -i).   Yo like the -io sound in prodigious.
45. Iu (medial -i).   Yiu as in view or the initial -u in union.

46. **Iung** (medial -i). Yung, in which an initial short -i as in 36 is followed by -ung sounded like -ong in mongrel, or as the Lancastrian pronounces the -ung in hungry.

47. **O.** Either -oa as in oar, soar, etc., or as in whoa !, the carter's " halt " to his horse.

48. **Ou.** Oe as in toe, foe, etc.

49. **U.** Oo as in choose, noose, etc.

50. **Ua** (medial ŭ). Wa like the -ua in suave.

51. **Uai** (medial ŭ). Wi as in wine, wide, etc.

52. **Uan** (medial ŭ). Wan, with the -an short as in man, can, etc.

53. **Uang** (medial ŭ). Wang, with the -a long as -ah in 25.

54. **Ui** (medial ŭ). Way, but approximating to the French oui (the difference between 31 and 54 lies here).

55. **Un.** Un as the Lancastrian pronounces the -un in hungry.

56. **Ung.** Ung as the Lancastrian pronounces the -ung in hungry.

57. **Uo** (medial ŭ). Wo as in woman, wooden, etc.

58. **Ü.** Ü as in French, as you would say " oo " with pursed lips, with the tip of the tongue close to the front teeth.

59. **Üan** (medial ü). U-an, the French -ü, followed by -an as in man.

60. **Üeh** (medial ü). U-eh, the French -ü, followed by -u as in butt.

61. **Ün** (medial ü). U-in, the French -ü, followed by -in with -i very short.

62. **Êrh.** Er as in earnest, the -r with a burr, thus distinguishing between this and 30.

III. Finals Used Independently

Eleven of the Final sounds as found in Section II are also used as rather independent sounds. But when so used some of them, as indicated below, are preceded by either an -ng or a -w in certain districts of China. In others there is no such modification, but as the modification is very common it is well to note it.

The eleven sounds referred to are as follows:—

63. A *or* Nga, as 25.
64. Ai *or* Ngai, as 26.
65. An *or* Ngan, as 27.
66. Ang *or* Ngang, as 28.
67. Ao *or* Ngao, as 29.
68. E *or* Nge, as 30.
69. En *or* Ngen, as 32.
70. I, as 34.
71. O *or* Ngo *or* Wo, as 47.
72. Ou *or* Ngou, as 48.
73. Erh, as 62.

INTRODUCTION TO THE DIALOGUES

NOTES ON THE TONES

The tones in Chinese are inflections of the voice, and the particular inflection of the voice when pronouncing a word determines the meaning. To put the matter in another way, tones serve the purpose of distinguishing one word from another. It is therefore important that attention should be paid to them.

As indicated in Dialogue No. 30, five tones are recognised in what used to be called Mandarin, or the official language of China. This is being gradually supplanted by the National language, " kuo yü ", but in pronouncing this National language, the five tones of the old Mandarin are still current. It is true that the tendency is for the " Ju shêng " (entering or fifth tone) to die out. But it is still in common use in many parts of China, particularly in the north-west, so it is just as well that the student should be prepared for it.

The names of the tones are—

1. Shang P'ing Shêng, or Upper even.
2. Hsia P'ing Shêng, or Lower even.
3. Shang Shêng, or Rising tone.
4. Ch'ü Shêng, or Departing tone.
5. Ju Shêng or Entering tone.

As commonly heard in the vicinity of Peking, the true home of the Mandarin language with its four tones (1–4), the first is a falling tone, uttered somewhat sharply; the second is a curt upper rising tone; the third is a long rising tone broken in the middle; while the fourth is what its designation more or less suggests, namely, a short finishing falling away intonation. The " Ju shêng ", as the writer is familiar with it, is a very abrupt intonation in which the vowel sounds are shortened and hardened. It is usual to show this by romanising the characters in this tone by a final " h ". *E.g.,* in Shansi the character " ch'u " 出 to go out, is spoken as a " Ju shêng " and pronounced " ch'ŭh ". " Cho tzu " 棹子 table, normally in the first tone, is pronounced " Chŭōh tzu " in the " Ju shêng ".

It is practically impossible to convey the actual sounds of these tones in writing, but try to find a Chinese to repeat the lessons with you, and observe the inflections of his voice as he pronounces the different words.

It should be noted that the tones alter in different combinations, and also that they vary considerably in different parts of China.

I have tried to indicate the character of the tones as pronounced in Peking and vicinity, with the addition of the " Ju shêng " as I am familiar with it in Shansi province.

THE DIALOGUES

DIALOGUE No. 1

A Friend Arrives

Host, *H.*   Visitor, *V.*   Servant, *S.*   Friend, *F.*

1. *H.* Men k'ou yu jên.   **1. There is someone at the door.**

The order of words in the sentence should be observed. You have heard of " pidgin English ", which is the coolie's attempt to say " Business " English. This is English as spoken by some Chinese servants and coolies on the China coast, who cast English words into Chinese sentence order. *E.g.*, if in this sentence we adopted a literal translation and kept the Chinese order of the words, we should get " Door mouth is (have) man ". The word " yu " may mean " to have ", or it may mean " There is, are ".

2. *S.* Shui.   **2. Who (is there)?**

3. *F.* Wo.   **3. It is I (expecting his voice to be recognised).**

4. *V.* Shih shui.   **4. Who is it?**

Note the order again, lit. " Is who? "

5. *H.* Pu chih tao.   **5. I don't know.**

The first personal pronoun is often omitted before verbs. " Chih " to know; " tao " to arrive. But the composite verb means " to know ". There are many verbs formed in this way, the second part indicating that the " goal " of the verbal action has been reached. There are parallels in colloquial English, *e.g.*, " Getting there ".

6. *V.* Wo ch'ü, k'an i   6. I will go to see (who k'an.   it is).

It is necessary to use the first personal pronoun here. If it were omitted, the " ch'ü " would be an order to someone else to go. K'an i k'an. Lit. " look one look ". A very common idiom.

7. *H.* Pu yung. Wo   7. No need (for that). I chiao Lung Fu   will tell Lung Fu ch'ü.   (the servant) to go.

Pu yung, no need. Note the absence of a verb to indicate " there is ". This is regarded as unnecessary. Chinese is something like the language we use in telegrams.

VOCABULARY OF DIALOGUE No. 1

第	Ti.⁴	Number, degree, used to introduce ordinal numbers.
一	I.¹	One.
課	K'o.⁴	Task, exercise.
1. 門	Mên.²	Door, gate.
口	K'ou.³	Mouth, opening.
有	Yu.³	There is, there are, has, have.
人	Jên.²	Man.
2. 誰	Shui.²	Who, whom.
3. 我	Wo.³	I, me.
4. 是	Shih.⁴	Is, are, am, etc.
5. 不	Pu.¹	No, not.
知	Chih.¹	To know.
道	Tao.⁴	Way, truth.
知道	Chih-tao.	To know.
6. 去	Ch'ü.⁴	To go.
看	K'an.⁴	To look, to look at.
看一看	K'an i k'an.	To look, see.
7. 用	Yung.⁴	Need, use.
叫	Chiao.⁴	To call, cause, order.

8. *H*. Lung Fu.   8. Lung Fu !

9. *S*. Ai.   9. Ai !   (the   servant's response).

10. *H*. Lai pa.   10. Come here !

" Pa " is used to add emphasis to the verb, especially when giving a command. It has other uses which will be explained later. But you should not use " pa " when addressing your equals or superiors, unless you are on extremely familiar terms with them.

11. *S*. Ai !   11. Yes !

12. *H*. Mên k'ou yu jên. 12. There is someone at
    Ni ch'ü, k'an i   the door. Go and
    k'an shih shui.   see who it is.

The use of " Ni " you, in addressing servants, etc., is permissible. Care should be exercised in using it in speaking directly to others. Sometimes the word " Nin " is used to address superiors.

13. *S*. Ai.   13. Right !

14. *S*. (*to friend at door*). 14. What is your name,
    Hsien shêng kuei   sir ?
    hsing.

" Kuei " honourable, the commonest form of polite epithet in addressing others. There are equivalents of question marks in Chinese, but in sentences like this they are unnecessary. See sentence 15 for an example.

15. *F*. Wo hsing Li. Wang 15. My name is Lee. Is
    Hsien shêng tsai   Mr. Wang at home ?
    chia ma.

I have said (see 5 above) that the first personal pronoun is often omitted. It is, however, more commonly used than, say, thirty years ago. There are at least three ways of replying to the question in sentence 14 : —

Chien hsing Li. Humble name Li.

Wo chien hsing Li. I humble name Li.

Pu kan tang, wo chien hsing Li. I am unworthy, I humble name Li.

Pu kan tang. Lit. " not dare bear (such honorific address) " is a very common reply to any complimentary or polite remarks. " Ma " is one of the Chinese marks of interrogation.

8. 隆福   Lung-Fu. A name (for the servant in this case).

9. 哎   Ai.[3] Exclamation.

10. 來   Lai.[2] to come.
   吧   Pa.[4] Final particle.

14. 先   Hsien.[1] Before, formerly, first.
   生   Shêng.[1] Born, to beget, life.
   先生   Hsien-shêng. Teacher, Mr., Mrs.
   貴   Kuei.[4] Honourable, dear, costly.
   姓   Hsing.[4] Surname, clan.

15. 李   Li.[3] A surname. Plum.
   王   Wang.[2] A surname. King, prince.
   在   Tsai.[4] At, in, on, present, living.
   家   Chia.[1] Home, house, family, class.
   嗎   Ma.[1] Interrogative.

16. *S.* Tsai chia. Ch'ing 16. **Yes he is. Pleas**
  chin lai.   **come in.**

17. *F.* **Hao.**   17. **Good (thank you).**

Here we might have used " pu kan tang " (see on 15 above)
instead of " Hao " which means good. But " hao " may be use
in expressing appreciation of favours offered.

18. *S.* (*to host*). Li Hsien 18. **Mr. Lee has come.**
  shêng lai lo (la).

" Lo " is short for " liao ", which denotes the completed action o
the verb (perfect tense).

19. *H.* **Ch'ing chin lai pa.** 19. **Ask him to come in.**

20. *H.* (*to friend*). Ya, 20. **Hello Mr. Lee, how**
  (ah) Li Hsien   **are you?**
  shêng hao ya
  (ah).

" Ah " or " ya " at the end of sentences has mainly euphoni
value, *i.e.*, it helps to round off the sentence smoothly.

21. *F.* Hao. Wang Hsien 21. **Quite well. Are you**
  shêng, C h a n g **Mr. Wang and Mr**
  Hsien shêng, tou **Chang, both well?**
  hao ya (ah).

" Tou " or " tu " both, all. Note that it follows nouns, or pro
nouns, to which it refers.

22. *H. and V.* Hao, hao. 22. **Quite well. Pleas**
  C h ' i n g t s o, **take a seat.**
  Ch'ing tso.

The duplication of polite forms of speech is very common.

23. *F.* **Hsieh hsieh.**   23. **Thank you, thank**
           you.

24. *H.* (*to servant*). P'ao 24. **Prepare tea !**
  ch'a.

16. 請   Ch'ing.[3] Invite, please, call, engage.
    進   Chin.[4] Enter, advance.
    進來   Chin-lai. To enter.
17. 好   Hao.[3] Good, well, complete.

18. 了   Liao.[3] Lo.[3] La.[3] To end, finish, sign of
         past tense.

20. 呀   Ya.[1] Particle, exclamation, initial or
         final.

21. 張   Chang.[1] A surname, also classifier of
         nouns.
    都   Tou,[1] tu.[1] Both, all, together.

22. 坐   Tso.[4] To sit, a seat.

23. 謝   Hsieh.[4] To thank, thanks.

24. 泡   P'ao.[4] To brew, soak, bubble, infuse.
    茶   Ch'a.[2] Tea.
    泡茶   P'ao ch'a. To make tea (in the teapot).

25. *S.* Shuo hua, chiu lai.

25. Coming in a moment. (Lit. "as you speak I come ").

" Chiu " is a word of many uses. Here it implies sequence, with a suggestion of immediacy.

26. *H.* Ch'ing Li Hsien shêng ho ch'a.

26. Take some tea Mr. Lee.

27. *F.* Pu kan tang.

27. Thank you. (Lit. " unworthy ").

28. *H.* (*as friend rises to leave*). Tsai tso i hui'rh.

28. (Can't you) stay a little longer.

Lit. Again sit awhile, " i hui erh " awhile. But in speech the hui and erh coalesce and are pronounced huerh.

29. *F.* Tui pu chu. Yu jên têng cho wo, tê hui ch'ü.

29. Sorry ! There is someone waiting for me. I must return.

" Tui pu chu "—a common phrase signifying regret or apology.
" Cho " is the sign of the present participle, and denotes the continuing action of the verb. " Têng " wait; " têng cho " waiting.
" Tê " must, or should, in the sense of ought.
" Hui " return, " ch'ü " go, another instance of the double verb, the second of which indicates completion of the action.

30. *F.* (*as host rises to see him off*). Pu sung, pu sung.

30. Stay where you are. (Lit. " don't escort me ").

31. *H. and V.* Na'erh ti hua.

31. Never heard of such a thing ! (Lit. " where does such talk come from ? ").

32. (*All together.*) Tsai chien, tsai chien.

32. Good-bye, good-bye. (Lit. " again see ").

25. 說　　　Shuo.¹ To speak, say, narrate.
　　話　　　Hua.⁴ Words, language, speech.
　　說話　　Shuo-hua. To speak.
　　就　　　Chiu.⁴ Immediately, then, so, etc.

26. 喝　　　Ho.¹ To drink.

27. 敢　　　Kan.³ Dare, presume.
　　當　　　Tang.¹ To bear, act as, ought.
　　不敢當　Pu-kan-tang. I am unworthy, I dare not
　　　　　　　presume, etc.

28. 再　　　Tsai.⁴ Again, repeat.
　　會　　　Hui.⁴ A time, a turn, able to, etc.
　　兒　　　Êrh.¹ Enclitic, added to nouns, suffix.
　　一會兒　I-hui-rh. Awhile, a little time.

29. 對　　　Tui.⁴ To face, pair, opposite.
　　住　　　Chu.⁴ To dwell, to stop.
　　對不住　Tui-pu-chu. To offend, apologise, regrets.
　　等　　　Têng.³ To wait, a class.
　　着　　　Cho.² Particle, sign of present, participle.
　　得　　　Tê.² Must, ought, get.
　　回　　　Hui.² To return, go back.
　　回去　　Hui-ch'ü. To return.

30. 送　　　Sung.⁴ To send, escort, accompany.

31. 那　　　Na.³ ⁴ Where, how, why?　There, that.
　　的　　　Ti.¹ Sign of possessive 's.

32. 見　　　Chien.⁴ To see, perceive.
　　再見　　Tsai-chien. Good-bye.

DIALOGUE No. 2

The Chinese Teacher Arrives

Lady, *L.*   Teacher, *T.*   Servant, *S.*

1. *S.* Wang Hsien shêng lai la.

1. Mr. Wang has come.

2. *L.* Ch'ing t'a chin lai.

2. Ask him to come in

3. *L.* Wang Hsien shêng hao ya.

3. How are you, Mr. Wang?

4. *T.* Hao. T'ai t'ai ch'ih kuo fan mei yu.

4. Well, (thank you) Have you Lady partaken of food?

This illustrates the full form of common questions in the Past or Perfect tenses. "Ch'ih liao (kuo) mo yu". Lit. Eaten—not have (eaten)? The object "food" comes between the two halves of the question form.

5. *L.* Ch'ih la. Hsien shêng ch'ih la ma.

5. Yes, have you (teacher) eaten?

Now you see that the interrogative sign "ma" is but a shortened form of "mo yu" or mei yu as used in sentence 4 (above).

6. *T.* Hai mei yu ch'ih (*or*) P'ien kuo la.

6. I have not yet eaten (*or*) Yes I have (I am ashamed to say).

Chinese avoids redundancy wherever possible. If the tense is otherwise indicated there is no need to add extra words to the verb to show the tense. Here the word "huan" pronounced "hai", yet, serves in that way. So it is unnecessary to use "la" or "liao" after "ch'ih".

Inquiries about food form the usual method of greeting, particularly in the earlier parts of the day.

The alternative in sentence 6. "p'ien kuo la" is the very polite form of reply, and means "I have deprived you of your share", or "I have acted in a selfish or improper manner".

7. *L.* Ch'ing Hsien shêng tso (*or*) Hsien shêng ch'ing tso.

7. Please (teacher) take a seat.

VOCABULARY OF DIALOGUE No. 2

二   Êrh.⁴ Two. Second.

2. 他   T'a.¹ He, she, it.

4. 太   T'ai.⁴ Too, very, superlative, exalted.
   太太   T'ai-t'ai. Madame, Lady.
   喫   Ch'ih.¹ To eat, used of tobacco as well as food.
   過   Kuo.⁴ Sign of past tense, to pass over.
   飯   Fan.⁴ Rice, food.
   沒   Mei,²mu, mo.⁴ Negative, used with the verb " yu " to have.

6. 還   Huan, hai.² Still, yet, precedes negative.
   偏   P'ien.¹ Deflected, on the contrary, prejudiced.

8. *T.* Ch'ing T'ai t'ai hsien tso.

8. Please (Lady) be seated first.

9. *L.* Hsien shêng t'ai k'o ch'i.

9. You (teacher) are much too polite (Lit. " too much guest's flavour ").

10. *T.* Pu k'o ch'i. Shih li tang ti.

10. Not at all. Noblesse oblige.

" Li " courtesy: " tang " ought: " ti " the possessive sign, used to turn verbal, adjectival or other phrases into composite noun clauses. Here, *e.g.*, it makes this sense—" It is something that courtesy demands ".

11. *L.* (*to servant*). K'o i kei Hsien shêng p'ao ch'a (*or*) ch'i ch'a.

11. Make tea for the teacher.

The " k'o i " modulates the sense of command, and so is appreciated by servants. Use it frequently if you want to get good service.

12. *S.* Ya. (Ah) Yü pei hao la.

12. Right, it is ready.

13. (*L. to teacher*). Ch'ing Hsien shêng ho ch'a.

13. Take a cup of tea (teacher).

14. *T.* Hsieh, hsieh.

14. Thank you, thank you.

15. *L.* Chung kuo hua, wo pu ta tung.

15. I don't understand Chinese very well.

Note the order of words. " Chung kuo hua ", lit. Middle Kingdom words, is placed first for the sake of emphasis.
" Ta " is used to qualify the verb and has adverbial use, " greatly ".

16. *T.* T'ai t'ai, chi shih tao pi kuo lai ti.

16. When did you (Lady) arrive in our country ?

Note that " lai " without " la " or " liao " indicates past tense, because that is obvious from the context.

9. 客   K'o.⁴ Guest, traveller.
   氣   Ch'i.⁴ Breath, air, vapour, flavour.

10. 理   Li.³ Right, principle, arrange, fitting.

11. 可   K'o.³ May, might, can, be able.
    以   I.³ To take, by means of.
    可以   K'o-i. May, can, will do.
    給   Kei. Chi.³ Give, for, to, sign of dative.
    泃   Ch'i.³ Infuse, brew, alternative for
          " p'ao ".

12. 預   Yü.⁴ Beforehand.
    備   Pei.⁴ Prepare, ready.
    預備   Yü-pei. To prepare, make ready.

15. 中   Chung.¹ Middle.
    國   Kuo.² Country, kingdom.
    中國   Chung-kuo. China, the Middle Kingdom.
    大   Ta.⁴ Big, great, much
    懂   Tung.³ To understand.

16. 幾   Chi.³ Many, interrogative how much?
          how many?
    時   Shih.² Time, season.
    幾時   Chi-shih. When?
    到   Tao.⁴ Arrive, reach.
    敝   Pi.⁴ Humble, my (polite).

17. *L.* Wo shih shang yüeh ts'ai tao kuei kuo lai ti.

17. I came to your country only last month.

" Ts'ai " is a connecting word, here indicating the definite point of time, with a certain qualifying sense of " only, just then ", etc.

18. *T.* T'ai t'ai ti Chung kuo hua, shuo tê hao.

18. But you (Lady) speak Chinese well (Lit. " Lady's China country words speak get well ").

19. *L.* Kuo chiang, kuo chiang.

19. You flatter me (Lit. " over-praise ").

20. *T.* Chên ti. Shih tsai hao.

20. It is the truth. (You speak) really well.

21. *L.* Chung kuo hua yung i hsüeh pu yung i hsüeh.

21. Is Chinese easy to learn?

22. *T.* Ping pu t'ai nan.

22. Not too difficult.

" Ping "—really—for emphasis.

23. *L.* Wo yüan i pa Chung kuo hua, hsüeh hao.

23. I should like to learn Chinese well.

24. *T.* Wo chin hsin ti chiao ni, chiu shih la.

24. Then I will do my best to teach you.

Lit. " I exhaust heart teach give you ".
" Chiu shih la "—a final rounding off phrase.

17. 上 Shang.⁴ The last in point of time, above, on, go up.

月 Yüeh.⁴ Month, moon.

才 Ts'ai.² Just, thereupon, scarcely.

19. 獎 Chiang.³ Praise, commend.

過獎 Kuo-chiang. Excessive praise, flattery.

20. 眞 Chên.¹ True, real.

實 Shih.² Solid, sincere, true, real.

實在 Shih-tsai. Truly, really.

21. 容 Yung.² Jung.² Easy, contain, face, looks.

易 I.⁴ Easy.

學 Hsüeh.² Learn.

22. 並 Ping.⁴ Together, abreast, all.

難 Nan.² Difficult.

23. 願 Yüan.⁴ Wish, willing.

意 I.⁴ Idea, wish, intention, meaning.

願意 Yüan-i. Willing, wish, desire.

把 Pa.³ Take, take hold. Introduces object of verb.

24. 盡 Chin.⁴ Limit, exhaust, utmost.

心 Hsin.¹ Heart, mind.

敎 Chiao.¹ Teach, instruct.

你 Ni.³ You.

DIALOGUE No. 3

Conversation with Teacher

Teacher, *T.*   Pupil, *P.*

1. *P.* Chê ko shih shih-   1. What is this?
mo.

Note the order of words, exactly the reverse of English. " This is what? "

2. *T.* Na shih i pên shu.   2. That is a book.

" Pên " is a classifier of the noun " shu ". There are many of these, such as pên, ko, kuan. " Ko ", a piece, is the most common, and may be almost universally used. But if you want to speak Chinese well, you must learn to use the appropriate classifier with its noun. A list of the more common classifiers is given in Grammar Lesson, p. 427.

3. *P.* Shih shih-mo shu.   3. What (kind of) book is it?

4. *T.* Shih i pên tzu tien.   4. It is a dictionary.

5. *P.* Na ko tung hsi   5. What is that (thing) chiao shih mo.   called?

6. *T.* Na shih i kuan   6. That is a pencil. ch'ien pi.

7. *P.* Wo mên k'o i tso   7. What shall we do? shih-mo.

Note the use of " k'o i ". Let us, we may, may we, shall we, etc., generally speaking of permissive significance.

VOCABULARY OF DIALOGUE No. 3

三	San.¹ Three.

1. 這 — Chê.⁴ This.
   個 — Ko.⁴ Piece, classifier of nouns.
   這個 — Chê-ko. This.
   甚什 — Shen.² Shih.² What, very, any, the second form being more commonly used.
   麼麼 — Mo.¹ Interrogative particle.
   什麼 — Shih-mo. What? anything.
2. 本 — Pên.³ Classifier of books, documents, root, source.
   書 — Shu.¹ Book.

4. 字 — Tzu.⁴ Word, written word.
   典 — Tien.³ Constant, rule, record
   字典 — Tzu-tien. Dictionary.
5. 東 — Tung.¹ East.
   西 — Hsi.¹ West.
   東西 — Tung-hsi. Thing, things.
6. 管 — Kuan.³ Tube, classifier of tubular things.
   鉛 — Ch'ien.¹ Lead (metal).
   筆 — Pi.³ Pen, pencil, brush.
   鉛筆 — Ch'ien-pi. Lead-pencil.
   們 — Mên.² Sign of plural.
7. 我們 — Wo-mên. We, us.
   作做 — Tso.⁴ To do, to make, to act.

8. *T.* Wo mên k'o i nien shu.	8. Let us read.
9. *P.* Wo mên k'o i nien shih-mo shu.	9. What book shall we read?
10. *T.* Wo mên k'o i nien chê ko tu pên.	10. Let us read this Reader.
11. *P.* Ch'ing hsien shêng nien, wo t'ing.	11. Will you please read (teacher). I will listen.
12. *T.* Na ko fa tzu pu ta hao.	12. That is not a very good method.

The verb " shih ", is, are, etc., is usually omitted in direct speech where no special emphasis is needed.

13. *P.* Na mo, hsien shêng hsien nien, wo chiu kên cho nien, hsing pu hsing.	13. Then will you (teacher) read first, and I will read after you. Will that do?

Na mo, a very common phrase in conversation, indicating connective logical sequence, as in English we say, " Then ", " That being so ", " In that case ", etc.

" Nien " usually indicates reading aloud. " Tu " or " k'an " which also mean to read, are used of reading to oneself.

" Hsing pu hsing ", a very common way of finishing up a sentence seeking, or assuming the approval of the person addressed.

14. *T.* Hsing. Chê ko fa tzu hên hao.	14. Yes, that's a very good method.
15. *P.* Yao shih wo nien ts'o la, ch'ing hsien shêng kao su wo.	15. You (teacher) will please tell me if I make mistakes in reading.

Your first introduction to the Conditional Mood. " Yao shih ", if.
The " la " is short for " Liao ", which latter is not often heard in colloquial. Here it indicates the future-perfect tense, as the act of reading wrongly would have been completed before the teacher would be called upon to correct.

8. 唸　　　Nien.⁴ To read aloud.
　 唸書　　Nien-shu. To study, read aloud.

10. 讀　　　Tu.² To read.
　 讀本　　Tu-pên. A reader (book).
11. 聽　　　T'ing.¹ To listen.
　 聽一聽　T'ing-i-t'ing. To listen.

12. 法　　　Fa.²³⁴ Method, way of doing things, law.
　 子　　　Tzu.³ Son, terminal of nouns, child.

13. 那麼　　Na-mo. Then, seeing that it is so.
　 跟　　　Kên.¹ To follow, accompany, the heel, with.
　 行　　　Hsing.² To go, to do.
　 行不行　Hsing-pu-hsing. Will that do? Is it possible?

14. 很　　　Hên.³ Extreme, very.

15. 要　　　Yao.⁴ If, necessary, want.
　 錯　　　Ts'o.⁴ Mistake, error, wrong.
　 告　　　Kao.⁴ Inform, accuse.
　 訴　　　Su.⁴ Inform, explain.
　 告訴　　Kao-su. Tell, inform.

16. *T.* Li tang, li tang.   16. (Certainly), that is my bounden duty.

This is a shortened form in duplicate of sent. 10, dial. 2.

17. *P.* Hsien tsai nien wan la shu, wo mên hai k'o i tso shih-mo.   17. Now that we have finished reading, what else shall we do?

The character " huan " in colloquial is almost always read " hai " indicating something that is not yet done. As we should say in English, " What else shall we do? "

18. *T.* Wo mên k'o i hsieh tzu.   18. We might write.

19. *P.* Hao. Wo hsi huan hsieh tzu.   19. Good. I like writing.

20. *T.* Hui hsieh tzu pu hui.   20. Can you write?

" Hui " is " to know *how* to do a thing ".

21. *P.* Pu hui, k'o shih wo yüan i hsüeh.   21. No, but I am willing to learn.

22. *T.* Na mo, wo chiu chin hsin ti chiao ni.   22. Then I will do my best to teach you.

23. *P.* Hsieh tzu, yung shih mo tung hsi.   23. What do we need for writing?

24. *T.* Wo men yung i kuan pi, i chang chih, i k'uai mo, ho i fang yen t'ai. Tsai chia shang i tie'rh shui, yen mo.   24. We need a pen (brush), a sheet of paper, a piece of ink (Chinese) and an ink slab. Then we must also have (lit. add) a little water to mix the ink. (Lit. rub the ink.)

7. 現   Hsien.⁴ Now, at present.
   現在   Hsien-tsai.   At present, now.   At this
                point.
   完   Wan.² To finish, complete, end.

8. 寫   Hsieh.³ To write.

9. 喜   Hsi.³ Joy, pleased, glad.
   歡   Huan.¹ Rejoice, take pleasure.
   喜歡   Hsi-huan. To rejoice, be pleased, happy.

1. 可   K'o.³ But.

4. 紙   Chih.³ Paper.
   塊   K'uai.⁴ Piece.
   墨   Mo. Mei.⁴ Ink.
   和   Ho.² ⁴ With, together, harmony.
   方   Fang.¹   Square, classifier of pieces of
                Chinese ink.
   硯   Yen.⁴ Ink-slab.
   台   T'ai.² Slab.
   硯台   Yen-t'ai. Slab for mixing Chinese ink.
   加   Chia.¹ To add.

25. *P.* Wo pa chê hsieh tung hsi na lai. Wo mên chiu hsieh tzu.

25. I will get these thing and we will (begi to) write.

26. *T.* Hao. Wo mên hsieh tzu pa.

26. Good, we will (begi to) write.

24. 點　　　Tien.³　A little, point, dot.
　一點兒　I tie'rh.　A little.
　水　　　Shui.³　Water.
　研　　　Yen.²　To grind, as ink on the slab.　To
　　　　　　inquire.
25. 把　　　Pa.³　To take, handle, grasp.
　些　　　Hsieh.³　A few, some, sign of plural, with
　　　　　　adjectives.
　拿　　　Na.²　To take.
　拿來　　Na-lai.　To bring.

DIALOGUE No. 4

Between two friends A and B who are learning Chinese together. This dialogue provides some basic rules of grammar in the form of useful sentences. Learn this lesson thoroughly, and you will be well repaid.

1. *A.* Chê ko tung-hsi chiao shih-mo.

1. What is this called?

Note again the order of the words. " This thing called what? "

2. *B.* Na shih i ko ch'a pei (wan).

2. That is a teacup.

It is not necessary to use " ko " after " na " if " ko " comes later in the sentence in reference to the same thing.

3. *A.* Ch'a pei ho ch'a wan yu shih-mo fên pieh.

3. What is the difference between a ch'a pei and a ch'a wan?

Notice carefully the framework of this sentence, " Cup with bowl have what difference? "

4. *B.* Ch'a pei yu pa'rh, ch'a wan mu yu pa'rh.

4. A ch'a pei has a handle while a ch'a wan has not.

5. *A.* Na shih shih-mo tung hsi.

5. What is that?

6. *B.* Na shih i ko (pa) ch'a hu.

6. That is a teapot.

" Pa " is the correct classifier of teapots, but " ko " is also used.

7. *A.* Ch'a hu ho shui hu, i yang pu i yang.

7. Is a ch'a hu the same as a shui hu?

Lit. " Teapot with (compared with) kettle one kind not one kind? "

8. *B.* Pu i yang. Ch'a hu shih p'ao ch'a yung ti, shui hu shih shao shui yung ti.

8. No. A teapot is used for making tea and a kettle for boiling water.

Note " ti " after " yung " making an adjectival phrase. " A teapot is making tea's use ". So " used for ".

VOCABULARY OF DIALOGUE No. 4

四   Ssu.⁴ Four.

2. 盃 Pei.¹ Cup, with or without handle, glass.
  碗 Wan.³ Cup, bowl, usually without handle.

3. 分 Fên.¹ ⁴ (1) Verbal form, to divide. (4)
      Part, tenth.
  別 Pieh.² To distinguish, also " do not ".
  分別 Fên-pieh. Difference.

4. 把 Pa.⁴ Handle, classifier of teapots, etc., also
      introduces object of verbs.

6. 壺 Hu.² Kettle, pot.
  茶壺 Ch'a-hu. Teapot.

7. 水壺 Shui-hu. Kettle.
  樣 Yang.⁴ Pattern, way, manner.
  一樣 I-yang. The same, similar.

8. 燒 Shao.¹ To burn, bake (to boil).

9. *A*. Chê hsieh yen   9. Whose are these cigar
     chüan'rh shih   ettes?
     shui ti.

Chê-hsieh, these. Na-hsieh, those. "Hsieh" is the sign of the plural with distinguishing or demonstrative adjectives.
Note order of words. "These cigarettes are whose?"

10. *B*. Na hsieh yen chüan'   10. Those cigarettes are
     rh shih wo ti.   mine!

11. *A*. Yu yang huo (huo   11. Have you any matches?
     ch'ai) mei yu.

Yu mo (mei) yu. Have you? (anything).

12. *B*. Yu, ni yao pu yao.   12. Yes, do you want some?

Yao pu yao. Do you want (anything). Note the use of "mo" and "pu" as negatives in questions of a direct character. Always use "mo" with "yu". "Pu" is used only in the present and future tenses. In the past tense you say "T'a yao la mu yu" Did he want?

13. *A*. Pu yao. Wo pu   13. No, I don't smoke.
     ch'ih (ch'ou) yen.

14. *B*. Chê liang kuan pi   14. Are these two pen
     shih ni ti ma.   yours?

"Liang" in sense of "two" is used when qualifying a noun. In complex multiple numbers and in ordinals you use "êrh".

15. *A*. Chê i kuan kang pi   15. This steel pen is mine
     shih wo ti.

16. *B*. Na i kuan ni.   16. And what about that
     one?

17. *A*. Na i kuan mao pi,   17. That Chinese brush i
     shih pu shih ni ti   yours, isn't it?
     ya.

Note the difference in tone of the two "na". In questions it is third, and in statements fourth, tone.

9. 這些　　Chê-hsieh.　These.

煙　　　Yen.[1]　Tobacco, snuff, smoke, opium.

捲　　　Chüan.[3]　A roll, to roll up.

煙捲兒　Yen-chüan-rh.　Cigarettes ("rh" being short for "êrh").

誰的　　Shui-ti.　Whose?

10. 那些　　Na-hsieh.　Those.

我的　　Wo-ti.　My, mine.

11. 洋　　　Yang.[2]　Foreign, the sea, over the sea, vast.

火　　　Huo.[3]　Fire.

柴　　　Ch'ai.[2]　Firewood, fuel.

火柴　　Huo-ch'ai.　Matches.

13. 喫煙　　Ch'ih-yen.　To smoke (lit. to eat smoke).

抽　　　Ch'ou.[1]　To draw, pull out.

抽煙　　Ch'ou-yen.　To smoke, as tobacco.

14. 兩　　　Liang.[3]　Two, preceding nouns.

15. 鋼　　　Kang.[1]　Steel.

鋼筆　　Kang-pi.　Steel pen.

16. 那一管　Na-i-kuan.　That one?

呢　　　Ni.[1]　Mark of interrogation, and final enclitic.

17. 毛　　　Mao.[2]　Hair.

毛筆　　Mao-pi.　The hair-brush, Chinese pen.

你的　　Ni-ti.　Your, yours.

18. *B.* Pu shih wo ti. Shih   18. No, it is not mine. It
    wo p'êng yu ti.   belongs to my friend.

There is no need to use " ti " the possessive after " wo " in the second half of this sentence. It would be too clumsy to say " Shih wo ti p'êng yu ti ". Where the sense is clear, Chinese prefer to avoid repetition of these small words.

19. *A.* Na i p'ing mo shui,   19. Is that bottle of ink his
    yeh shih t'a ti ma.   too ?

20. *B.* Pu shih t'a ti, shih   20. No, it belongs to the
    hsien shêng ti.   teacher.

21. *A.* Chê hsieh yen   21. Are these good cigar-
    chüan'rh hao pu   ettes ?
    hao.

22. *B.* Pu ta hao.   22. Not very good.

23. *A.* Ni tsai na'rh mai ti.   23. Where did you buy
                                     them ?

Notice carefully the two words spelled the same " mai ", but meaning respectively " buy " and " sell ". In the Chinese character (see Chinese exercises at end of book) these two words are written differently. But the tones for " buy " and " sell " are different. For " buy " use the third tone, and for " sell " the fourth.

24. *B.* Tsai shih ch'ang   24. In the market.
    shang mai ti.

25. *A.* Tsai chê li yu mai   25. Are there any on sale
    ti mei yu.   here ?

26. *B.* Tsai chê li mei yu   26. No, there are none on
    mai ti.   sale here.

27. *A.* Tsai na li yu mai   27. Where are there any on
    ti ni.   sale ?

28. *B.* Shang ta chieh   28. If you go on to the
    shang ch'ü, huo   main street, you may
    che k'o i mai.   be able to buy some.

18. 朋   P'êng.² Companion, friend, mate.
    友   Yu.³ Intimate acquaintance, friend.
    朋友   P'êng-yu. Friend, mate.

19. 瓶   P'ing.² Bottle.
    也   Yeh.³ Also.

23. 那兒   Na ³ 'rh. Where?
    買   Mai.³ To buy.
24. 市   Shih.⁴ The market.
    場   Ch'ang.² An open place, square.
    市 場   Shih-ch'ang. The public market.

25. 裡。裏 Li.³ In, inside, within.
    這裡   Chê-li. Here.
    賣   Mai.⁴ To sell. (Notice the tone is 4; cf.
          with mai 3, to buy.)
    買賣   Mai-mai. Business, trade.
27. 那裡   Na-li. Alternative for " na'rh ", where?,
          tone 3.
28. 街   Chieh.¹ Street.
    或   Huo.⁴ Perhaps, if, someone.
    者   Che.³ Particle, to form adverbs, abstract
          nouns, etc.

29. *A*. Tsa men lia, k'o i   29. Let us two go on the
     shang chieh ch'ü,   street to buy a few.
     mai chi ko pa.

Tsa-men is a friendly familiar form for "wo-men", "we". Tsa-men-lia is a shortened form for "Tsa-men-liang-Ko".

30. *B*. Hao. Tsa mên i   30. Right, let us go to-
     k'uai'êrh ch'ü.   gether.

I-k'uai-êrh. Lit. one piece, so together.

29. 咱   Tsa.² We (familiar).
    倆   Lia.³ Two.
    咱們倆 Tsa-mên-lia. We two.
30. 一塊兒 I-k'uai-êrh. Together (all one piece).

DIALOGUE No. 5

Between two friends A and B, comprising a series of short sentences, to be fired at one another in quick rotation, and illustrating grammatical rules of a basic character.

1. *A*. T'a lai la mei yu.
1. Has he come?

2. *B*. T'a mei yu lai.
2. No he has not.

3. *A*. Ni lai pu lai.
3. Are you coming?

4. *B*. Wo lai.
4. Yes, I am coming (in reference to the place where they are standing).

5. *A*. Tso t'ien t'a mên lai la ma.
5. Did they come yesterday?

6. *B*. T'a men lai la.
6. Yes, they did.

7. *A*. Ming t'ien ni mên lai pu lai.
7. Are you coming to-morrow?

8. *B*. Ming t'ien wo mên pu lai.
8. No, we are not coming to-morrow.

9. *A*. Chin t'ien ni ch'ü pu ch'ü.
9. Are you going to-day?

10. *B*. Wo ch'ü.
10. Yes, I am going.

11. *A*. Ming t'ien ni hui lai pu hui lai.
11. Are you coming back to-morrow?

12. *B*. Ming t'ien pu hui lai.
12. No, I shall not come back to-morrow.

13. *A*. Ming t'ien t'a (f) hui ch'ü pu hui ch'ü.
13. Will she go back to-morrow?

Note that expressions of time usually precede everything else in simple direct questions and answers.

14. *B*. Shih ti, ming t'ien t'a hui ch'ü.
14. Yes, she will go back to-morrow.

VOCABULARY OF DIALOGUE No. 5

五　　　Wu.³　Five.

5. 昨　　Tso.³　Yesterday.
　 天　　T'ien.¹　Day, Heaven
　 昨天　Tso-t'ien.　Yesterday.
7. 明　　Ming.²　The dawn, also bright, clear, open.
　 明天　Ming-t'ien.　To-morrow.

9. 今　　Chin.¹　Now, the present.
　 今天　Chin-t'ien.　To-day.

11. 回來　Hui-lai.　To return (here).

13. 她　　T'a.¹　She.　Note feminine form of character.

12. 是的　Shih-ti.　Yes, affirmation.　Often expressed by " shih " alone.

15. *A.* Ni shang na li ch'ü. **15.** Where are you going?

Note that the verb ch'ü comes last in these sentences. That is because it is part of the composite verb shang-ch'ü. Sometimes this verb is put first, *e.g.*, 18. '' Ni ch'ü kan shem-mo ''.

16. *B.* Wo shang chieh ch'ü. **16.** I am going on the street.

17. *A.* Wo yeh ch'ü. **17.** I am going too.

18. *B.* Ni ch'ü kan shih mo. **18.** What are you going for?

19. *A.* Wo ch'ü mai tung hsi. **19.** I am going to buy some things.

20. *B.* Mai shih mo tung hsi. **20.** What are you going to buy?

21. *A.* Mai i ting mao tzu, ho i shuang hsieh. **21.** A hat and a pair of shoes.

Note '' ting '', the classifier of '' mao-tzu ''.

22. *B.* Tao kuo Pei-ching mei yu. **22.** Have you ever been to Peking?

Pei-ching (Northern Capital), styled Pei-p'ing (Northern Peace) since the old Pei-ching was captured by Chiang K'ai Shek in 1926, when Nanking (Southern Capital) became the new capital of all China.

23. *A.* Mei yu tao kuo. **23.** No, I have never been.

24. *B.* Ch'i lai, wo mên tsou pa. **24.** Get up, let us go.

Tsou is simply to go, without any goal being indicated. If you use '' ch'ü '', some idea of a goal is implied.

25. *A.* Têng i têng, tê na chi ko ch'ien. **25.** Wait a bit, I must get some money.

26. *B.* Na pu yao chin, wo tai tê yu ch'ien. **26.** That doesn't matter, I have some money on me.

The '' tê '' in '' tai tê '', followed by '' yu '', which some would consider redundant, is really equivalent to '' la '', the past tense.

18. 幹   Kan.⁴ To do, manage, ability.

21. 頂   Ting.³ The classifier of hats, caps, etc.,
              top, button.
    帽   Mao.⁴ Hat, cap.
    雙   Shuang.¹ A couple, both, pair.
    鞋   Hsieh.² Shoe.
    一雙鞋   I-shuang-hsieh. A pair of shoes.
22. 北   Pei.³ North.
    京   Ching.¹ Capital city.
    北京   Pei-ching. Old name for Peking, now
              called Peiping.

24. 起   Ch'i.³ To get up, rise, mount.
    起來   Ch'i-lai. To get up, rise.
    走   Tsou.³ To walk, to go (without reference
              to a specific goal).
25. 等一等   Têng-i-têng. To wait a bit.
    錢   Ch'ien.² Money.
26. 緊   Chin.³ Tight, pressing.
    要緊   Yao chin. Important (lit. want urgent).
    帶   Tai.⁴ To carry on the person.

27. *A*. K'o shih chieh jên   27. But borrowing other
    ti ch'ien pu ta   people's money is not
    hao.   a very good (habit).

" Chieh " means both to borrow and to lend, and there is no difference in tone to help in differentiating the two meanings. You have to look to the context to discover the difference. As a help, sometimes " chieh-lai " is used for " to borrow ", and " chieh-ch-ü " for " to lend ". " Chieh-kei " is also used in the latter sense.

28. *B*. Na yao k'an ch'ing   28. That depends on cir-
    hsing tsên yang.   cumstances.

" Yao ", must, need to.

" K'an " is used in the sense of " depends on ", as well as of " look at ".

29. *A*. Yu ti shih hou hao,   29. Sometimes it is all right,
    yu ti shih hou pu   sometimes not, isn't
    hao, shih pu shih.   it ?

" Yu ti shih hou ", sometimes. Lit. " There are times ".

30. *B*. Tui la.   30. Right.

Note how " tui " means " right " as well as agreeing, etc.

27. 借   Chieh.⁴ To borrow anything, also means
                to lend !

28. 看   K'an.⁴ To look at, regard, depends (in the
                sense as translated).
   情   Ch'ing.² Facts, affairs, feelings, nature.
   形   Hsing.³ Form, appearance.
   情 形 Ch'ing-hsing. Circumstances.
   怎   Tsên.³ How? In what way?
   怎 樣 Tsên-yang. How? In what way, manner,
                etc.
29. 時   Shih.² Time, season.
   候   Hou.⁴ A time or period, to wait, expect.
   時 候 Shih-hou. Time, season, time of day.

30. 對   Tui.⁴ Right, to agree with.

DIALOGUE No. 6

Mistress and Servants discuss domestic matters.

Mistress, *M.*   Servant(s), *S.*

1. *S.* T'ai t'ai chiao wo pa.

1. Did you (Lady) call me?

2. *M.* Shih ti. Chiao ch'u tzu ho k'an mên ti (mên fang) lai, wo yao ho ni mên shuo chi chü hua.

2. Yes, call the cook and gate-man. I want to say something to you (lit. say a few sentences to you).

3. *S.* T'a mên chiu lai. Ai, lai la.

3. They will be along shortly. Ah, here they come!

4. *M.* Tso hsia pa.

4. Sit down!

5. *S.* (In a body.) Pu yung tso. Wo mên chan cho ti hao.

5. No need for us to sit. It is more fitting that we stand.

Servants naturally expect to stand in the presence of their mistress.

6. *M.* Chin t'ien wo hên mang, yao ta chia pang mang.

6. I am very busy to-day and want you all to help.

" Ta-chia ", a frequently used expression for " All of you ".

7. *S.* T'ai t'ai chiao wo mên tso shih-mo. Wo mên chao pan chiu shih la.

7. What do you want us to do? We will do as you say (lit. according do just so).

" Chao-pan ". According—act. Do as you say.

8. *M.* Hsien pa ch'ih fan ti chia chü na lai, wo yao k'an i k'an.

8. First bring the cutlery and crockery (lit. the eating utensils) and let me see them.

VOCABULARY OF DIALOGUE No. 6

六   Liu.⁴ Six.

2. 厨   Ch'u.² Kitchen, cook.
   房   Fang.² Room, house, with preceding
                     means, kitchen, or cook.
   句   Chü.⁴ Sentence, phrase.

4. 下   Hsia.⁴ Down, beneath, below.
5. 站   Chan.⁴ To stand, station, post, etc.

6. 忙   Mang.² Busy.
   家   Chia.¹ Home, family.
   大家 Ta-chia. All, everybody.
   帮   Pang.¹ Help, assist.

8. 傢   Chia.¹ Utensils.
   具   Chü.⁴ Utensils.

9. *S.* T'ai t'ai shih chiao wo mên pa tao tzu, ch'a tzu, t'iao shih ho shao tzu, tou yao na lai ma.

9. Do you want us to bring the knives, forks, spoons and ladles, the whole lot?

Notice the position of " tou ", meaning all. It follows the enumeration of the things which form the compound subject, gathering them all up as it were.

10. *M.* Shih ti, yeh yao na ch'a pei, wan, tieh tzu ho p'an tzu.

10. Yes, I also want you to bring the tea-cups, bowls, saucers and plates.

The " ho ", meaning " and ", usually precedes the last of a number of items enumerated together.

11. *S.* Chê hsieh tung hsi na lai la, chiao wo mên fang tsai na li ni.

11. When we have brought them, where do you want us to put them?

12. *M.* Pa t'a mên tou fang tsai cho tzu shang.

12. Put them all on the table.

" T'a-men ", here applied to inanimate things.

13. *S.* T'ai t'ai chin t'ien wan shang, pu shih ch'ing k'o ma.

13. Aren't you inviting some guests to-night?

14. *M.* Pu shih wan shang ch'ing k'o, shih chin t'ien hsia wu ch'ing chi ko jên lai ho ch'a.

14. No, not this evening. I am asking a few folk to tea this afternoon.

15. *S.* Na mo, t'ai t'ai tê chiao ch'u fang to k'ao mien pao ho tien hsin.

15. Then you should tell the kitchen (cook) to bake a lot of bread and cakes.

Note the position of " to ", meaning more. It precedes the verb.

刀 Tao.¹ Knife, blade.
叉 Ch'a.¹ Fork.
調 T'iao.² To stir, mix.
匙 Shih.² Ch'ih.² Spoon, key.
勺 Shao ² (tzu). Scoop, ladle.

碟 Tieh ² (tzu). Plate, saucer.
盤 P'an ² (tzu). Plate, dish.

放 Fang.⁴ Put, place.

桌 Cho ¹ (tzu). Table.

晚 Wan.³ Evening, late.

午 Wu.³ Noon.
下午 Hsia-wu. Afternoon.

多 To.¹ Much, many, how (in figures).
烤 K'ao.² To bake, roast.
麵 Mien.⁴ Flour, bread.
包 Pao.¹ Parcel, wrap, with the preceding, a loaf, bread.

16. *M.* Huang yu ho kuo tzu chiang, to pu to.

16. Is there a fair quantit of butter and jam (i the house)?

17. *S.* Chê hsieh, tou kou shih lai ko k'o jen ch'ih.

17. There is enough of thes for about ten guest

" Lai ", come, is used in multiples of ten, to indicate roughly th number.

18. *M.* Chia chü, yeh kou shih lai ko jén yung ma.

18. Are the table utensi (crockery, cutlery etc.), sufficient f about ten people?

19. *S.* Pu ta kou. Yao shih tao tzu, ch'a tzu pu kou ti shih hou, k'o i yü pei k'uai tzu, chiao t'a mên shih.

19. Not quite enougl (But) if the kniv and forks are insuf cient, we might ha chopsticks ready f them to use.

20. *M.* Chih p'a yu ti jên pu hui shih k'uai tzu.

20. My fear is that son of them will not able to use cho sticks.

" Chih p'a ". Only fear, A mental reservation.

21. *S.* Na tao mei yu fa tzu la.

21. Then there is nothi we can do.

15. 點　　Tien.³　A dot, mark out, with the next,
　　　　　cakes, pastry.

　　心　　Hsin.¹　Heart, with the preceding, cakes,
　　　　　pastry.

16. 黄　　Huang.²　Yellow, with the next, butter.

　　油　　Yu.²　Oil, with preceding, butter.

　　果　　Kuo³ (tzu).　Fruit, consequences, etc.,
　　　　　with the next, jam, preserve.

　　醬　　Chiang.⁴　Thick, paste, etc., with preceding, jam, preserve.

17. 够　　Kou.⁴　Enough, sufficient.

　　十　　Shih.²　Ten.

　　十來個　Shih-lai-ko.　About ten.

9. 筷　　K'uai⁴ (tzu).　Chopsticks.

　　使　　Shih.³　To employ, use.

0. 只　　Chih.³　Only.

　　怕　　P'a.⁴　To fear.

1. 倒　　Tao.⁴　On the contrary, used for emphasis
　　　　　as, then in that case.

DIALOGUE No. 7

Between a Chinese villager, *V.*, and a foreigner, *F.*, meeting for the first time.

The student will note that in Chinese, as in many other languages, there are different ways of addressing a person according to his education or social status. In this dialogue alternatives are offered for a number of sentences. These are marked respectively C. for common, and P. for polite. You can never go wrong in using the polite form of speech, even to the most rusticated. But if you find that they are embarrassed you can readily adopt the more common and familiar form.

1. *F.* Hsien shêng hao ma.

1. Good morning sir, are you well?

2. *V.* Hsieh hsieh, hsien shêng ni hao. (C.)
Ch'êng wen. Ch'êng wen. (P.)

2. Thank you, I hope you are well?
(Thank you) I have received your inquiry.

3. *F.* Hsien shêng (nin) ch'ih la fan mei yu.

3. Have you eaten?

4. *V.* Ch'ih la. Hsien shêng (nin) ch'ih la ma. *or*
Hai mei yu ch'ih. Hsien shêng (nin) ch'ih la ma.

4. Yes, have you had your meal?

No, not yet; have you had your meal?

5. *F.* P'ien kuo la. (P.)

5. Yes, I am ashamed to say.

6. *V.* Kuei hsing. (P.)
Hsing shih mo. (C.)

6. What is your name?

VOCABULARY OF DIALOGUE No. 7

七   Ch'i.[1]   Seven.

2. 承   Ch'êng.[2]   To receive.

    問   Wên.[4]   To inquire, ask, a question.

    承問   Ch'êng-wên.   Used together politely, in reply to any personal inquiry.

3. 您   Nin.[2]   Polite form of Ni—You, Sir.

7. *F.* Chien (pi) hsing Wang. (P.)
Wo hsing Wang. (C.)

7. My humble name is Wang.
My name is Wang.

8. *V.* T'ai fu. (P.)

8. What is your honourable appellation?

9. *F.* Ts'ao tzu Ch'ing Chang. (P.)

9. My unworthy (lit. grass) name is Ch'ing Chang.

10. *V.* Ming tzu chiao shih mo. *or*
Shih mo ming tzu. (C.)

10. What is your name?, *i.e.*, given or Christian name.

11. *F.* Ming chiao Ch'ing Chang. *or*
Ch'ing Chang. (C.)

11. My name is Ch'ing Chang.
Ch'ing Chang.

The Chinese usually have at least two names, in addition to the surname, one for everyday use and the other for special occasions.

12. *V.* Hsien shêng to ta nien chi. *or*
Hsien shêng to ta sui shu. (C.)

12. How old are you sir?

Note the expression " to ", introducing questions about quantities, size, age, distance, etc., equivalent to our " how ". " Ma " is sometimes added, *e.g.*, " to ma yüan ", how far?

13. *F.* Wu shih' wu. *or*
Wu shih wu sui.

13. Fifty-five.
Fifty-five years (old).

7. 賤   Chien.⁴ Humble, mean, low, cheap.

8. 甫   Fu.³ Designation, title or rank, etc., surname.

9. 草   Ts'ao.³ Grass, so humble, used as a term
of self-depreciation.

字   Tzu.⁴ The ordinary character for a name,
used here in contrast with the very
honourable appellation used by the
inquirer.

清   Ch'ing.¹ Clear, used as a name.

長   Chang.² Old, used as a name.

10. 名   Ming.² Name, not surname, fame.

12. 多   To.¹ Much, many, how many. With
"mo" means How much, how many?

大   Ta.⁴ Big, great.

多大   To-ta. How big, great, etc.

年   Nien.² Year, years.

紀   Chi.⁴ To record.

年紀   Nien-chi. One's age.

歲   Sui.⁴ The year, years.

數   Shu.⁴ Number, to count, etc.

歲數   Sui-shu. One's age.

14. *V.* Hsien shêng kuei 14. What is your esteemed
     kêng. *or*   age?
     Hsien shêng kuei
     chia tzu. (P.)

A question like "kuei chia tzu" might elicit a cryptic reply, as the person asked might indicate the animal which presides over the year of birth. There is a clear question relating to this, *viz.*, "Hsien shêng shu shêmmo ti": "What (animal) do you belong to?" The "chia tzu" refers to the ten stems, which, with the twelve branches combined in pairs, give the Chinese sexagenary cycle (sixty years). Cf. Tennyson's lines in Locksley Hall: "Better fifty years of Europe than a cycle of Cathay." I wonder whether Tennyson knew there was only ten years' difference between the two! The older Chinese were very fond of guessing ages by means of the "animal" system. There are twelve animals, corresponding to the twelve "branches" or horary characters referred to above. The animals, in order of sequence, are: rat, ox, tiger, hare, dragon, serpent, horse, sheep, monkey, cock, dog, boar. These again correspond with certain constellations, and ultimately the calculation of age is based on the particular constellation which was paramount at the time of birth.

15. *F.* Hsien shêng kao 15. What is your exalted
     shou. (P.)   age sir?
16. *V.* Hsiung ti hai hsiao, 16. I (younger brother) am
     hsü tu la wu shih   still young. I have
     wu sui. (P.)   lived vainly for fifty-
                                 five years.

17. *V.* Hsien shêng kuei 17. Which is your honour-
     kuo. *or*   able country?
     Kuei kuo shih na i
     kuo. *or*
     Kuei kuo shih na   Where is your honour-
     li. (P.)   able country?
18. *F.* Pu kan tang. Pi 18. My humble country is
     kuo Ying Kuo.   England.
     (P.)

Ying-kuo is England. Ta Ying-kuo is Great Britain.

14. 庚   Kêng.[1] Age, used only in polite language.
    甲子   Chia-tzu. The first term of the Sexagenary
            cycle, which the Chinese use for the
            reckoning of time. Here it is a
            honorific.

15. 高   Kao.[1] High.
    壽   Shou.[4] Age, old age, long life.
16. 兄   Hsiung.[1] Elder brother.
    弟   Ti.[4] Younger brother.
    兄弟   Hsiung-ti. Younger brother. Used in self-
            depreciation.
    小   Hsiao.[3] Small, young.
    虛   Hsü.[1] In vain, empty, useless.
    度   Tu.[4] To ford, pass over, pass.
17. 英   Ying.[1] Brave, illustrious. Used for Eng-
            land.

19. *V.* Hsien shêng shih na li lai ti. (C.)

19. Where do you hail from ? *or*

    Where have you come from ?

20. *F.* Wo shih Nan Ching lai ti.

20. I (have) come from Nanking.

21. *V.* Hsien shêng kuei ch'u. *or*

    Fu shang tsai na li. (P.)

21. Where do you reside ?

22. *F.* Pu kan tang. Pi ch'u Peip'ing. (P.)

22. Unworthy, my humble abode is at Peip'ing.

23. *V.* Peip'ing li chê li to yuan. (C.)

23. How far is Peip'ing from here ?

    Lit. Peip'ing distant here how far ?

24. *F.* San pai to li lu.

24. Over three hundred li.

25. *V.* Hsien shêng wang na li ch'ü.

25. Where are you going sir ?

26. *F.* Wo shang Han k'ou ch'ü.

26. I am going to Hankow.

27. *V.* Ko hsia shih tsou shui lu, hai shih tsou han lu lai ti ni.

27. Did you travel by sea or overland sir ?

28. *F.* Wo mei yu tsou shui lu, yeh mei yu tsou han lu, wo shih tso fei chi lai ti.

28. I travelled neither by sea nor by land. I came by plane.

20. 南   Nan.² South.
    南京   Nan-Ching. Nanking. Lit. Southern Ca-
            pital.
21. 處   Ch'u.⁴ Place, dwelling place.
    府   Fu.³ Home, residence (polite).
    府上   Fu-shang. Residence.
    平   P'ing.² Peace, level, tranquil, ordinary.

23. 離   Li.² Apart from, separated from.
    遠   Yüan.³ Far, distance, distant.

24. 百   Pai. Po.³ ² ⁴ Hundred.
    里   Li.³ The Chinese measure of distance.
            "Li" about one-third of a mile.
    路   Lu.⁴ Road.
25. 往   Wang.³ ⁴ Towards, synonym for "Shang".

26. 漢   Han.⁴ The word for ancient Chinese dy-
            nasty. Part of Hankow.
27. 閣   Ko.² Council, title of respect. With next
            means Sir.
    閣下   Ko-hsia. Sir.
    旱   Han.⁴ Dry, dry land.

28. 飛   Fei.¹ To fly.
    機   Chi.¹ A machine, opportunity.
    飛機   Fei-chi. Aeroplane.

29. *V*. Tsou la chi t'ien ti   29. How many days were
    kung fu.   you en route?

30. *F*. I kung ssu t'ien ti   30. Four days in all.
    kung fu.

31. *V*. Ai ya, fei ch'ang ti   31. I say, that *is* quick.
    k'uai.

29. 工   Kung.[1] Work. With the next means time.
    夫   Fu.[1] A man. With the preceding means
                time.
    工 夫   Kung-fu. Time in which to do things.
30. 一 共   I-kung. Altogether.

31. 非   Fei.[1] Not. With the next means unusual.
    常   Ch'ang.[2] Usual, ordinary. With the pre-
                ceding means unusual, extraordinary.
    非 常   Fei-ch'ang. Unusual, extraordinary.
    快   K'uai.[4] Quick, lively.

DIALOGUE No. 8

1. *F.* Chia li yu chi ko jên.
1. How many are there in your family?

2. *V.* T'ung kung liu ko.
2. Six in all.

3. *F.* Fu mu hai tsai ma.
   or
   Fu mu tou tsai pu tsai.
3. Are your parents living?

4. *V.* Fu ch'in tsai, mu ch'in pu tsai la.
4. My father is living, but my mother is dead.

5. *F.* Ling tsun kao shou. (P.)
5. What is the exalted age of your esteemed father?

6. *V.* Pa shih erh sui.
6. Eighty-two.

7. *F.* Ling t'ang ch'ü shih, shih to ta nien chi.
7. What was the age of your honoured mother when she died?

8. *V.* Wu shih liu sui.
8. Fifty-six.

9. *F.* K'o hsi. K'o hsi.
9. How sad! (what a pity).

10. *V.* Hsien shêng yu pao chüan mei yu.
10. Have you a family? (precious wife).

11. *F.* Hai mei yu ch'êng chia.
11. I have not yet set up a home (not yet married).

VOCABULARY OF DIALOGUE No. 8

八   Pa.[1] Eight.

2. 統   T'ung.[2] Together, connected.

       共   Kung.[4] Together, combined.

       統共   T'ung-kung. All together.

3. 父   Fu.[4] Father.

       母   Mu.[3] Mother.

       父母   Fu-mu. Parents.

       在   Tsai.[4] Note special meaning of " to be living ".

4. 親   Ch'in.[1] Close relationship, especially in family or clan.

       父親   Fu-ch'in. Father.

       母親   Mu-ch'in. Mother.

5. 令   Ling.[4] Honourable, used in ceremonious language.

       尊   Tsun.[1] Honourable, used in ceremonious language.

       令尊   Ling-tsun. Your honourable father.

7. 堂   T'ang.[2] The hall, principal room, honorific for mother.

       令堂   Ling-t'ang. Your mother.

       世   Shih.[4] The world, this life, generation.

9. 惜   Hsi.[1] To pity, sympathise.

       可惜   K'o-hsi. What a pity ! pitiable.

10. 寶   Pao.[3] Precious, valuable.

       眷   Chüan.[4] Family, wife.

       寶眷   Pao-chüan. Your family, or wife.

11. 成   Ch'êng.[2] Complete, finish, accomplish, become.

12. *V.* Hsien shêng ting la   12. Are you engaged?
    hun mei yu.
13. *F.* Ting la.   13. Yes.

Alternative questions and answers to the foregoing.

14. *V.* Hsien shêng chieh   14. Are you married?
    la hun ma.

" Ch'ü ch'in " is still heard for " to marry ". But " chieh hun " is more up to date.

15. *F.* Chieh la hun la.   15. Yes, I am.
16. *V.* Hsien shêng yu chi   16. How many children
    ko hai tzu.   have you?
17. *F.* Ssu ko.   17. Four.
18. *V.* Nan ti yu chi ko   18. How many boys?
    [wei. (P.)].
19. *F.* Liang ko nan ti,   19. Two boys and two girls.
    liang ko nü ti.
20. *V.* Hao fu ch'i.   20. You have great happi-
                         ness.
21. *F.* T'o fu, t'o fu. (P.)   21. My happiness is due to
                         you.

The expression " t'o fu " is frequently used after a person has been congratulated, the idea being that such felicity as has been gained is due to the other person's merit.

22. *V.* Hsien shêng ling   22. How many boys (noble
    lang chi wei.   princes) have you?
23. *F.* Hsiao ch'üan liang   23. Two (small puppies).
    ko.
24. *V.* Ling ai yu chi wei.   24. How many daughters
    (P.)   (esteemed loved
                         ones).

These sentences are included here for the convenience of the student. They are not often heard in China now. But it is just possible they may be used, and it is well to be ready for the emergency.

2. 訂　　Ting.⁴ Fix, settle, become engaged to be
　　　　　　　married.
　　婚　　Hun.¹ Marriage, marry.
　　訂婚　Ting-hun. To be engaged to be married.

4. 結　　Chieh.² To tie a knot, join together.
　　結婚　Chieh-hun. To marry, to be married.

6. 孩　　Hai.² Child, children.
　　男　　Nan.² Male (of human beings).
　　位　　Wei.⁴ Classifier of persons (polite).

9. 女　　Nü.³ Female (of persons).

10. 福　　Fu.² Happiness, felicity.
　　福氣　Fu-ch'i. Happiness, felicity.
11. 托　　T'o.¹ᐟ Rely upon, due to, depend on.
12. 郎　　Lang.² Prince, your son.

13. 犬　　Ch'üan.³ Dog, pup.

14. 嬡　　Ai, ngai.⁴ Loved, beloved, used of other
　　　　　　　people's daughters.

24A. *F.* Hsiao nü liang ko.　24A. Two.

25. *V.* Hsien shêng kuei
　　　　kan. *or*

25. What is your business?

　　　Hsien shêng yu shih
　　　mo ch'ai shih. *or*

What administrative
post have you?

　　　Hsien shêng pan
　　　shih mo kung
　　　kan. *or*

What public work are
you on?

　　　Hsien shêng kan
　　　shih mo shih.
　　　(C.)

What do you do?

The difference between " kan ", " ch'ai shih " and " kung kan "
is as indicated in the vocabulary and dialogue.

26. *F.* Wo shih ko shang
　　　　jen. *or*

26. I am a commercial man.

　　　Wo tso mai mai.

I am in business (buy
sell).

27. *V.* Hsien shêng fêng la
　　　chiao mei yu.

27. Have you joined the
Church? *or*

Are you a member of
the Church?

" Chiao " here is a special use of the term, which originally means
" instruction ".　But it is applied to any of the various religions of
the country.　However, when speaking with foreigners the inquiry
would refer specifically to one of the " foreigners' " religions, Protestant or Roman Catholic Churches.

28. *F.* Tsai chiao.

28. I belong to the Church.

29. *V.* Shih Yeh su Chiao
　　　hai shih T'ien
　　　Chu Chiao ni.

29. Are you a Protestant or
a Roman Catholic?

30. *F.* Wo shih Yeh su
　　　Chiao. *or*
　　　Chi Tu Chiao.

30. I am a Protestant.

25. 差　　Ch'ai.[1] Commission, send.
　　事　　Shih.[4] Affair, matter, business.
　　差事　Ch'ai-shih. Commission, public work, appointment.
　　辦　　Pan.[4] To do, manage, transact.
　　公　　Kung.[1] Public, official.

26. 商　　Shang.[1] Commerce.

27. 奉　　Fêng.[4] To join, attach oneself to.
　　教　　Chiao.[4] Instruction, church.

29. 耶穌　Yeh[1]-su.[1] Jesus.
　　基督　Chi[1]-tu.[1] Christ, Christian, Protestant.
　　主　　Chu.[3] Lord, used of Christ.
　　天主　T'ien[1]-chu.[3] Roman Catholic (lit. Heaven's Lord).

31. *V.* Chê li yu Yeh su Chiao t'ang. *or* Chê li yu fu yin t'ang.

31. There is a Protestant Church here (Gospel hall).

32. *F.* Yu mu shih, nü chiao shih, tsai chê li ma.

32. Is there a pastor or a woman missionary here ?

" Chiao-shih " is a term that is commonly used of all foreigners in office in the Church, both men and women. " Chiao-hsi " is teacher. used of those in school work. But " nü ", female, is usually prefixed to indicate the women.

33. *V.* Yu chiao shih, mei yu mu shih.

33. There is a woman missionary, but no pastor.

34. *V.* Hsien shêng shih mo shih hou tao ti Chung Kuo.

34. When did you come to China ?

35. *F.* Wo shih san ko yüeh i ch'ien lai ti.

35. I came over three months ago.

36. *V.* Ai ya. Hsien shêng shuo ti Chung Kuo hua chên hao.

36. My ! you speak Chinese really well.

37. *F.* Kuo chiang, kuo chiang. Wo pu kuo hui chiang chi chü.

37. You flatter me. I can speak only a few sentences.

" Chiang " is the usual term for " preaching ". But as here indicated it also means to speak, perhaps intelligibly !

38. *V.* and *F.* Tsai chien, tsai chien.

38. Good-bye, good-bye.

31. 堂　　　T'ang.² Hall, church.
　　音　　Yin.¹ Sound.
　　福音　Fu-yin.　Gospel.

32. 牧　　　Mu.⁴ Shepherd, pastor.
　　師　　Shih.¹ Teacher.
　　士　　Shih.⁴ Scholar, teacher.
　　教士　Chiao-shih.　Teacher (used of missionaries).

35. 前　　　Ch'ien.² Before, formerly.
　　以前　I ch'ien.　Before, ago.

37. 不過　Pu-kuo.　But.
　　講　　Chiang.³ Expound, preach, say.

DIALOGUE No. 9A

THE NUMERALS

I. CARDINALS

A. The numbers one to ten are as follows:—

1. One. I.
2. Two. Erh. Liang.
3. Three. San.
4. Four. Ssu.
5. Five. Wu.
6. Six. Liu.
7. Seven. Ch'i.
8. Eight. Pa.
9. Nine. Chiu.
10. Ten. Shih.

Note that "erh" and "liang" both mean "two". Amongst the numerals "liang" is used with 2,000, *i.e.*, "liang ch'ien", and 20,000, which is "liang wan". In most other cases "erh" is used.

However, when "two" is used as a numeral adjective, *i.e.*, when it precedes nouns in a qualifying sense, "liang" is the correct form, *e.g.*:—

11. Two men. Liang ko jen.
12. Two books. Liang pen shu.

B. The numbers eleven to nineteen are made up of 10 plus the digit, *e.g.*:—

13. Eleven. Shih i. *i.e.*, ten-one.
14. Seventeen. Shih ch'i. *i.e.*, ten-seven, etc.

C. Exact multiples of ten, *i.e.*, 20–90, are made up by the reverse process, *viz.*, the digit followed by 10, as follows:—

15. Twenty. Erh shih. *i.e.*, two-ten.
16. Eighty. Pa shih. *i.e.*, eight-ten, etc.

VOCABULARY OF DIALOGUE No. 9A

9. 九   Chiu.³   Nine.

D. Hundreds and compound numbers above a hundred (pai) are as follows:—

17. One hundred. I pai.
18. Six hundred. Liu pai.
19. Nine hundred. Chiu pai, etc., for the exact hundreds.
20. 110. I pai i shih. (*or*) i pai i.
21. 112. I pai i shih erh.
22. 115. I pai i shih wu.
23. 170. I pai ch'i.
24. 768. Ch'i pai liu shih pa.

Now exercise yourself and your fellow-student in these numbers, using the following sentence:—

25. Che ko shu mu tzu, fan   25. How do you translate
    ch'u lai, shih tsen   this number?
    yang ti nien ni.

E. Where a "nought" comes in the middle of the figures, it is usual, though not the universal practice, to insert "ling", *e.g.*:—

26. 105. I pai ling wu.
27. 209. Erh pai ling chiu.

To leave out the "ling" in combinations of this kind would lead to confusion, as "i pai wu" would be 150.

F. "Thousand" is "ch'ien". Compounds and multiples of thousands follow these examples, *viz.*:—

28. 2,000. Liang ch'ien (erh ch'ien is sometimes used).
29. 1,089. I ch'ien *ling* pa shih chiu. *or* I ch'ien pa shih chiu.

There is no possibility of confusion in this instance, so the use of "ling" is optional.

30. 3,903. San ch'ien chiu pai ling san ("ling" is necessary).
31. 3,930. San ch'ien chiu pai san (cf. 30).
32. 10,000. I wan.

25. 目　　Mu.⁴ Index, list, eye.
　　　　　Shu-mu-tzu. Number(s), figures.
　　繙　　Fan.¹ To translate, turnover.

26. 零　　Ling.² Nought, cipher.

28. 千　　Ch'ien.¹ Thousand.

32. 萬　　Wan.⁴ Ten thousand, myriad.

33. 11,042. I wan i ch'ien *ling* ssu shih erh.
34. 30,056. San wan *ling* wu shih liu.
35. 40,007. Ssu wan *ling* ch'i ko. *or*
             Ssu wan *ling ling* ch'i.

The device of adding " ko " in the first of these two alternatives serves to indicate that " seven " is a digit. Only multiply the " ling " when it is absolutely essential for clarity. In reading out complex numbers for records more frequent use is made of " ling ".

II. ORDINALS

These are formed by the simple expedient of preceding the Cardinal numbers by " ti ", as follows:—

36. The first. Ti i.
             T'ou i ko. (This is a common alternative,
                  lit. Head one piece.)
37. The eighteenth. Ti shih pa.
38. The 135th. Ti i pai san shih wu, etc.

III. FRACTIONS

39. A half. I pan. (One and a half is " i ko pan ".)
40. A tenth. Shih fên chih i.
41. Three-quarters. Ssu fên chih san.
42. Seven-eighths. Pa fên chih ch'i.

All fractional numbers are formed in this way, *i.e.*, by putting the greater number, *i.e.*, the denominator, first, add " fên ", which means " part ", follow this by " chih ", which is a possessive, and then finish by the smaller number, *i.e.*, the numerator. *E.g.*, a tenth is " ten parts one ", or one out of ten, etc.

36. 頭   T'ou.² Head, first, beginning.

39. 半   Pan.⁴ Half.
40. 分   Fên.¹, ⁴ A tenth, part, to divide.
　　之   Chih.¹ Sign of possessive, like "ti", etc.

DIALOGUE No. 9B

1. *A*. Tsai ti hsia yu chi chien tung-hsi.

1. How many things are there on the floor?

2. *B*. Têng i **têng**, wo shu shu pa.

2. Wait a moment while I count them.

3. *A*. Tung hsi kou shu pu kou shu ni.

3. Are there any things missing? (lit. are the full number of things there)?

" Kou shu ", enough number, so the full number.

4. *B*. Wo k'an shao (ch'a, tuan) cho i ko.

4. I think there is one short.

5. *A*. Na mo t'a mên pi hsü pu shang.

5. Then they must make it up.

6. *B*. Chin t'ien shih hsing ch'i (li pai) chi.

6. What is the day of the week to-day?

" Hsing ch'i chi ". Note how the " chi " comes at the end, What is the number? (Lit. Day of the week how many?)

7. *A*. Chin t'ien shih hsing ch'i (li pai) san.

7. To-day is Wednesday.

" Li pai san ". Here again note the position of " san ", three.

8. *B*. Chin t'ien ch'u chi. Chin t'ien shih-chi. Chin t'ien êrh shih chi.

8. What day of the month is it to-day (applies only from first to tenth), 2. from eleventh to twentieth, 3. to the rest.

9. *A*. Chin t'ien shih ch'u pa.

9. It is the eighth.

" Ch'u pa ". The expression " ch'u " applies to the first ten days of the month.

VOCABULARY OF DIALOGUE No. 9B

1. 地   Ti.⁴ Earth, floor, locality.

4. 少   Shao.³ Few, little, short of.

5. 必   Pi.⁴ Must, certainly, necessary.
   須   Hsü.¹ Necessary, must, wait, a moment.
   補   Pu.³ Patch, repair, mend, make up for.

6. 星   Hsing.¹ Star, spark.
   期   Ch'i.² Date, appointed time, expect. Hsing-ch'i, week.

   禮   Li.³ Ceremony, courtesy, politeness.
   拜   Pai.⁴ Worship, pay respect. Li-pai, week.

8. 初   Ch'u.¹ Beginning, first.

10. *B.* T'ou i ko yüeh chiao chêng yüeh, mo i ko yüeh (huo ti shih êrh ko yüeh) chiao la yüeh.

10. The first month of th year is called Chen Yueh, and the las month (or the twelfth is called La Yueh.

11. *A.* Ch'i yü na chi ko yüeh chiao shêm-mo.

11. What are the rest of th months called?

" Ch'i yü ", the remainder. " Ch'i " is equal to " the ", " that " etc.

12. *B.* Êrh yüeh, san yüeh, ssu yüeh i chih tao shih i yüeh tou shih i yang (tou shih chao li ti).

12. The second, third fourth, up to th eleventh are the sam (or follow the sam rule).

" I chih tao ", up to, in a series.
Note that in speaking of the months the numeral precedes, ju contrary to what has been said above regarding the days of the wee

13. *A.* K'o shih shih i yüeh yeh chiao tung yüeh.

13. But the eleventh mont is also called Tun Yueh (Winte month).

14. *B.* Nien ti shih shêm-mo i ssu.

14. What is meant b " nien ti "?

15. *A.* Nien ti chiu shih la yüeh tsui hou chi t'ien ti i ssu.

15. It means the last fe days of the twelft month.

Compare the expressions for the first and the last. " T'ou " is use for the former and " mo " for the latter. " T'ou chi t'ien ", the fir few days. " **Hou** chi t'ien ", the last few days, when the reference to a fraction of the whole.

16. *B.* Kuo nien shih shêm-mo i ssu.

16. What does " kuo nien mean?

10. 月   Yüeh.⁴ Moon, month.
    正   Chêng.⁴ Right, correct, chief, chêng¹ first
           month.
    末   Mo.⁴ Last, end, dust, not, branches.
    腊   La.⁴ Twelfth moon, winter sacrifice.

11. 其   Ch'i.² He, she, it.
    餘   Yü.² Surplus. Ch'i yü, the remainder,
           surplus.

12. 至   Chih.⁴ Reach, reach to, send.
    隨   Sui.² Comply with, according to, follow.
    一直   I¹ chih.³ Straight.

    例   Ii.⁴ A regulation.

13. 冬   Tung.¹ Winter.

14. 思   Ssu.¹ Think on, ponder, thought.

17. *A.* "Kuo nien" chiu shih hsin nien, t'ou i t'ien ti i ssu.

17. That is the first day of the New Year.

18. *B.* Pa chê hsieh wan i êrh, fen k'ai kei hai tzu wan.

18. Divide these toys up and give them to the children to play with.

19. *A.* Pa chê hsieh t'ang yeh 'fên kei t' amen.

19. Divide this toffee amongst them too.

20. *B.* K'o i, mei i ko jên kei t'a i fên.

20. Yes, let each have a portion.

21. *A.* Wo i ching fên la liang tz'u.

21. I have divided it twice already.

7. 新　　Hsin.[1] New.

8. 玩　　Wan.[2] Enjoy, amuse, play.
　　藝　　I.[4] Skill, craft.
　　玩藝兒　Wan-i-crh. Playthings, toys.
　　要　　Shua.[3] To play, sport, joke.
9. 糖　　T'ang.[2] Sugar, sweets.

10. 每　　Mei.[3] Each, every.
　　份　　Fên.[4] A portion.
11. 經　　Ching.[1] Pass through, manage.
　　已經　　I Ching. Already.

DIALOGUE No. 10

Time by the clock, and other temporal expressions.

1. *A*. Ni shên shang tai la piao mei yu.

1. Have you a watch wit you?

2. *B*. Mei yu. Tan shih tui mie'rh yu chung.

2. No, but there is a cloc opposite.

3. *A*. Ni k'an yu chi tien chung.

3. What time is it? *o* See what time it is.

4. *B*. Wo chin shih yen, k'an pu ch'ing ch'u.

4. I am short-sighted, an cannot see clearly.

" K'an pu ch'ing ch'u ", an illustration of two words being us together, with the negative in between to denote a qualification of t verbal action—" see . . . not clear ".

5. *A*. Wo k'an chien la. Hsien tsai shih (yu) i tien chung.

5. I can see. It is on o'clock now.

" Shih ", is, *or* " yu ", have, are both in common use for expressio of time.

6. *B*. Ai. Wo yo la i ko p'êng yu, shih êrh tien pan chung chien mien. I ching tan wu la.

6. Oh dear! I made a appointment with friend to see him 12.30. I am alread late.

" Tan shih " *or* " k'o shih " for " but " might be included befo " i ching tan wu liao ". But, as has been frequently hinted, Chine are disinclined to use extra words if the sense is already clear.

7. *A*. Yeh hsü t'a hai tsai, têng ni.

7. Perhaps he is still ther waiting for you.

VOCABULARY OF DIALOGUE No. 10

1. 身   Shên.[1] Body, self.
   身上   Shên-shang. On one's person.
   表   Piao.[3] Watch.
2. 面   Mien.[4] Face, front, side, aspect.
   對面   Tui-mien. Opposite, the opposite side.
   鐘   Chung.[1] Clock, bell.
3. 點   Tien[3]. A stroke, mark, dot.
   幾點鐘   Chi-tien-chung. What is the time?
4. 近   Chin.[4] Near.
   視   Shih.[4] See, look.
   近視眼   Chin-shih-yen. Near-sighted.
   眼   Yen.[3] Eye, the eye.

5. 見   Chien.[4] To see, perceive.

6. 約   Yüeh.[1] Yo.[1] To make an appointment,
                  covenant, bind, agree.
   見面   Chien-mien. To see anyone, interview.
   已   I.[3] Particle used as sign of perfect tense
                  already.
   經   Ching.[1] Pass through, pass.
   已經   I-ching. Already, past action.
   耽   Tan.[1] Obstruct, prevent, delay.
   誤   Wu.[4] To thwart, hinder, delay.
7. 許   Hsü.[3] Perhaps, may be.
   也許   Yeh-hsü. Perhaps, implying a certain
                  doubt, but not too strong a doubt.

8. *B.* K'ung p'a t'a têng pu tao wo, tsou la.

8. I fear he will not have been able to wait and will have gone.

" Teng pu tao ", cannot wait. Lit. wait not arrive. " Pu tao " is commonly used with verbs to express inability.

9. *A.* Hsien tsai chi tien chung.

9. What time is it now?

10. *B.* I tien kuo i k'o. *or* I tien i k'o.

10. A quarter past one.

11. *A.* Yao shih shih êrh tien i k'o, wo hai k'o i kan tê shang.

11. If it were a quarter past twelve I could still be there in time.

" Kan tê shang ". Lit. catch up get up. Notice the use of " shang ", which with " tê " is commonly used for ability to do this or that. Cf. note 8 above.

12. *B.* Yao shih shih êrh tien ch'a i k'o, na chiu kêng hao.

12. If it were a quarter to twelve, it would be better.

" Kêng ", more, is the most common form of expressing the comparative degree.

13. *A.* Hsien tsai chi tien chung.

13. What time is it now?

14. *B.* I tien êrh shih wu fen.

14. Twenty-five minutes past one.

15. *A.* Na mo, tsai têng shih fên chung, chiu shih liang tien ch'a êrh shih wu fên, shih pu shih.

15. Then in ten minutes time (lit. again wait ten minutes), it will be twenty-five minutes to two, won't it?

Note " liang " for two. The other form " erh " is used with most numeral expressions. " Liang " is commonly used before nouns.

" Shih pu shih ", is not is, right not right, commonly used at the end of statements to throw what precedes into question form, like the French n'est ce pas, and many other Continental languages.

8. 恐   K'ung.³ Fear.
   怕   P'a.⁴ Fear, afraid.
   恐怕   K'ung-p'a. Fear, I fear.

10. 刻   K'o.⁴ A quarter, fifteen minutes.

11. 趕   Kan.³ To catch up, pursue, drive.

12. 更   Kêng.⁴ Sign of comparative, more, more
              so.
    差   Ch'a.¹ Short of, to err, differ, also read
              Ch'ai¹, to send.

16. *B.* Pu ts'o, pu ts'o.   16. Quite so (lit. not wrong).

"Pu ts'o", not wrong, a common alternative to "tui la", right, and used in same sense.

17. *A.* Ch'ü nien hsia t'ien, ni shang na'erh pi shu ch'ü ti.   17. Where did you go last Summer, to avoid the great heat?

18. *B.* Ch'ü nien wo mên na'erh yeh mei yu ch'ü. Ch'ien nien wo mên tao Lao Shan ch'ü, pi shu ti.   18. We did not go anywhere last year, but the year before last we went to Lao Shan to escape the heat.

"Na'erh yeh mei yu ch'ü", "anywhere also have not gone", so "we went nowhere". This is a very common idiom. Cf. sentence 20 for another example.

19. *A.* Ni ts'ung Lao Shan hui lai i hou, tso la shih mo.   19. What did you do after you returned from Lao Shan?

"I hou", after, like "i ch'ien", before (see 11 29) follows the verb to which it refers.

20. *B.* Shih mo yeh mei yu tso, wo tsai chia li hsien cho.   20. I did nothing. I just remained idly at home.

21. *A.* Ts'ung ch'ien ni pu shih ai ta wang ch'iu ma.   21. Weren't you fond of tennis at one time?

22. *B.* Na ko shih hou, ta wang ch'iu, t'i tsu² ch'iu, tou shih wo hsi huan ti.   22. In those days I liked both tennis and football.

16. 錯   Ts'o.⁴ Wrong, fault.

17. 夏   Hsia.⁴ Summer.
    避   Pi.⁴ Avoid, escape, flee.
    伏   Fu.² Summer heat.
    暑   Shu.³ Summer heat.
18. 前   Ch'ien.² Before.
    前 年   Ch'ien nien. The year before last.
    嶗   Lao.³ Name of hill.
    山   Shan.¹ Hill, mountain.

19. 從   Ts'ung.² From, follow, obey.
    後   Hou.⁴ After, behind.

20. 閒   Hsien.² Leisure, idle.

21. 愛   Ai.⁴ To love, to like.
    打   Ta.³ To beat, strike, to play at . . .
    球   Ch'iu.² Ball.
    打 球   Ta ch'iu. To play with a ball, tennis.
    打 網 球   Ta wang ch'iu. Tennis, to play tennis.
22. 網   Wang.³ Net; see the last.
    足   Tsu.² Foot.
    足球   tsu²-ch'iu.² Football.
    踢   T'i.¹ To kick.
    喜   Hsi.³ Joy, glad, pleased.

23. *A.* Na mo, ni hou t'ien
    lai, ho wo ta wang
    ch'iu, hao ma.

23. Then come and play
    tennis with me the
    day after to-morrow;
    does that appeal?

24. *B.* Ta hou t'ien hsing
    pu hsing.

24. Will three days hence
    do?

25. *A.* Pu kan shuo, yin
    wei ch'ien t'ien
    wo ho i ko p'êng
    yu yo hao, ta hou
    t'ien ho t'a ta
    p'ai.

25. I can't say. The day
    before yesterday I
    fixed up with a friend
    to play cards with
    him three days hence.

26. *B.* Na mo, chiu shih
    hou t'ien pa.

26. Then let it be the day
    after to-morrow.

27. *A.* Hao, ni tai liang ko
    ch'iu p'ai tzu lai.

27. Good, bring two rac-
    quets with you.

22. 歡   Huan.¹ Rejoice, pleased.
    喜歡   Hsi-huan. To be pleased.
23.   Hou-t'ien. The day after tomorrow.
24. 大後天   Ta-hou-t'ien.   Three days hence.

25. 因   Yin.¹ Cause, because.
    爲   Wei.⁴ Because, do, make, be.
    朋   P'êng.² Friend, comrade, associate.
    友   Yu.³ Friend.
    定   Ting.⁴ Fix, settle, certain.
    規   Kuei.¹ Rule, fix.
    定規   Ting-kuei. To have arranged, settled, settle,
               fix.
    牌   P'ai.³ Cards, dominoes.
    打牌   Ta p'ai. To play cards, etc.
27. 拍   P'ai.¹ To beat, clap, etc.
    球拍子   Ch'iu-p'ai-tzu. Tennis racquet.

DIALOGUE No. 11

More about watches, and expressions of time.

1. *A.* Ni yu piao mei yu.
1. Have you a watch?

2. *B.* Mei yu. Tan shih wo chia li yu i tso chung.
2. No, but there is a clock at home.

Note that expressions of place or time tend to come early in Chinese sentences. Here " tsai chia li ", *or* " chia li ", at home, comes first, whereas in English we put such expressions last.

" Tso ", a classifier for clock, bell, etc.

3. *A.* Na ko chung tui pu tui.
3. Is the clock right?

4. *B.* Pu tui, na ko chung tsou tê man.
4. No, that clock is slow (lit. goes slow).

5. *A.* Wo ti piao tsou tê k'uai.
5. My watch gains (lit. goes fast).

6. *B.* Na mo, tê pa k'uai man kai i kai.
6. Then you must alter the regulator.

" K'uai man ", lit. quick, slow, a good illustration of the way in which adjectives of opposite meaning are joined together to express the abstract noun connected with the idea of both. Here, *e.g.*, " k'uai man " means speed, regulator.

7. *A.* Kai la, yeh mei yu yung.
7. I have altered it, but without effect.

8. *B.* Tsên yang mei yu yung ni.
8. How is that?

9. *A.* Wo ti piao tsou ti mei yu chun.
9. My watch is unreliable (goes without a standard).

10. *B.* Na mo, ni ti piao tê hsiu li.
10. Then your watch should be repaired.

VOCABULARY OF DIALOGUE No. 11,

2· 座　　Tso.⁴　The classifier of clocks, bells, etc.

4. 走　　Tsou.³　To go, walk, movement of any kind.
　　慢　　Man.⁴　Slow.
5. 快　　K'uai.⁴　Quick, quickly.
　　快慢　K'uai-man.　The speed, speed.
6. 改　　Kai.³　Alter, change.

7. 用　　Yung.⁴　Use, usefulness.

9. 準　　Chun.³　Standard, a standard.
　　能　　Nêng.²　Can, able.
　　替　　T'i.⁴　For, instead of, substitute.
10. 修　　Hsiu.¹　Repair, put in order.
　　理　　Li.³　Adjust, arrange.

11. *A.* Pu ts'o. K'o shih   11. Quite right, but I do
         pu chih tao shui   not know who can
         nêng t'i wo hsiu   repair it for me.
         li.

" T'i " *or* " kei " are used for the Dative Case, to do anything for anyone.

12. *B.* Wo jên tê i ko chung   12. I know a watch and
         piao chiang.   clock maker.

" Jên tê ", to know a person. " Chih tao ", to know, is used mostly of things and affairs.

13. *A.* Hao, ni na wo ti   13. Good, would you be
         piao, chiao t'a   good enough to take
         k'an k'an, hao pu   my watch and let
         hao.   him see it ?

" Hao pu hao ", lit. good not good, used at end of statements, like " shih pu shih " above (see Dialogues 10, 15) to throw statement into polite form of question.

14. *B.* K'o i. Pu kuo chin   14. Certainly, but I have
         t'ien shang wu,   no time this morning.
         wo mei yu kung
         fu.

15. *A.* Hsia wu ni yu kung   15. Will you have time this
         fu mei yu.   afternoon ?

16. *B.* Pu i ting. Ni pa   16. I am not sure. But
         piao kei wo, Yao   give me the watch,
         shih hou pan t'ien   and if I have time
         yu kung fu, wo   this afternoon I will
         chiu kei ni sung   take it for you.
         ch'ü.

17. *A.* Lao chia, lao chia.   17. Thank you very much
                                      Sorry to trouble you

18. *B.* Na mei yu shih mo.   18. That's nothing.

0. 修理   Hsiu-li.   To repair.

1. 能   Nêng.³   Can, able.
    替   T'i.⁴   For, instead of.

2. 認 -   Jên.⁴   To recognise, to know, acknowledge.
    認 得   Jên-tê.²   To recognise, be acquainted with, to know.
    匠   Chiang.⁴   An artisan.
    鐘表匠   Chung-piao-chiang.   A watch-maker.

3. 拿   Na.²   To take, take hold of.

4. 午   Wu.³   Noon.
    上午   Shang-wu.   Forenoon.
    工   Kung.¹   Work, task.
    工夫   Kung-fu.   Time, leisure.

5. 下   Hsia.⁴   Below, beneath.
    下午   Hsia-wu.   Afternoon.

6. 定   Ting.⁴   Fix, settle, certain.
    一定   I-ting.   Certainly, without doubt.
    要   Yao.⁴   In the sense of " if ", introducing the Conditional mood.
    後   Hou.⁴   After, afterwards, later.
    後半天   Hou-pan-t'ien.   Afternoon (later half day).

7. 勞   Lao.²   To trouble, hinder.
    駕   Chia.⁴   Chariot, progress.

19. *A.* Chin t'ien wan shang, wo ch'ing chi ko p'êng yu ch'ih fan. Ni nêng lai pu nêng lai.

19. I am inviting a fe friends to dinner th evening. Can yo come?

" Nêng lai pu nêng lai ", lit. can come no can come ", the usual fo of verbal question.

20. *B.* Pu kan tang. Wo hai yu shih.

20. Thank you, but I hav something else on.

21. *A.* Ni tsui hao nêng lai. Wo ch'ing ni p'ei k'o.

21. I do hope you can com I want you to help entertain the gues (lit. best you ca come, I want, etc.

22. *B.* Ch'ih fan yao chi ko chung t'ou.

22. How long will the me last?

" Chung t'ou " is actual hours of protracted time. " Tien " " tien chung " is used of hours of time by the clock.

23. *A.* Ta kai yung liang ko chung t'ou.

23. Probably about tw hours.

" Ta-kai ", probably, on the whole, etc. " Kai " means a summa of anything. " Ta " is big, so big summary, summarising the matte

24. *B.* Ch'ih la fan i hou, yao ta p'ai ma.

24. Are you going to pl cards after dinner

25. *A.* Sui pien. Wo tzu chi tao hsiang hsia chi p'an ch'i.

25. Just as you please. F myself I should li a few games of che

7. 勞駕   Lao-chia. Polite expression of thanks. Lit.
         I have hindered your chariot.

9. 晚上   Wan-shang. Evening.

1. 最   Tsui.⁴ Most, every.

陪   P'ei.² To accompany, entertain, help to
         entertain.

陪客   P'ei-k'o. Help to entertain guests.

2. 鐘頭   Chung-t'ou.² An hour, an hour's time.

概   Kai.⁴ All, general.

3. 大概   Ta-kai. Probably, presumably.

5. 便   Pien.⁴ Convenient; read p'ien, cheap.

隨便   Sui-pien. Suit your own convenience, be
         at ease.

自   Tzu.⁴ Self, natural, from.

己   Chi.³ Self, personal.

自己   Tzu-chi. Oneself.

盤   P'an.² Plate, board, classifier of games of
         chess.

下   Hsia.⁴ To play (chess), with the following.

棋   Ch'i.² Chess.

26. *B*. Ni mên hsia ch'i, ta chia k'o i ch'u ch'ü, kuang i kuang.

26. You play chess, the rest (lit. all) will go out for a stroll.

27. *A*. Na tao pu hsing. Nü k'o k'o i tso chên hsien, nan k'o ch'ih yen, t'an t'an pa.

27. That won't do. The ladies can get on with their sewing, while the gentlemen smoke and chat.

Here " tao " comes in again—meaning " on the contrary ".

28. *B*. Tsə mên pu tao pan yeh i ch'ien, pu hui fên shou ti.

28. (In that case) we shall not be able to break up before midnight.

" Fên shou ", lit. divide or separate hands, is used of " taking one's leave or departure ".

29. *A*. Shih i tien chung i ch'ien, hui ch'ü chiu hao.

29. If you leave before eleven, that should be all right.

6. 大家　　Ta-chia. All together, the group.
　　逛　　Kuang.⁴ Stroll, visit.
　　逛逛　　Kuang-kuang. To take a stroll.

7. 倒　　Tao.⁴ A strong adversative, but, never-
　　　　　theless, on the contrary, to fall. ⁸
　　鍼　　Chên.¹ Needle, needle-work (with the
　　　　　next).
　　線　　Hsien.⁴ Thread, needle-work (with the
　　　　　last).
　　鍼線　　Chên-hsien. Needle-work.
　　男　　Nan.² Male.
　　客　　K'o.⁴ Guest, traveller.
　　喫煙　　Ch'ih-yen. To smoke.
　　抽煙　　Ch'ou-yen. To smoke.
　　譚　　T'an.² To chat, talk, gossip.
　　譚譚　　T'an t'an. To have a chat.

8. 夜　　Yeh.⁴ Night.

DIALOGUE No. 12

Between Master and Servant on domestic matters, suc.
as windows, doors, boxes, buckets and the well.

Master. *M.*   Servant, *S.*

1. *M.* Pa ch'uang hu kuan shang.

1. Close the window.

Note again that " pa " introduces the object of the verb, and tha
the main verb comes after the object in this construction.

2. *S.* K'ung p'a kuan pu shang.

2. I fear I cannot close it

Here we have another illustration of the rule of a negative comin
between the two parts of a composite verb to express " impossibility
of the action being performed.

3. *M.* Tsê-mo kuan pu shang.

3. How is that ?

4. *S.* Yu mao ping.

4. There is somethin wrong.

" Mao " is a fault—a defect.
" Ping " is a positive flaw—like a sickness.
" Mao ping " together equals " something wrong ".

5. *M.* Yu shih mo mao ping.

5. What is wrong with it

6. *S.* Chê chi t'ien, t'ien ch'i fa ch'ao, chiao ch'uang hu k'uang tzu tsou la fêng.

6. The weather has bee very damp the la few days, and th window-frame h become warped.

" T'ien "—notice the various uses of this one word—day, weathe
heaven, the heavens, etc.
Learn to use " fa " in the sense of " to be ", " to become ", "
be in a state of "; *e.g.*, " hsin li fa mên "—I am sad. Literally-
In my heart is produced sadness.
" Chiao "—to cause, causing, equivalent to our English " so that "
and when used with a verb forming the passive voice.

VOCABULARY OF DIALOGUE No. 12

1. 窗   Ch'uang.[1] Window.
   戶   Hu.[4] A hole, opening, screen.
   窗戶   Ch'uang-hu. Window.
   關   Kuan.[1] To close, bar, put to.

4. 毛   Mao.[2] Defective, hair, surface.
   病   Ping.[4] Disease, illness.
   毛病   Mao-ping. Fault, defect, flaw.

5. 氣   Ch'i.[4] Atmosphere, air, etc.
   天   T'ien.[1] Heaven, the upper air.
   天氣   T'ien-ch'i. The weather.
   發   Fa.[1] To produce, become.
   潮   Ch'ao.[2] Damp, dampness, humid, tide.
   框   K'uang.[4] Frame.
   縫   Fêng.[2] A seam, split, crack.

7. *M.* Na mo, tê chiao mu chiang lai, hsiu li, hsiu li.

7. Then we had better cal in a carpenter to put it right.

The Chinese are fond of repetition of the verb, especially when positive action is to be expressed.

8. *S.* Shih ti. Wo chiao Li Ssu fu lai, k'an i k'an.

8. Yes, I will call in Crafts- man Lee to come and look at it.

" Shih ti "—equal to " right ! ", " yes ! ", etc.

9. *M.* Ch'ien mên so shang la mei yu.

9. Is the front door locked ?

10. *S.* So shang la. *or* So pu shang. Na ko so shang la hsiu.

10. Yes, it is locked. *or* I can't lock it. The lock is rusty.

" Shang la hsiu ". " Shang " is " to add to ", " become " " hsiu " is rust. So " add rust "—rusty.

11. *M.* Na yao shih lai, shih i shih.

11. Bring the key and le us try it.

You could say " Pa yao shih na lai ". Both constructions are common and equally correct.

" Shih i shih "—try a try—one the verbal form, the other a noun

12. *S.* Tsui hao hsien t'u i tie'rh yu.

12. We had better try a little oil first.

" Tsui hao "—literally " the best "—indicating that any course of action other than the one suggested would be inferior—so " It would be best to do . . . so and so ".

13. *M.* Ni shuo ti tui, hsien t'u i tie'rh yu pa.

13. You are right, first pu a little oil on.

" Ni shuo ti " is a shortened form of the relative clause " Ni so shu ti "—what you have said.

14. *M.* Pa hou mên k'ai k'ai pa.

14. Open the back door.

" K'ai k'ai ". You could also use " K'ai i k'ai "—" open an oper ing."—on lines of 11 above.

7. 木　　　Mu.⁴ Wood, timber.
　　木匠　　Mu-chiang. Carpenter, joiner.

8. 司　　　Ssu.¹ Master, manager, control.
　　夫　　　Fu.¹ A master of craft.
　　司夫　　Ssu-fu. A leading workman, foreman,
　　　　　　　　skilled artisan.
9. 前　　　Ch'ien.² Front, before.
　　鎖　　　So.³ Lock, to lock.
10. 銹　　　Hsiu.⁴ Rust, to rust.

11. 鑰　　　Yao.⁴ Yo.⁴ A key.
　　匙　匙　Shih.² A key, a spoon.
　　鑰匙　　Yao-shih. A key.
　　試　　　Shih.⁴ To try, to test, experiment.

12. 塗　　　T'u.² To grease, to oil, smear.
　　油　　　Yu.² Oil, fat, grease.

14. 開　　　K'ai.¹ To open.

15. *S.* Na ko mên wo i ching k'ai la.

15. I have already opened it.

" I ching "—already passed—so " already ", the commonest expression for things already done.

16. *M.* Pu yao tsai kuan shang.

16. Keep it open (lit. don't close it again).

17. *S.* Yao shih pa mên ch'ang k'ai, k'ung p'a hsiao t'ou chin lai, t'ou tung hsi.

17. But if we leave the door wide open, I fear that thieves might come in and steal some things.

" Yao " usually means " want ", and so it may be interpreted here —" *if* you want " to leave, etc., and so it becomes a sign of the Conditional mood.

18. *M.* K'o pu shih ma. Pu ju pa mên kuan shang.

18. That is so. You had better close the door.

" K'o pu shih ma "—But is it not so? so That is so!

19. *S.* Chê ko p'ing tzu ti sai tzu, wo ch'ü pu ch'u lai.

19. I can't extract the cork out of this bottle.

" Ch'ü pu ch'u lai "—literally take not come out.

20. *M.* Na shih yin wei mei yu ho shih ti tung hsi. Tê yung i ko lo ssu chuan.

20. That is because you haven't a suitable gadget. You must use a corkscrew.

16. 關   Kuan.[1] To close, bar, put to.

17. 敞   Ch'ang.[3] To open, wide open, disclose.
    偷   T'ou.[1] To steal, a thief.

19. 瓶   P'ing.[2] Bottle, vase.
    塞   Sai[1, 4]. Cork, stopper. Sê.[4] Obstruct.
    取   Ch'ü.[2] To take off or out.

20. 因   Yin.[1] Cause, reason.
    爲   Wei.[4] Because, on account of.
    因爲   Yin-wei. Because.
    式   Shih.[4] Pattern, shape, fashion.
    合式   Ho-shih. Suitable.
    螺   Lo.[2] Conch, small screw.
    絲   Ssu.[1] Wire, thread.
    轉   Chuan.[3] To turn—*re*, again.
    螺絲轉   Lo-ssu-chuan. A corkscrew.
21. 箱   Hsiang.[1] Box.
    匣   Hsia.[2] Small box, crate.

Pa chê ko hsia tzu ta k'ai. | Open this small box.

Pa chê ko ho tzu ta k'ai. | Open this tin.

Pa chê ko t'ung tzu ta k'ai. | Open this tin, bucket, etc.

22. *S.* K'ai chê ko hsiang tzu, hên fei shih. | 22. This box is hard to open.

23. *M.* Tsên yang fei shih ni. | 23. What is the trouble?

Note " ni " at the end of a question which already contains an interrogative word or phrase; here " tsên-ni "—how?

24. *S.* Ting tzu t'ai to, ch'üan tou shang hsiu la. | 24. There are too many nails and they are all rusty.

Note position of " tou "; it always comes " second ". At any rate it never occupies the first place in a sentence or clause.

25. *M.* Na ko hao pan. Ni shang Wang hsien shêng na li ch'ü, chieh t'a ti ch'ien tzu. | 25. That's a small matter (lit. easy to manage). Go over to Mr. Wang's and borrow his pincers.

You cannot say " Ni shang Wang hsien shêng ch'ü ". You must add the " na-li " after the name to express motion towards a person.

26. *S.* Yao shih Wang hsien shêng pu tsai chia, wên shui ch'ü chieh ni. | 26. But suppose Mr. Wang is not at home, whom shall I ask for the loan of them?

Note " pu tsai chia " for not at home. Do not say " pu tsai " or " pu tsai la ", as that would mean " he is dead ".
" Wên ", " **ken** " or " ho " are all permissible—meaning " of " or " from " whom.

27. *M.* T'a chia li tsung yu yung jên, chiu hsiang t'a chieh, hao la. | 27. There must be a servant at home, ask him for the loan (of the pincers).

" Tsung yu " or " pi shih yu " for " there must be ".

21. 盒   Ho.² A tin or box, casket.
    筒   T'ung.² A tin, container.

22. 費   Fei.⁴ Waste, expend.
    費事   Fei-shih. A wasteful affair, difficult.

24. 釘   Ting.¹ A nail, to nail.
    全   Ch'uan.³ All.

25. 鉗   Ch'ien.² Pincers, tongs.

27. 用人   Yung-jên. Servant, one used.
    總   Tsung.³ Certainly.
    佝   Hsiang.⁴ Towards, of, etc.

28. *S.* Shih ti, wo chiu ch'ü.

28. Right, I will go along.

29. *M.* Ni ching kuo yüan tzu ti shih hou, k'an k'an shui ching, kai shang la mei yu.

29. As you pass through the garden (yard), just look to see if the well is covered.

Note this circumlocutory clause with the "when" represented by "ti-shih-hou" at the end. Literally "your passing over the yard's time".

30. *S.* Wo chin t'ien ch'ing tsao, ta wan la shui, chiu pa ching kai shang la.

30. I covered the well, after I had finished drawing water, early this morning.

31. *M.* Ni na chi ko t'ung tzu, tou ch'êng (tao) man la shui ma.

31. Have you filled all those buckets with water?

32. *S.* Chia li so yu ti t'ung tzu, wo tou ch'êng man la shui.

32. I have filled all the buckets there are in the house with water.

"So yu ti" = "what there are", equal to "all that there are".

33. *M.* Yüan tzu li na ko ta shui kang, chuang ti shih tsang shui, ni tao ch'u ch'ü la mei yu.

33. That big water butt in the garden was full of dirty water. Have you poured it all out?

After "yuan tzu li" you don't need to add "ti", the possessive, although the sense seems to require it. The "na ko" takes the place of the "ti".

29. 圍　　Yüan.² Courtyard, garden.
　　井　　Ching.³ A well.
　　蓋　　Kai.⁴ To cover.

30. 清　　Ch'ing.¹ Dawn, daybreak.
　　早　　Tsao.³ Early.
　　打　　Ta.³ To draw up.
　　完　　Wan.² To finish, complete.

31. 桶　　T'ung.³ A bucket, barrel.
　　盛　　Ch'êng.² To fill, fill up; to contain. Also
　　　　　　read sheng⁴, abundant, flourishing.
　　滿　　Man.³ Full, to fill.

32. 所　　So.³ The relative pronoun. That which,
　　　　　　those which, etc.
　　所有的 So-yu-ti. What there is.

33. 缸　　Kang.¹ Butt, large vessel for water, etc.,
　　　　　　cistern.
　　裝　　Chuang.¹ To contain—fill in, load, pack.
　　髒　　Tsang.¹ Dirty, filthy.
　　倒　　Tao.⁴ To pour, upset.
　　倒出去 Tao ch'u ch'ü. To pour away.

34. *S.* Wo pa na ko tsang shui, wan ch'üan tao ch'u ch'ü la, i tie'rh yeh mei yu liu.

34. I have emptied that dirty water out completely. There is not a drop left.

The repetition for the purposes of emphasis of " wan ch'üan ", in the form " wan wan ch'üan ch'üan ti ", is very common.

" Tao ch'u ch'ü "—the " ch'ü " suggests throwing *away from* you. If it were " tao ch'u lai " that sense would not necessarily be implied.

Note position of " i tie'rh " for emphasis—" *even one* drop is not left ".

35. *M.* Wo pa i chien shih ch'ing wang chi la.

35. I have forgotten something.

36. *S.* Shih shih mo shih ch'ing.

36. What is that?

37. *M.* Tsa mên ching li pie'rh ti shui, shih k'u ti, hai shih t'ien ti ni.

37. Is the water in our well bitter or sweet?

38. *S.* Shih t'ien ti, k'o i yung lai chu fan, p'ao ch'a.

38. Sweet, usable for cooking or making tea.

34. 完全   Wan-ch'üan.   Complete, perfect.
     全   Ch'üan.²   Perfect, complete, the whole.
     留   Liu.²   To leave, retain, keep.

35. 忘   Wang.⁴   To forget.
     記   Chi.⁴   To remember.
     忘記   Wang-chi.   To forget, *sic*. forget to remember !
     件   Chien.⁴   An article, item, classifier.
37. 苦   K'u.³   Bitter.
     甜   T'ien.²   Sweet.

38. 煮   Chu.³   To boil, cook.

DIALOGUE No. 13

Talk with Servant on domestic matters—*continued*.

1. *M.* Pa chê i chang cho tzu pan tao lou shang ch'ü.

1. Take this table upstairs.

Note "chang" as the classifier of tables, benches, etc., also tha verbs of movement usually carry an auxiliary, like "tao", to arrive

2. *S.* I ko jên pan pu tung, tê chiao chi ko jên lai pang mang.

2. But one man can't move it. I must get a few men to help

The positive of "pan pu tung"—"can't move it"—is "pan tung la"—can be moved, or can move it; so with all expressions of thi kind.

3. *M.* Yao chi ko jên pang mang.

3. How many men wil you need to help?

"Pang mang"—literally "help busy".

4. *S.* Chih shao yao san ko jên.

4. Three men at least.

5. *M.* Ku san ko jên lai t'ai cho tzu, ching chi pu shang suan.

5. But to hire three men solely for this is no economical.

"Pu shang suan"—"not up reckon"—no advantage.

6. *S.* K'o chên pu shang suan. Pu ju ku t'a men i t'ien ti kung fu, hai k'o i chiao t'a mên tso pieh ti shih ch'ing.

6. Truly it is not econo mical. We had bette hire them for th day so that we ca give them othe things to do as well

"Chiao" is "to cause" give them to do.
"Pieh ti"—something different.

VOCABULARY OF DIALOGUE No. 13

1. 張   Chang.[1]   Classifier of tables, etc.
   桌   Cho.[1]   Table.
   搬   Pan.[1]   To move, remove, transport.
   樓   Lou.[2]   A second storey, tower, upper storey,

2. 幫   Pang.[1]   Help, assist.
   忙   Mang.[2]   Busy.
   動   Tang.[4]   To move.

4. 至   Chih.[4]   Extreme, reach to, utmost.
   少   Shao.[3]   Few, little (of quantity).
5. 雇   Ku.[4]   To hire.
   經   Ching.[1]   To manage.
   濟   濟   Chi.[4]   To help, save, up to the mark.
   經   濟   Ching chi.   Economic.
   算   算   Suan.[4]   To reckon, calculate.
   上   算   Shang suan.   To be of advantage, economical. Lit. reckon on top side.
6. 別   Pieh.[2]   Other, another, extra, part from, separate.

7. *M.* Na shih tzu jan ti. Hai yu shêm-mo shih, chiao t'a mên tso ni.

7. That is naturally so (quite so). What other things can we give them to do?

8. *S.* Shih ch'ing tao pu shao. T'a mên k'o i ta sao yüan tzu, shou shih ch'u fang.

8. There are many things to do. They can sweep the yard, and put the kitchen straight (tidy up).

" Shih ch'ing tao pu shao "—" affairs on contrary not few ". " Tao " is used to express something different from what has been proposed, either explicitly or implicitly.

9. *M.* Ku chê chung jên, i t'ien tê kei to shao kung ch'ien.

9. How much in wages will this type of man want if hired?

" I t'ien "—one day—also a whole day. " Tê to shao."—ought how much?

10. *S.* Chê yang ti jên tu suan hsiao kung. I t'ien kei t'a liu mao ch'ien chiu hsing.

10. This type of man counts as a labourer (small workman). To hire one such man for a day would take 60 cents.

11. *M.* Ku liang ko jên pu kou ma.

11. Wouldn't two men be enough?

12. *S.* Pu kou. Chê ko cho tzu hên chung, liang ko jên t'ai pu tung.

12. No, the table is very heavy, and two men couldn't carry it.

" T'ai "—to carry—is used when two or more people are employed For one person to carry on one's shoulder " tan " or " t'iao " is used

13. *M.* Na mo chiu ku san ko jên pa. T'a mên chi tien chung shang kung.

13. Then hire three men What time will they start work?

"Shang kung"—go up to work. Note the verbal use of "shang" —it is in the fourth tone when used as a verb.

7. 自　　　Tzu.⁴ Natural, self, from.
　 自 然　Tzu-jan. Naturally.

8. 掃　　　Sao.³ To sweep.
　 打 掃　Ta sao. Sweep, big sweep.
　 收　　　Shou.¹ To receive, collect, gather.
　 拾　　　Shih.² Arrange, pick up.
　 收 拾　Shou-shih. Arrange, tidy up.
　 厨　　　Ch'u.² Cook (house)—kitchen cook.
　 房　　　Fang.² A room.
　 厨 房　Ch'u-fang. Kitchen.
　 院　　　Yuan.⁴ A court-yard.

10. 都　　　Tu.¹ Tou. All, both, altogether.
　 工　　　Kung.¹ Work, labour.
　 小 工　Hsiao-kung. Coolie, labourer (lit. small
　　　　　　　labour).
　 毛　　　Mao.³ A ten cent. coin, ten cents.

11. 夠　　　Kou.⁴ Enough, sufficient.

12. 重　　　Chung.⁴ Heavy, cumbersome.
　 抬　　　T'ai.² Lift, carry between two, or on
　　　　　　　shoulders.

14. *S.* Tsao shang liu tien chung shang kung, wan shang liu tien chung hsia kung.

14. They will start at si a.m. and finish a six p.m.

15. *M.* Hsiu hsi chi ko chung t'ou.

15. How many hours o for rest?

" Chung t'ou "—not " chung tien "—the latter being confined time by the clock. If you want to use " chung tien " you must ad " ti kung fu "; *e.g.*, " hsiu hsi chi . . . tien chung ti kung fu ".

16. *S.* Chung wu t'a mên yao hsieh I ko pan chung t'ou.

16. They will rest an hou and a half at noo

One and a half—" i ko pan ".

17. *M.* Chiu chê yang ti pan pa.

17. Then we will procee along these lines.

18. *M.* Pa chê chi pa i tzu pan tao na pien ch'ü.

18. Move these chairs that side.

19. *S.* Na pien mei yu k'ung ti, wo hsiang fang tsai wai t'ou hao.

19. There is no room ov there. I think it w be good (better) put them outside.

20. *M.* K'o shih pa i tzu lao tiu tsai wai pien, pu ta hao, hai pu ju na tao ti yin tzu li mien ch'ü.

20. But to leave chairs ou side for any leng of time (lao) is n very good. It wou be better to ta them into the cell

14. 早上   Tsao³ shang.   Early in the morning.

    下   Hsia.⁴   Down, to put down, to go down.

15. 休   Hsiu.¹   Rest, recuperate, relax.

    息   Hsi.²   Rest, to rest.

    鐘頭   Chung-t'ou.   Hour, of protracted time.

16. 中午   Chung-wu.³   Mid-day, noon.

    歇   Hsieh.¹   To rest, ease off.

18. 把   Pa.³   Classifier of chairs, etc.

    椅   I.³   Chair, couch.

    到   Tao.⁴   To arrive, get to, at.

    邊   Pien.¹   Side, one side.

19. 地   Ti.⁴   Ground, floor, etc.

    空   K'ung.¹   Empty.

    空地   K'ung-ti.   Room, in the sense of space. Lit. empty ground.

    想   Hsiang.³   To think, reflect.

    放   Fang.⁴   To put, place, set down, to let go.

    外   Wai.⁴   Outside, foreign.

    外頭   Wai-t'ou.   Outside, in the open.

20. 老   Lao.³   A long time, old.

    丟   Tiu.¹   To leave.

    外邊   Wai-pien.   Outside, out of doors.

    窨   Yin.⁴   A Cellar.

    地窨子   Ti-yin-tzu.   The Cellar, basement.

21. *S.* Wo hsiang ch'i i ko hao fa tzu **lai.**

21. I have thought of a better idea.

"Hsiang ch'i . . . lai" is the usual expression. Note how much comes between the parts of this compound verb—the whole subject of thought.

22. *M.* Shih shêm-mo fa tzu.

22. What is your plan?

23. *S.* Hsien pa chê i t'iao ch'ang cho tzu, pan tao k'o fang li ch'ü.

23. First take that long table into the guest room.

24. *M.* Shih ti, i hou tsai tso shêm-mo ni.

24. All right, and what will you do after that?

25. *S.* Tsai pa chê i t'iao têng tzu tiao kuo lai, chiu yu ti fang, fang chê chi pa i tzu la.

25. Then turn this bench (form) round, and there will be room for these chairs.

26. *M.* Shih ti, chiu chê yang ti pan pa.

26. Good, do it that way.

27. *S.* Hsien-shêng tê hsien jang wo pa cho tzu shang ti tung hsi pan tsou.

27. But you must first allow me to move the things (from the table).

28. *M.* Tzu jan. Tsai huan i chang kan ching ti cho pu.

28. Naturally. After that change the table cloth for a clean one.

"Chang"—classifier of table-cloth.

29. *S.* Wan shang ch'ing k'o pu ch'ing k'o.

29. Are you inviting any guests to dinner to night?

30. *M.* Ch'ing ssu wei k'o, so i yao shou shih fan t'ing.

30. Yes, four. So you must put everything tidy in the dining room.

"So i", generally speaking, is equivalent to our "so", "and so", "therefore", etc.

21. 起   Ch'i.³ To rise, arise, get up, spring up.
    想起   Hsiang-ch'i. To think of a thing.
    法   Fa.³ Method, manner, rule.
    法子   Fa-tzu. Method, way of doing things.

23. 先   Hsien.¹ First, in the front.
    條   T'iao.² Classifier of long things, like long
                   tables, benches, etc.
    客房   K'o-fang. Guest-room, drawing-room.
    裡   Li.³ Inside, within.
24. 以後   I-hou. Afterwards, behind.

25. 凳   Têng.⁴ Form, bench, long-seat.
    掉   Tiao.⁴ To change round, turn round, twist
                   round.
    掉過來   Tiao-kuo-lai. To turn around.

26. 辦   Pan.⁴ To do, transact, manage.

27. 讓   Jang.⁴ To allow, permit.

28. 換   Huan.⁴ To change.
    乾   Kan.¹ Dry, clean.
    淨   Ching.⁴ Clean.
    乾淨   Kan-ching. Clean.
    布   Pu.⁴ Cloth.

30. 所以   So-i. Therefore, so (logical conclusion).
    廳   T'ing.¹ Court, hall.
    飯廳   Fan-t'ing. Dining-room.

31. S. Ta-ssu-fu hsiao pu hsiao tê.

31. Does the cook know (about this)?

" Ta-shih-fu "—the cook, often the senior member of domestic staff —chêf.

Note " hsiao pu hsiao tê ", but often the whole compound verb is duplicated.

32. M. Hsiao tê. Wo tso t'ien fên fu la t'a.

32. Yes, he knows. I gave him his orders yesterday.

33. S. Na mo, wo chiu hao hao êrh ti yü pei.

33. Then I will prepare everything in apple-pie order.

" Hao hao êrh ti "—thoroughly, very well.

34. M. Hao. Ti t'an yao sao i sao; hsi tzu yao fan kuo lai; ch'i chü yao hsi kan ching; tuan fan ti-shih hou, yao ling li, shih-mo tou yao chêng chêng ch'i ch'i ti.

34. Good, sweep the carpet; turn over the mats; wash the crockery, etc., quite clean; and when you are serving up the food, do it smartly. Everything must be in proper order.

" Shih-mo tou yao ", lit. " anything all want ", equal to " everything should be ".

35. S. Shih ti, t'ing hsien-shêng ti fên fu.

35. Right, I will carry out your instructions.

" T'ing "—to listen—has the sense of " obey " when coupled with words which imply an order or advice, etc.

31. 大師傅   Ta-shih-fu. The skilled person, ganger, cook.
    曉   Hsiao.³   To know.
    曉得   Hsiao-tê   To know (concerning affairs), not persons.

32. 吩   Fên.¹   To order, command.
    咐   Fu.⁴   To commission, order.
    吩咐   Fên-fu.   To order, command, instruct (in the sense of issuing an order).

33. 預   Yü.⁴   Beforehand, prepare.
    備   Pei.⁴   Get ready, prepare.
    預備   Yü-pei.   To prepare, to get ready.

34. 毯   T'an.³   Carpet, felt.
    席   Hsi.²   Mat, reed mat.
    翻   Fan.²   To turn over.
    器具   Ch'i⁴-chü.   Utensils, furniture.
    洗   Hsi.³   To wash, bathe, rinse.
    端   Tuan.¹   To serve, as a waiter, put on the table.
    伶   Ling.²   Clever, active, adjust.
    俐   Li.⁴   Lively, quick, smart.
    整齊   Chêng³-ch'i.²   In good order, straight, orderly, arranged.

DIALOGUE No. 14

Exercise on Weights and Measures

Weights.

A Chinese catty, " chin ", is equal to about 21 ozs. (English), but consists of 16 " liang " (oz.). The " liang " is again divided into " ch'ien ", each of which is a tenth of a " liang ". Below that the metric system continues into several divisions, the " fên " being a tenth of a " ch'ien " and the " li " being a tenth of a " fên ". Other extremely fine measures of weight need not bother us here. The picul, in China about 133 lbs., is used for heavier articles. The word for this is " tan ".

1. Chê ko tung hsi yu to chung.

    1. What is the weight of this?

" Yu to chung "—has how much weight? Alternative expressions are " Yu to shao fên liang ", " Fên liang to chung ", " Yu to ma ch'ing chung ".

2. I tan chiu chin pan.

    2. One picul nine and a half catties.

3. Ch'ing ni kei wo ch'êng i ch'êng chê ko pao kuo. Mei yu kuo chung pa.

    3. Please weigh this parcel for me. It isn't overweight is it?

4. Kuo la chung la.

    4. Yes it is overweight.

5. Chiu ching yu to chung.

    5. How heavy is it then?

" Chiu ching "—really, getting to the heart of the matter.

6. Pa chin ch'i liang pa ch'ien.

    6. Eight catties seven ozs. and eight drams.

In measuring grain the Chinese use standard vessels, called " tan ", " tou ", " shêng ", etc. The " tan ", which for want of a better term we will call bushel, is equal to ten " tou " (peck), and the " tou " again is equal to ten " shêng ", which we will call pint.

VOCABULARY TO DIALOGUE AND
EXERCISE No. 14

2. 擔   Tan.⁴ A load, picul, tan¹ to carry.
   斤   Chin.¹ A catty, one and a third lbs.
3. 稱   Ch'êng.¹ To weigh, call, style.
  稱一稱 Ch'êng-i-ch'êng. To weigh on the scales.
   裹   Kuo.³ To bind, wrap.
  包裹   Pao-kuo. A parcel.

5. 究竟 Chiu⁴-ching.⁴ **Really.**
   兩   Liang.³ Ounce, tael.
   錢   Ch'ien.² Coin, mace, tenth of an ounce.

7. Chê ko k'ou tai li yu to shao liang shih.

7. How much grain is there in this sack?

8. Yu i tan, liu tou, ch'i shêng.

8. One " tan " six bushels and seven pints.

Tan, tou, shêng. It is difficult to give exact equivalents in English of these Chinese measures of capacity. **But see note p. 140.**

Measures of length in the shorter ranges are on the decimal system. The foot varies in length according to the material that is to be measured. There are ten inches to the foot, and ten feet make a " chang ". The inch is divided into ten " fên ". Other commonly used measures are the " pu ", which is five feet, and the " li ", about a third of the English mile, which consists of 180 " chang ".

9. Tsai t'an i t'an ch'ih ts'un pa.

9. Let us further discuss measures of length.

10. Na taò jung i ming pai. Shih fên chiu shih i ts'un; shih ts'un chiu shih i ch'ih; shih ch'ih chiu shih i chang.

10. That is easy to understand. An inch has ten parts; a foot is ten inches, and a " chang " ten feet.

11. K'o shih yu ti shih hou, wo t'ing jên shuo, chi pu, chi pu. Chê shih shih mo i ssu.

11. But sometimes I hear people say, " so many ' pu ', so many ' pu ' ". What does that mean?

12. Ai, shih ti. I pu chiu shih wu ch'ih.

12. Ah, yes. A " pu " i five feet.

13. Na mo, liang pu yeh shih i chang, shih pu shih.

13. In that case, two " pu " also make a " chang " ?

7. 袋　　　Tai.⁴ Bag, sack.
　 口袋　 K'ou-tai. Bag, sack, pocket.
　 糧　　　Liang.² Grain, food.
　 糧食　 Liang-shih. Grain, food.

8. 斗　　　Tou.³ A peck.
　 石　　　Tan.⁴ Bushel.
　 升　　　Shêng.¹ A pint.

9. 尺　　　Ch'ih.³ A foot.
　 寸　　　Ts'un.⁴ An inch.
　 尺寸　 Ch'ih-ts'un. Measure of length, length.
10. 白　　　Pai.²⁴ White, clear, in vain.
　 明白　 Ming-pai. To comprehend, understand.
　 丈　　　Chang.⁴ Ten feet, husband.

11. 步　　　Pu.⁴ Pace, step, five feet.
　 意　　　I.⁴ Idea, intention, meaning, wish.
　 思　　　Ssu.¹ Think on, ponder, thought.
　 意思　 I-ssu. Meaning.

14. Pu ts'o. Hai tê chih tao, i pai pa shih chang, chiu shih i li.

14. And you should also know that 180 " chang " make a " li ".

15. Na mo, san li chiu shih ch'a pu to, ho i Ying li i yang yüan.

15. Then three Chinese " li " are about equal in length to an English mile?

" Ch'a pu to "—different not much. A very popular expression for " nearly ", " about ", etc.

" I yang yüan "—the same distance. " Yüan " is used in longer measurements of length.

16. Ch'a pu to.

16. Just about.

17. Tso i t'iao k'u tzu tê yung to shao ts'ai liao.

17. How much material is required to make a pair of trousers?

18. Na k'an ts'ai liao ti k'uan hsia.

18. That depends on the width of the material.

" Na k'an "—that depends (lit. that looks).

19. Pi fang shuo, ts'ai liao shih êrh ch'ih k'uan, yung to shao.

19. For example, say the material is two feet wide, how much would be needed?

" Pi fang shuo "—equal to our e.g., for illustration, etc.

20. Êrh ch'ih k'uan ti ts'ai liao, tê yung i chang êrh ch'ih ti pu.

20. In material two feet wide, twelve feet will be needed.

21. I ko jên p'ao i hsiao shih (i tien chung), nêng p'ao to yüan.

21. How far can a man run in an hour?

" I hsiao shih "—an hour's time, alternative for " i tien chung tê kung fu ", " i ko chung t'ou ".

22. Ch'üan shih chieh tsui k'uai ti chi lu, chiu shih shih ying li.

22. The world's record is about ten miles.

" Chi lu "—record, adapted for the best achievement in any sphere

17. 褲　　K'u⁴ (tzu).　Trousers.
　　一條褲子I-t'iao-k'u-tzu.　A pair of trousers.

18. 材　　Ts'ai.²　Materials.
　　料　　Liao.⁴　Materials, calculate, etc.
　　材料　Ts'ai-liao.　Materials, material.
　　寬　　K'uan.¹　Wide, broad, easy.
　　狹　　Hsia.²　Narrow.
　　寬狹　K'uan-hsia.　Width.

19. 比方　Pi-fang.　For illustration, comparison, etc.

20. 布　　Pu.⁴　Cloth, to spread.

21. 跑　　P'ao.³　To run, to gallop.
　　一小時　I-hsiao-shih.　An hour.

22. 世　　Shih.⁴　The world, a generation.
　　界　　Chieh.⁴　The world, boundary.
　　世界　Shih-chieh.　The world.
　　紀　　Chi.⁴　To record, year.

23. Ai ya. I ko jên hsiang p'o la chê ko chi lu, hên fei shih.

23. I say! A man who thinks of breaking that record has a hard task.

" P'o chi lu "—to break the record, also an adaptation from the West.

24. Pu ts'o, pu ts'o.

24. Quite right.

22. 錄	Lu.⁴	To record, copy.
紀錄	Chi-lu.	Record.
23. 破	P'o.⁴	Break, solve.

DIALOGUE No. 15

A talk with the Cook.

Mistress, *M.*   Cook, *C.*

1. *M.* Ming t'ien chung wu, wo yao ch'ing san ko k'o.

1. I am inviting three guests for to-morrow noon.

Notice again how expressions of time come early in the sentences.

2. *C.* T'ai-t'ai hsiang ch'ih shih-mo fan.

2. What food would you like to eat?

" Hsiang " means " to think ", but the sense is as translated.

3. *M.* Hsien yü pei chi ko hsiao tieh tzu.

3. First prepare some assorted appetizers.

4. *C.* Yao jou t'ang pu yao.

4. Will you want soup?

5. *M.* Yao chi t'ang.

5. Yes, we'll have chicken soup.

6. *C.* T'ai-t'ai ch'ih shêm-mo jou. Hsien tsai yang jou kuei i tie'rh.

6. What meat would you like? Mutton is rather dear just now.

7. *M.* Chê chi t'ien t'ien ch'i jê, ch'ih liang ts'ai yeh hsing, pi ju huo t'ui, chi p'ien, niu shê t'ou têng têng.

7. It has been rather hot these days. Cold viands would be all right, like ham, chicken, tongue, etc.

" Têng têng "—sort-sort, equal to our et cetera.
" Shem mo ti " is another way of saying et cetera.

VOCABULARY OF DIALOGUE No. 15

3. 碟   Tieh.[2][5] Saucer.

4. 肉   Jou.[4] Ju.[4] Meat.
   湯   T'ang.[1] Soup, gravy.
   肉湯   Jou-t'ang. Soup, gravy, sauce.
5. 雞   Chi.[1] Chicken.
   魚   Yü.[3] Fish.
   猪   Chu.[1] Pig, pork. ⎫
   排   P'ai.[2] Chops.   ⎬ Alternatives for use in this dialogue.
   骨   Ku.[3] Chops.   ⎭
6. 羊   Yang.[2] Sheep.
   羊肉   Yang-jou. Mutton.

7. 熱   Jê.[4] Hot.
   天   T'ien.[1] Heaven, used for weather with the next.
   天氣   T'ien-ch'i. Weather.
   涼   Liang.[2] Cool, pleasant.
   火   Huo.[2] Fire.
   腿   T'ui.[3] Leg, thigh, ham.

8. *C*. Tsai chia t'u tou, po ts'ai.

8. And potatoes, an spinach, etc.

There are many words for potatoes, such as " ti-tan ", " shan-yü " " yü t'ou ".

9. *M*. K'o shih tê pa ts'ai, chu (shu) shou la.

9. But see that the vege ables are well cooked

10. *C*. T'ai-t'ai yeh yao ch'ih t'ien ti ma.

10. Will you also be want ing a sweet ?

11. *M*. Shih ti, yü pei ping ch'i lin, ho tien hsin pa.

11. Yes, prepare ice-crear and cake.

12. *C*. Yao nai-ping ho ping-kan pu yao.

12. Will you want chees and biscuits ?

13. *M*. Yao, mo-liao hai yao ho chia-fei.

13. Yes, and finally w shall want to drin coffee.

" Mo liao "—at the end—sometimes expanded, *e.g.*, " mo mo lia erh ti "—finally.

7. 火腿　　Huo-t'ui. Boiled ham.
   片　　　P'ien.⁴ Sliced, a slice, a strip.
   牛　　　Niu.² A cow.
   舌　　　Shê.² Tongue.
   牛舌頭　Niu-shê-t'ou. The tongue of an ox, ox-
   　　　　 tongue.
   等　　　Têng.³ Class, kind, etc.
   等等　　Têng-têng. Et cetera.
8. 加　　　Chia.¹ To add, to increase.
   再　　　Tsai.⁴ Again, repeat.
   土　　　T'u.³ Earth.
   豆　　　Tou.⁴ Beans.
   土豆　　T'u tou. Potatoes.
   菠　　　Po.¹ ² Spinach.
   菠菜　　Po-ts'ai. Spinach, etc.
9. 煮　　　Chu.³ To boil.
   熟　　　Shou.² Shu.² Ripe, soft, properly cooked.

11. 冰　　　Ping.¹ Ice.
    淇淋　　Ch'i²-Lin.² Transliteration of English " jelly ".
    冰淇淋　Ping-ch'i-lin. Ice-cream.
    點　　　Tien.³ Dot, etc., with next used for cakes,
    　　　　 sweetmeats.
    心　　　Hsin.¹ The heart, the mind.
12. 奶　　　Nai.³ Milk, curdled milk, cheese.
    餅　　　Ping.³ Cake, slab.
    奶餅　　Nai-ping. Cheese.
    餅乾　　Ping-kan. Biscuits (kan is dry). Kan is
    　　　　 added to fruits when dried.
13. 末　　　Mo.⁴ The end, at the last.
    末了　　Mo-liao. At the end, to finish with.
    咖啡　　Chia¹-fei¹. Transliteration for coffee.

14. *C*. T'ai-t'ai pu yao shui kuo ma.

14. Won't you want fresh fruit?

15. *M*. Mai p'in kuo, li, p'u t'ao pa.

15. Buy some apples, pears and grapes.

16. *C*. Hai yao ho chiu ma.

16. Shall I put on wine?

17. *M*. Huang chiu chiu hsing, yeh yao lü-sung yen.

17. Yellow wine will suffice, and put on some cigars.

" Lü-sung "—Luzon, the large southern island of the Philippines.

18. *C*. Yeh hsü yu i liang wei k'o jên shih chieh chiu ti, tsui hao hsien yü pei chi p'ing ch'i shui.

18. Perhaps one or two of the guests may be teetotal; we had better prepare some minerals (soft drinks).

" Chieh chiu "—abstain from wine.

19. *M*. Pu ts'o.

19. All right.

20. *C*. Pai cho tzu tê chao i ko pang mang ti.

20. I suppose I had better get a man to help with the table.

21. *M*. Ni k'o i chao lao ma, tao ch'u fang pang mang hao la.

21. You can tell the amah to help in the kitchen.

22. *M*. Ling wai yü pei shui yen tai, yeh hsü yu jên hsiang ch'ou shui yen.

22. And, in addition, prepare a water pipe, as probably someone will want to smoke.

14. 果   Kuo.³ Fruit in general.
   水果   Shui kuo. Fresh fruit.
15. 蘋   P'ing.² P'in.² Apple.
   梨   Li.² Pears.
   葡萄   P'u-t'ao.² Grapes. Cf. Greek, Putos, the
                     vine.

16. 酒   Chiu.³ Wine.
17. 黃   Huang.³ Yellow.
   呂宋   Lü-sung. Luzon, Philippines.
   呂宋煙 Lü-sung-yen. Cigars.

18. 戒   Chieh.⁴ Forbid, prohibit.
   瓶   P'ing.² A bottle.
   汽水   Ch'i-shui. Aerated waters.
20. 擺   Pai.³ To spread, to lay on table.

21. 老媽   Lao-ma. Nurse, "old mother".

22. 另   Ling.⁴ Separate.
   外   Wai.⁴ Outside, additional.
   另外   Ling-wai. In addition.
   袋   Tai.⁴ Pipe, bag.
   抽   Ch'ou.¹ To smoke, draw.

23. *C.* Cho tzu shang yeh
yao pai t'ang, niu
nai, yen, hu chiao
mien, ts'u, chiang
yu, ho chieh mo
pa.

23. And (I suppose) I
should put sugar and
milk, salt, pepper,
vinegar, sauce, and
mustard on the
table?

The "pa" at the end of the sentence carries the sense of "I suppose". This is a common idiom.

24. *M.* Ya ch'ien yeh pu
yao wang la.

24. And the tooth-picks
must not be for-
gotten.

23. 糖   T'ang.²   Sugar.

    奶   Nai.³   Milk, breasts.

    鹽   Yen.²   Salt.

    胡   Hu.²   Pepper.

    椒   Chiao.¹   Pepper.

    胡椒麵   Hu-chiao-mien.   Pepper.

    醋   Ts'u.⁴   Vinegar.

    醬油   Chiang-yu.   Sauce.

    芥   Chich.⁴   Mustard.

    芥末   Chieh-mo.⁴   Mustard.

24. 牙   Ya.²   Tooth, teeth.

    籤   Ch'ien.¹   Bamboo-slip.

    牙籤   Ya-ch'ien.²   Tooth-pick.

DIALOGUE No. 16

Hiring a Rickshaw

Mistress, *M.*   Servant, *S.*

1. *M.* Chieh shang yu yang ch'ê (huang pao ch'ê) mei yu.

1. Are there any rickshaws on the street?

" Yang ch'ê "—foreign cart, rickshaw, also called " jên li ch'ê "—equal to jinrickshaw.   In the north, Peking and Tientsin, etc., " chiao p'i " is a favourite term.   It simply means " rubber ", referring to the tyres.   Another alternative is " huang pao ch'ê ", referring to the yellow covering of many rickshaws.

2. *S.* Yu shih yu, pu kuo pu hên to.

2. Yes, there are, but not many.

Note the phrase " yu shih yu "—have yes have !—the implication being that there are not many.

3. *M.* Ni kan k'uai ch'ü, kei wo ku i liang.

3. Hurry and hire one for me.

" Liang " is the classifier of carts.   It may be used by itself when the subject, cart, etc., is obvious.

4. *S.* T'ai t'ai shang na li ch'ü.

4. Where are you going Madam ?

5. *M.* Wo yao shang Li t'ai t'ai na li ch'ü.

5. I am going to Mrs. Lee's.

6. *S.* T'ai t'ai yao ku lai hui ch'ê ma.

6. Do you wish to hire the rickshaw for the return journey ?

7. *M.* Ku yang ch'ê, shih lun li shu, hai shih lun chung tien ni.

7. Do you hire a rickshaw by distance or by the hour ?

" Li shu "—miles, number, distance.

VOCABULARY OF DIALOGUE No. 16

1. 洋   Yang.² Foreign.
   車   Ch'ê.¹ Cart, carriage, vehicle.
   洋車   Yang-ch'ê. Rickshaw.

3. 趕   Kan.³ Hurry, chase.
   趕 快 Kan-k'uai. Speedily, hasten.
   僱   Ku.⁴ Hire.
   輛   Liang. Cart.

6. 來回   Lai-hui. Come-go, a return journey.

7. 論   Lun.⁴ To discuss, according to.
   里數   Li-shu. Distance.
   鐘點   Chung tien. Hours—time.

8. *S.* To pan shih lun chung tien.

8. Mostly by the hour.

" To pan " *or* " to-i-pan "—more than a half, mostly, probably.

9. *M.* Na mo, tsui hao ku t'a san ko chung t'ou.

9. Then it will be best to hire him for three hours.

10. *S.* T'ai t'ai yao wo ho t'a chiang chia ch'ien ma.

10. Do you want me to discuss the price with him? (the rickshaw coolie).

11. *M.* I ko chung t'ou, ying kai kei t'a to shao ch'ien.

11. How much ought one to give per hour?

12. *S.* Wo shuo pu chun. I ko chung t'ou, ta kai kai kei t'a wu mao ch'ien.

12. I can't say for certain, but probably one ought to give him fifty cents.

" Ta kai "—probably, on the whole. See p.114.

13. *M.* Wo i wei wu mao ch'ien t'ai to la i tie'rh. Ni ho t'a chiang chia ti shih hou, tsui hao hsien shao kei t'a i tie'rh.

13. In my opinion, fifty cents is a trifle too much. When you discuss the price with him, it will be best to offer him less at first.

" Wo i wei "—I think, often " I wo k'an lai "—literally " In my seeing come ", in my opinion.

14. *S.* Na pu yung shuo. Wo mên tso mai mai, chiu shih chê yang.

14. Needless to say we do business just along those lines.

15. *M.* K'o shih wo t'ing shuo, Chung Kuo shang chieh, hsien tsai, tou shih " yen pu êrh chia ".

15. But I have heard that in Chinese commercial circles now, the prices are fixed (lit. words have not two prices).

8. 多半　To pan.　Probably (lit. more a half).

10. 講　　Chiang.³　To expound, explain, discuss, bargain.
    價　　Chia.⁴　Price, value.
    價錢　Chia-ch'ien.　Price.
11. 應　　Ying.¹　Ought.
    該　　Kai.¹　Ought, should.
12. 準　　Chun.³　Standard, certainty, fixed.
    說不準　Shuo-pu-chun.　Can't say for certain.

15. 商　　Shang.¹　Commerce.
    界　　Chieh.⁴　World, sphere.
    商界　Shang-chieh.　The commercial world.
    言　　Yen.²　Words, speech.

16. *S.* Ta shang tien to pan   16. The big stores all have
       tou shih ting chia,   fixed prices, but
       k'o shih hsiao   small shopkeepers
       mai mai, hai shih   still bargain in the
       chao chiu chiang   old way.
       chia.

" Chao chiu "—according to old (practice).

17. *M.* Na mo, ni k'uai i   17. Then off you go as
       tie'rh ch'ü, chia   quickly as you can,
       ch'ien yüeh shao   the lower the price
       yüeh hao.   the better.

" Yüeh . . . yüeh "—a very common idiom, *e.g.*, " yüeh k'uai yüeh
hao ", the quicker the better.

18. *S.* Na pu yung shuo,   18. Needless to say I will
       wo chin li chiu   do my utmost.
       shih la.

19. *M.* Yeh pu yao tan wu   19. And don't loiter, come
       kung fu, k'uai   back quickly.
       k'uai ti hui lai
       pa.

20. *S.* Wo chin li ti pan.   20. I will do my best. If
       Nêng tsao hui lai   I can get back early
       wo chiu tsao hui   I will do so.
       lai.

Note construction of second half of this sentence.

16. 照   Chao.[4] According to.
    照舊   Chao-chiu.[4] As of old, as formerly.

17. 越   Yüeh.[4][5] The more, comparative sign.

19. 耽   Tan.[1] Obstruct, prevent, delay.
    誤   Wu.[4] Forget, careless, miss.
    耽誤   Tan-wu. Delay, waste time, loiter.

20. 能   Nêng.[2] Can, able.

DIALOGUE No. 17

An interesting discussion between two friends on an intimate personal matter.

1. *A.* Chao hsiao chieh ni jên tê pu jên tê.

1. Do you know Miss Chao?

" Jên-tê " and " jên-shih " are synonymous—both may be applied to persons.

2. *B.* Jên shih jên tê, k'o shih pu ta shu shih.

2. I may be said to know her, but I am not at all intimate with her.

3. *A.* T'a to ta sui shu, ni chih tao pu chih tao.

3. Do you know how old she is?

" Chih tao " cannot be used in reference to knowing persons.

4. *B.* Pu chih tao, wo ts'ai t'a shih shih liu sui shang hsia.

4. I don't really know, but I guess she is about sixteen.

" Shang-hsia "—up-down, thereabouts, roughly speaking.

5. *A.* T'a ti fu mu tou tsai shih ma.

5. Are both her parents living?

6. *B.* T'a fu ch'in hai tsai, pu kuo mu ch'in tsao ch'ü shih la.

6. Her father is still alive but her mother died some time ago.

" Tsai " used alone in this connection means " alive ".
" Ch'ü shih "—left the world, died.

7. *A.* T'a tsao chi nien ch'ü ti shih, ni chi tê pu chi tê.

7. Do you remember how many years ago she died?

" Ch'ü ti shih "—an adjectival phrase=one's leaving the earth An alternative is " ch'ü shih la ", verbal form in past tense.

VOCABULARY OF DIALOGUE No. 17

1. 趙   Chao.[4]   A common surname.
   小姐   Hsiao chieh. Miss, a single woman.
   認   Jên.[4]   Recognise, know (of persons).
   認得   Jên-tê. To know, mainly persons.

2. 認識   Jên-shih. To know, to recognise, an alter-
                 native for jên-tê.
   識   Shih.[4]   To know, recognise.
   熟   Shu.[2]   Intimate, very friendly.
   熟識   Shu-shih. Very intimate acquaintance.

3. 知道   Chih-tao. To know, of things and affairs.

4. 猜   Ts'ai.[1]   To guess.
   上下   Shang-hsia. Round about, roughly speak-
                 ing.

5. 世   Shih.[4]   The earth.
   在世   Tsai-shih. On the earth, alive, living.

6. 去世   Ch'ü-shih. To have left the earth, dead,
             to die.

7. 記   Chi.[4]   To remember, bear in mind.
   記得   Chi-tê. To remember.

8. *B.* Pu ta ch'ing ch'u,
wo hsiang t'a shih
wu liu nien ch'ien,
ch'ü ti shih.

8. I am not quite clear
about that, but I
think she died about
five or six years ago.

You may also say " chi pu ta ch'ing ch'u ".   Note that if an
adverbial phrase qualifies the verb only the main part of a composite
verb is used: " ' chi '—not ' chi tê ' pu ta ch'ing ch'u ".

9. *A.* Na mo, Chao hsiao
chieh shih k'o
lien ti.

9. Then Miss Chao is to
be pitied.

10. *B.* Shih tsai k'o lien.

10. Truly pitiable.

11. *A.* T'a chia li i kung
chi ko jên.

11. How many are there in
her family?

12. *B.* T'ung kung pa ko
jên.

12. Eight altogether.

13. *A.* T'a ti hsiung chi
wei.

13. How many brothers
has she?

There is no possessive " ti " after " t'a ", as it is clear from the
sense.

14. *B.* San ko ti hsiung,
san ko tzu mei.

14. Three brothers and
three sisters.

15. *A.* Chao hsiao chieh
shih hang chi.

15. What is her place
(where does she
come) in the family?

" Hang chi "—place on a list—the common way of inquiring about
one's place in the family.

16. *B.* T'a hang êrh. T'a
yu i ko ko ko,
liang ko hsiung
ti, liang ko mei
mei.

16. She comes second. She
has one elder bro-
ther, two younger
brothers, and two
younger sisters.

8. 清   Ch'ing.[1] Clear, pure.
   清楚 Ch'ing-ch'u. Clear, intelligent.
   前   Ch'ien.[2] Before, age, formerly.

9. 憐   Lien.[2] Pitiful, pity, sympathise.
   可憐 K'o-lien. Pitiable, to be pitied.

2. 通   T'ung.[1] Together with, altogether.
   共   Kung.[4] All, together.
   通共 T'ung-kung. Taken together, altogether.

3. 弟   Ti.[4] Younger brother.
   兄   Hsiung.[1] Elder brother.
   弟兄 Ti-hsiung. Brothers.
   位   Wei.[4] Classifier of persons, especially those of rank or position. Also a person of that kind.

4. 姊   Tzu.[2] Elder sister.
   妹   Mei.[4] Younger sister.
   姊妹 Tzu-mei. Sisters.

5. 行   Hang.[2] Grade, place in a list, position, order.
   行幾 Hang-chi. An inquiry as to one's place in the family.

6. 哥   Ko.[1] Elder brother.
   哥哥 Ko-ko. Elder brother.
   兄弟 Hsiung-ti.[4] Younger brother.
   妹妹 Mei-mei.[4] Younger sister.

17. *A.* Na mo, chao ni ti
    hua, t'a yeh mei
    yu chieh chieh,
    yeh mei yu mu
    ch'in.

17. Then, according to yo
    statement, she ha
    neither elder siste
    nor mother.

18. *B.* Pu ts'o. T'a tsao
    chiu tan fu chia
    li pie'rh ti tsê-jén,
    yeh hên tung chia
    shih.

18. That is so. Early c
    she had to assun
    domestic responsib
    lities, and she is ve
    conversant wit
    matters of the hom

" Tan fu . . . tsê-jên "—carry responsibility, the details of t
responsibility coming in between the verb and the noun.

19. *A.* Chao hsiao chieh
    kên jên ting la
    hun mei yu.

19. Is Miss Chao engaged

" Kên " is a colloquial alternative for " ho "—with.

20. *B.* Pu chih tao, wo k'o
    i kei ni ta t'ing.

20. I don't know, but I w
    inquire for you.

21. *A.* Wo hên hsi huan
    t'o ni t'i wo pan
    chê chien shih.

21. I am very happy to e
    trust you to mana
    this affair for me.

22. *B.* P'an wang wo nêng
    pan ti t'o tang,
    pu kei ni tiu lien
    chiu shih la.

22. I hope I shall be ab
    to put it throu
    satisfactorily, wit
    out causing you
    lose face.

23. *A.* Tsa mên lia shih to
    nien ti lao p'êng
    yu, ni yeh hên
    tung li mao, wo
    k'an ni pu hui
    chiao wo tiu lien
    ti.

23. We two are old friend
    and you understa
    etiquette thoroughl
    I think it impossib
    for you to let n
    down (lit. cause n
    to lose face).

17. 照   Chao.⁴ According to.
    姐姐   Chieh-chieh. Elder sister.

18. 擔負   Tan fu.⁴ To bear, carry, as responsibility.
    責   Tsê.² Chai.² Burden of office, responsi-
                   bility.
    任   Jên.⁴ Office, the care and burden of office.
    擔負責任   Tan-fu-chai-jên. To carry responsibility.

19. 訂婚   Ting⁴ hun. To become engaged to be
                   married, fix, settle.

20. 打聽   Ta-t'ing. To make inquiries.

21. 托   T'o.¹ Commission, to entrust to (pretext).

22. 妥   T'o.³ Satisfactory.
    妥當   T'o-tang. Satisfactory.
    丟   Tiu.¹ To lose.
    臉   Lien.³ Face.
    丟臉   Tiu-lien. To lose face.
    盼望   P'an.⁴ Wang.⁴ Hope, expect.
23. 貌   Mao.⁴ Appearance, form.
    禮貌   Li-mao. Courtesy, ceremony, etiquette.

24. *B*. Ch'i kan, ch'i kan. K'o shih t'a ch'in ch'i pu shao, pu tê tsui i liang ko jên, shih pu yung i na.

24. I am honoured (lit. how dare I accept such compliments). Bu^t her relations are numerous, and it wil^l not be easy to avoid giving offence to one or two of them.

25. *A*. Wu lun ju ho, ni pu yao shuo huang. Yao shih ni p'êng chien shih mo nan ch'u, k'ung p'a kuo pu ch'ü ti shih hou; ni hui lai, hsiang hsiang hsi hsi ti kao su wo, chiu tê la.

25. But whatever happens you must not tell any untruths. If you meet with difficultie^s which cannot be sur mounted, come and inform me as to the details, and leave it at that.

26. *B*. Ni na yang ti ch'u chu i, wo hen p'ei fu, wo pu hui tui ni shih hsin ti.

26. I admire you for voicing your opinion in that way. (Have no fear I will not break faith with you.

27. *A*. Hao, shih ch'ing pan ch'êng la, wo chiu hao hao êrh ti ch'ou hsieh ni.

27. Good. When the affair is completed, I shall gratefully reward you.

24. 登   Ch'i.³ How, how can it be? with the next
         a common term of polite usage.

    敢   Kan.³ Dare.

    戚   Ch'i.⁴ Relatives.

    親戚   Ch'in-ch'i. Relatives.

    罪   Tsui.⁴ Sin, crime, offence, offend.

    得罪   Tê-tsui. To offend a person.

25. 論   Lun.⁴ To discuss.

    無論   Wu²-lun.⁴ No matter, however that may
         be.

    何   Ho.² How, why.

    如何   Ju-ho. How, why.

    謊   Huang.³ Lies, false.

    碰   P'êng.⁴ To meet with, come across, hit
         upon.

    碰見   P'êng-chien. To meet with, come across,
         hit upon.

    難處   Nan-ch'u. Difficulties.

    詳   Hsiang.² Details.

    細   Hsi.⁴ Fine, delicate.

    詳細   Hsiang-hsi. Details, in detail.

26. 主   Chu.³ Opinion, lord, master.

    主意   Chu-i. Opinion.

    佩   P'ei.⁴ Wear at waist, respect.

    服   Fu.² Submit, serve, show deference.

    佩服   P'ei-fu. Respect, admire.

    失   Shih.¹ To lose, to err.

    失信   Shih-hsin.⁴ Be unfaithful, break faith.

27. 成   Ch'êng.² To complete, finish, become.

    酬   Ch'ou.² Reward, bestow.

    謝   Hsieh.⁴ To confer, make a gift.

28. *B.* Pieh t'i na ko. Wo pu kuo shih chin li, pang p'êng yu ti mang, pa la.

28. Say nothing about that. I am simply doing my best to help a friend in an emergency.

28. 提   T'i.[2]   To mention.

DIALOGUE No. 18

Between two friends, illustrating expressions of Comparison, and other common idioms.

1. *A.* Chê ko tung-hsi hao.

1. This is a good article.

2. *B.* Tan shih chê-ko pi na-ko hao.

2. But this is better than that.

" Pi " is compare—lit. " this compare that good " (see 10 below).

3. *A.* So i wo-mên shuo chê-ko kêng hao.

3. So we say " this is better ".

4. *B.* Chü wo k'an chê shih tsui hao ti tung-hsi.

4. I consider this is a very fine article.

" Chü wo k'an "—lit. " according to my seeing ".

5. *A.* Yeh k'o i shuo shih ting (t'ing) hao.

5. You may also say it is " the best ".

6. *B.* Chê ko pu pu hao, k'o shih ho na ko i pan hao.

6. This cloth is inferior, but it is as good as that.

7. *A.* Chê yang ti pu, pu ju na ko hao.

7. This kind of cloth is not as good as that.

" Pu ju na ko hao "—lit. " not as that good ".

8. *B.* Yeh k'o i shuo chê ko kêng pu hao.

8. It is also possible to say, " this is even worse ".

9. *A.* Hai yu i ko shuo fa, chiu shih chê ko pi na ko huai (tai).

9. There is another way of speaking, *i.e.*, this is worse than that.

10. *B.* K'o shih t'ou i ko shuo fa pi ti êrh ko shuo fa ch'iang.

10. But the first way of saying it is superior to the second.

" T'ou-i-ko " and " ti-i-ko " are synonymous.

VOCABULARY OF DIALOGUE No. 18

2. 比   Pi.³ ⁴ To compare, illustrate.

4. 據   Chü.⁴ According to.
   最   Tsui.⁴ Most, very, sign of superlative.

5. 頂   Ting.³ Top, head, sign of superlative.
   挺   T'ing.³ To stick out, stiff.

6. 布   Pu.⁴ Cloth.
   般   Pan.¹ Exactly alike.

9. 壞   Huai.⁴ Bad, vicious, ruined.

10. 強   Ch'iang.² Strong, so superior, violent.

11. *A*. Na chê i k'uai pu   11. Compare these two
    ho na i k'uai pi   pieces of cloth.
    i pi.

" Pi-i-pi "—compare a compare, make a comparison—a common
verbal form.

12. *B*. Yao chiao wo pi i   12. In what respect do you
    pi na i fang mien   want me to compare
    ni.   them ?

" Na i fang mien "—" na " is third tone representing the question
—which?

13. *A*. Hsien pi i pi ch'ang   13. First compare them as
    tuan, tsai pa pu   to length, then as
    ti hao tai pi i pi,   to quality, and then
    tsai pi i pi yen   again as to colour
    shai, tiao shai pu   especially as to the
    tiao shai.   dye being fast or not.

Note this interesting way of forming abstract nouns—long-short
equals length ; good-bad equals quality.
" Shai "—colour ; also pronounced " sê " or " sei ". " Tiao shai "
—to lose colour.

14. *B*. Chê ko pu t'ai kuei,   14. I can't afford to buy
    wo mai pu ch'i.   this cloth, it is too
        dear.

" Mai pu ch'i "—buy not rise—just as we say can't rise to it, can't
afford.

15. *A*. Chê ko hsiang tzu   15. This box is too heavy,
    t'ai chung, wo no   I can't move it.
    pu tung.

" No pu tung "—move not move, can't move it.

16. *B*. Chiu shih wo-mên   16. Even if we two thought
    liang hsiang t'ai,   of lifting it between
    yeh t'ai pu tung.   us, I fear we couldn't

" T'ai pu tung "—carry not move, can't carry it.
The positive of all these expressions is to add " la " to the composite verb : " mai ch'i la "—can afford ; " no tung la "—can move
it, etc.

12. 面   Mien.⁴ Face, aspect.
    方面   Fang-mien. A certain aspect of any matter,
             one side.

13. 長   Ch'ang.² Long.
    短   Tuan.³ Short.
    長 短   Ch'ang-tuan. Length.
    歹   Tai.³ Bad.
    好 歹   Hao-tai. Quality.
    顏   Yen.² Colour, face.
    色   Shai. Sê.⁴ Colour, beauty.
    掉   Tiao.⁴ Drop, fall, lose.

15. 動   Tung.⁴ Move, stir.

17. *A.* Chê li yu kên kun tzu, pu kuo shih t'ai ts'u, wo-mên na pu chu.

17. There is a short pole here, but it is too thick, and we shall find it hard to grasp.

" Ts'u "—thick; of round long things.
" Hou " is the word for thick when applied to flat things.

18. *B.* Wo-mên mai ti tung-hsi t'ai to, i ko hsiao ch'ê chuang pu hsia.

18. We have bought too many things, one barrow cannot take them all.

" Chuang pu hsia "—pack not down, can't get them on.

19. *A.* Huo wu shih tsai t'ai to, liang ko ma ch'ê yeh la pu tung.

19. We really have too many things, even two carts couldn't pull them.

" La pu tung "—pull not move, can't pull them.

20. *B.* Wo-mên hui tao chia ti shih-hou, k'ung p'a i ko wu li, yeh fang pu hsia chê hsieh tung hsi.

20. When we get home I fear that one room will be too small to take all these things.

" Yeh "—still. " Even the *whole* room, is *still* insufficient."

21. *A.* Pa t'a mên tui ch'i lai yeh hsü chiu chuang tê hsia la.

21. If we pile them up we can probably get them all in.

" Chuang tê hsia ". Note this alternative to what has been suggested in 16 above, to express the positive.

22. *B.* K'o shih tê hsiao hsin, pa tung-hsi tui ch'i t'ai kao, k'ung p'a kou pu chao.

22. But take care. If you put things too high I fear you might not be able to reach them.

17. 根　　Kên.[1] Classifier of sticks.
　　 棍　　Kun.[4] Staff, stick.
　　 挪　　No.[2] To move.
　　 粗　　Ts'u.[1] Broad, thick (of round things like columns).

18. 小車　Hsiao[3]-ch'e. Wheelbarrow.
　　 裝　　Chuang.[1] To pack, lead into, dress.

19. 貨　　Huo.[4] Goods, wares.
　　 物　　Wu.[4] Things, goods.
　　 貨物　Huo-wu. Goods, wares.
　　 馬　　Ma.[3] Horse.
　　 拉　　La.[1] To pull, drag.
20. 屋　　Wu.[1] Room in a house, house.

21. 堆　　Tui.[1] Heap, pile, to pile up.

22. 高　　Kao.[1] High, eminent.
　　 够　　Kou.[4] To reach to a height, put a thing high up.
　 够不着　Kou pu chao. I can't reach up to it.

23. *A.* Pu kuo chan tsai i tzu shang, huo shih hsiao t'ai tzu shang, chiu kou chao la.

23. But if you stand on a chair or on the small steps you can reach them all right.

" Huo shih "—or.

24. *B.* Yu t'ai tzu chê mo kao yeh chiu hsing.

24. If you have steps as high as this that will do.

" Chê mo kao "—as high as this, a very common idiom.

25. *A.* K'o shih yeh tê k'an t'ai tzu ti k'uan hsia tsên yang.

25. But we must also take note of the width of the steps.

" K'uan chai " is a common alternative to the text.

26. *B.* Yao shih ni pi wo hsien tao chia, k'o i ho yung jên shang liang, tsêm-mo pan tsêm-mo hao.

26. If you get home before me, talk the matter over with the servants, and whatever you do will be all right.

" Tsêm-mo . . . tsêm-mo "—" however . . . thus ".

27. *A.* Yao shih wo pi ni wan tao tsên yang ni.

27. If I arrive later than you what then ?

28. *B.* Yao shih wo pi ni hsien tao chia, pi shih yin wei ni tsou ts'o la lu.

28. If I get there before you it must be because you have taken the wrong road.

29. *A.* Na mo, shui hsien tao, shui pan chiu shih la.

29. Then whoever gets there first will put the business through.

" Shui . . . shui "—" whoever . . . he ".

23. 站   Chan.[4] To stand, stand up, a post (on a journey).

或   Huo.[4] Or, perhaps, someone.

台   T'ai.[2] Terrace, platform.

台子   T'ai-tzu. Steps.

25. 寬   K'uan.[1] Wide.

狹   Hsia.[2 5] Narrow (unusual).

寬狹   K'uan-hsia. Width.

26. 商   Shang.[1] Discuss, deliberate, consult.

量   Liang.[2] Measure, plan, to consider (with the preceding).

28. 路   Lu.[4] Road, way.

DIALOGUE No. 19

Shopping at the Drapery Store

Shopkeeper, *S.*   Customer, *C.*

1. *C.* Chang kuei ti, kung hsi fa ts'ai.

1. Good-day manager. I hope business is brisk and returns good.

" Kung hsi "—a common congratulatory expression conveying " good wishes ".

" Fa ts'ai "—get rich, special greeting to merchants, etc.

2. *S.* T'o fu. Mei yu shêm-mo shêng-i.

2. Thanks to you. But business is practically nil.

3. *C.* Wo yao mai ch'ou tzu, yu mei yu.

3. I am wanting silk. Have you any?

4. *S.* Yu. Hsien shêng yao shêm-mo yang'erh ti ch'ou tzu. Yao hao ti, hai shih yao tz'u i tie'rh ti ni.

4. Yes. What kind of silk do you want? Do you want good quality or something not quite so good?

" Tz'u "—something not of the first grade.

5. *C.* Yao hao ti. Ch'ou tzu shih tsên yang mai ti, shih lun ch'ih, hai shih lun chin.

5. I want good quality. How do you sell silk, by the foot or by the pound?

" Lun "—to discuss, how things are sold.

VOCABULARY OF DIALOGUE No. 19

1. 掌   Chang.[3] To control, palm of hand.
   櫃   Kuei.[4] Shop-counter, cupboard.
   掌櫃的   Chang-kuei-ti. The shop manager.
   恭   Kung.[1] Respectful feeling, reverence, offer.
   喜   Hsi.[3] Joy, felicity.
   恭 喜   Kung-hsi. To wish you joy, happiness, etc.
   財   Ts'ai.[2] Wealth, riches.
   發 財   Fa-ts'ai. To get rich.
2. 福   Fu.[2] Happiness, well-being.
   托 福   T'o-fu. Dependent upon you for my well-being.
   生   Shêng.[1] Produce, life, living, a living.
   意   I.[4] Idea, wish, intention.
   生 意   Shêng-i. Business, occupation.

3. 綢   Ch'ou.[2] Manufactured silk.

4. 次   Tz'u.[4] Inferior, second-rate, etc., next.

5. 尺   Ch'ih.[3] A foot of linear measure.

6. S. Ch'ou tzu shih lun
　　　ch'ih mai ti, ch'a
　　　yeh shih lun chin,
　　　hsin fêng shih lun
　　　ko mai ti.

6. Silk is sold by the foot
　　tea by the poun
　　and envelopes by th
　　piece.

7. C. Ling chiao, ling
　　　chiao. Jang wo
　　　k'an chi yang
　　　ch'ou tzu pa.

7. Thank you for your in
　　formation. Let m
　　see a few samples o
　　silk.

8. S. Chê ko ch'ou tzu
　　　ting hao, ts'ai
　　　liao nai chiu, yeh
　　　pu tiao shai.

8. This is excellent silk
　　the material is dur
　　able and of fast dye

" Shai "—colour, also pronounced " sê " or " sei ".

9. C. To shao ch'ien i
　　　ch'ih.

9. How much is it a foot

10. S. Ch'i mao ch'ien i
　　　ch'ih.

10. Seventy cents a foot.

11. C. Wei mien shao wei
　　　kuei la i tie'rh.
　　　Hai yu pi chê ko
　　　chien i tie'rh ti
　　　(p'ien i i tie'rh ti)
　　　mei yu.

11. But that is a trifle dear
　　Have you anythin
　　a little cheaper?

" Wei mien shao wei ", bookish rather, unavoidably a little,
courteous phrase designed to save the vendor's face.

12. S. Yu shih yu. K'o
　　　shih pieh wang
　　　la, " I fên chia
　　　ch'ien i fên huo ".

12. Yes we have. Bu
　　don't forget " Th
　　quality of the good
　　depends upon th
　　price you pay ".

" Pieh "—short for " pu yao "—do not.
" I fên chia ch'ien i fên huo "—one of China's innumerable pr
verbs; a chapter of the popular ones follows (see Dialogue 38).

6. 茶   Ch'a.² Tea.
    茶葉   Ch'a² yeh.⁴ Tea leaves (dried).
    信   Hsin.⁴ Letter, news, faith, believe.
    封   Fêng.¹ Classifier of letters, cover, seal, envelope.
    信封   Hsin-fêng. Envelope.
    各   Ko.⁴ Each, every, individual.
7. 領   Ling.³ Receive, lead.
    教   Chiao.¹ Instruction, teaching, to teach.

8. 材   Ts'ai.² Materials, material (cloth, silk, etc.).
    料   Liao.⁴ Materials.
    耐   Nai.⁴ Endure, bear.
    久   Chiu.³ Old, long time.
    耐久   Nai-chiu. Durable.

11. 未   Wei.⁴ Not yet.
    免   Mien.³ Avoid, remit, avoidable.
    稍   Shao.¹ Somewhat, slight.
    微   Wei.¹ Small, minute, slight.
    便   P'ien.² Cheap.
    宜   I.² Right, suits, fits.
    便宜   P'ien-i. Cheap, reasonable of price, advantageous to buyer.
12. 別   Pieh.² Do not, probably short for "pu yao".

13. *C.* Wo sui shih shê pu tê hua na mo to ti ch'ien, pu kuo chê ko ch'ou tzu ti ts'ai liao, kên yen shai tou hên hao, kei wo liang i chang wu pa.

13. Although I really cannot afford to spend so much money, the material and the colour of this silk is so fine, that I will take fifteen feet (lit. measure for me fifteen feet).

" Shê pu tê "—let go cannot get, can't spend (that much).
" Liang "—to measure, used of purchasing lengths of cloth, etc.
" Wu " is five and refers to " feet "; " chang "—ten feet; " ch'ih " —foot; " ts'un "—inch.

14. *S.* Ts'ai fêng tso hao la, t'ai t'ai ch'uan shang shen, i ting shih hên hao k'an ti.

14. After the tailor has made it up, and you put it on, it will certainly look fine.

" Ts'ai fang "—cutting out shop—tailor—is sometimes used for " ts'ai fêng ", " fêng " being " to sew ".

15. *C.* Kuei shang yu to shao jên.

15. How many assistants have you?

" Kuei shang "—lit. " on the counter ", but meaning is " in your store ".

16. *S.* Yu êrh shih to, tou shih lan ti.

16. Over twenty, but all lazy.

17. *S.* (*to assistant*). Na ch'ih lai, liang i liang chê ko ch'ou tzu.

17. Bring the rule and measure this silk.

18. *C.* Ni yu mei yu tso wên chang ti ts'ai liao.

18. Have you any material suitable for mosquito curtains?

19. *S.* Yu na, shang, chung, hsia, san têng tou yu. T'ai t'ai hsi huan na i chung ni.

19. Yes, we have three grades, top, medium and lower. Which kind would you like to see?

13. 捨　　　Shê.³　Let go, relinquish.
　　捨不得　Shê-pu-tê.　Can't afford, etc., unwilling to part with.
　　花　　　Hua.¹　To spend, flower.
　　丈　　　Chang.⁴　Measure of length, distance, etc., equal to ten English feet.
　　量　　　Liang.²　To measure, consider.
　　雖　　　Sui.²　Although.

14. 裁　　　Ts'ai.²　To cut, to cut out, plan.
　　裁縫　　Ts'ai-fêng.　The tailor.
　　穿　　　Ch'uan.¹　To wear, put on.

16. 懶　　　Lan.³　Lazy, slack.

18. 蚊　　　Wên.²　Mosquito.
　　帳　　　Chang.⁴　Curtain, net for bed.
　　蚊帳　　Wên-chang.　Mosquito-net.

20. *C.* K'an k'an chung têng ti pa. Chê ko ts'ai liao yeh k'o i tso lien tzu ma.

20. I will look at the medium grade. Is this material suitable for curtaïns?

21. *S.* Fên liang ch'ing la i tie'rh. Tsai chung i tie'rh ti ts'ai liao hao.

21. The material is a little light for that. A little heavier material would be advisable (good).

22. *C.* Wo hai yao chi chang nai shih i tie'rh ti, tso p'u kai.

22. I also want several yards of somewhat stronger (cloth) to make bedding.

" P'u kai "—spread, cover, so bedding.

23. *S.* Na tao hao pan. Wo-mên yeh yu hên chieh shih ti pu, tso ju tzu hên ho shih.

23. That we can easily manage. We also have some very strong cloth which is suitable for mattresses.

24. *C.* Chiao wo k'an k'an pa. K'o shih ni mên k'uai yao kuan tien mên, pu shih ma.

24. Let me see it. But you will be closing shortly won't you?

25. *S.* Na mei kuan hsi. Kuan la tien mên, hai tê ch'ing suan tang t'ien ti chang.

25. That doesn't matter. When the shop is closed, we have still the day's accounts to do.

" Ch'ing suan "—clearly reckon.
" Tang t'ien "—that particular day, the same day. Note this special use of " tang ".

20. 簾　　　Lien-²(tzu). Curtain.

21. 分量　　Fên-liang. Weight.
　　輕　　　Ch'ing.¹ Light.

22. 鋪　　　P'u.¹ To spread.
　　蓋　　　Kai.⁴ To cover, build.
　　鋪蓋　　P'u-kai. Bedding (lit. cover and spread)

23. 結　　　Chieh.¹ Solid, strong, reliable, real.
　　實　　　Shih.² Solid, strong, reliable, real.
　　褥　　　Ju.⁴ Mattress.

25. 關　　　Kuan.¹ Concern, involve.
　　係　　　Hsi.⁴ Connected with, concern, involve.
　　關係　　Kuan-hsi. Concern.
　　賬　　　Chang.⁴ Account, bill.

DIALOGUE No. 20

Shopping at the Shoe Shop

Shopkeeper, *S*.   Customer, *C*.

1. *C*. Yao i shuang hsieh.
" I shuang "—a pair, also " i tui ".

1. I want a pair of shoes.

2. *S*. Ch'ing tso. Yao ti shih chi hao.

2. Please take a seat. What size do you want?

3. *C*. Ta kai shih pa hao.

3. Probably size eight.

4. *S*. Hsien shêng yao p'i hsieh, hai shih pu hsieh ni.

4. Do you want leather or cloth shoes?

5. *C*. Yao p'i hsieh. Ch'uan pu hsieh pu nêng tang ni shui.

5. I want leather shoes. Cloth shoes don't resist mud and water (so well).

6. *S*. Pu ts'o. K'o shih tsai chia li hsien cho, ch'uan pu hsieh shih hên shu fu ti.

6. Correct. But cloth shoes are very comfortable when you are at leisure at home.

" Hsien cho "—the " cho " is a participle, indicating continuation of the action " while you are at leisure ", " resting ".

7. *C*. Hsien pa p'i hsieh na lai, shih i shih pa.

7. Bring (some) leather shoes first, for me to try on.

8. *S*. Chê i shuang, wo k'an ta hsiao ho shih.

8. I should think this pair is right for size.

" Ta-hsiao "—big-small, so " size ", another illustration of the way abstract nouns are formed.

9. *C*. T'ai chin. Tsai shih i shuang ta i tie'rh ti.

9. This is too tight. Let me try a little larger pair.

VOCABULARY OF DIALOGUE No. 20

1. 雙   Shuang.¹ A pair, double, both.
   鞋   Hsieh.² Shoes, slippers.

2. 號   Hao.⁴ Mark, sign.

4. 皮   P'i.² Leather, skin.

5. 泥   Ni.² Mud, slush.
   擋   Tang.³ To resist.
   閒   Hsien.² At ease, leisure.
6. 舒   Shu.¹ Comfortable, at ease.
   服   Fu.² Accord with.
   舒服   Shu-fu. At one's ease, comfortable.

8. 大小   Ta-hsiao. Size.

9. 緊   Chin.³ Tight, restricted, important.

10. *S.* Hao.   Chê shuang
      chêng ho shih.
      Shu fu pu shu fu.

10. Very good. This pair
      is just right. Are the
      shoes comfortable ?

" Chèng ho shih "—just according to style.

11. *C.* Shu fu. Wo chiu
      na chê i shuang.
      Tsai na'erh k'o i
      mai ling tzu, ling
      tai ho mao tzu.

11. Yes, comfortable. I
      will take this pair.
      Where can one buy
      collars, ties and hats ?

12. *S.* Tsai tui mie'rh.
      Hsing Lung Chi
      shang tien.

12. Across the way, at
      the Hsing Lung Chi
      store.

13. *C.* Ni nêng kou pa
      chê shuang hsieh,
      sung tao wo ti
      chia li ch'ü ma.

13. Can you send the shoes
      to my home ?

14. *S.* Hsing. Hsien shêng
      fu shang tsai
      na'rh.

14. Certainly, what is your
      address ?

" Fu shang "—a polite term for " residence ".

15. *C.* Shang Ma Chieh,
      ssu shih liu hao.

15. No. 46 Shang Ma
      Chieh.

16. *S.* Na pu yüan. Wo
      chiu ta fa i ko
      huo chi, kei hsien
      shêng sung ch'ü.

16. That is not far. I will
      send one of the assist-
      ants with them.

" Ta fa "—used of sending *persons*. " Fa " alone used of sending
things. " Sung " means to escort a person or send things for a
person.

17. *C.* Chiao t'a tso yang
      ch'ê, wo kei t'a
      k'ai ch'ê fei.

17. Tell him to take a rick-
      shaw. I will give
      him his expenses.

" Ch'ê fei "—used of travelling expenses when a conveyance is
used.

10. 正   Chêng.⁴ Just, exactly, correct.

11. 領   Ling.³ Collar.
    帶   Tai.⁴ Girdle, belt, tie, tape.
    帽   Mao.⁴ Hat, cap.

12. 興   Hsing.¹ Rise, prosper.
    隆   Lung.² Eminent, abundant.
    記   Chi.⁴ Sign, record.

16. 遠   Yüan.³ Distant.
    打   Ta.³ An auxiliary verb denoting action.
    發   Fa.¹ To send, transmit.
    打發   Ta-fa. To send a man.
    夥   Huo.³ Assistant, band, company.
    計   Chi.⁴ To reckon, calculate.
    夥計   Huo-chi. Shop assistant, apprentice.

17. 費   Fei.⁴ Expenses, what is spent.
    車費   Ch'ê-fei. Travelling expenses (lit. cart
                        expense).

18. S. Pu pi. Kei t'a chi   18. There is no necessity to
ko chiu ch'ien   do that. Give him
chiu tê la.   a little wine money
                                   (tip), that will be all
                                   right.

" Chiu ch'ien "—wine money, tip. The more scrupulous use " ch'a shui ch'ien "—tea-water money.

18. 必   Pi.⁴ Necessary, must.
    酒錢   Chiu-ch'ien. Wine money, a pourboire, tip.

DIALOGUE No. 21

Domestic Conversation on Lighting, Heating, etc.

Master, *M*.   Servant, *S*.

1. *M*. Ni k'an i k'an chê ko ti t'an, kan ching pu kan ching.

1. Look at this carpet, is it clean?

2. *S*. Chê wu tzu t'ai an, wo k'an pu ta ch'ing ch'u.

2. This room is too dark, I can't see very clearly.

Note that " pu ", the negative, follows the main verb when qualified by an adverb.

3. *M*. Pa têng tien shang, chiu k'an tê ch'ing ch'u la.

3. Light the lamp, and then you will be able to see clearly.

4. *S*. Chê i chan têng li mei yu yu, tien pu liang.

4. There is no oil in this lamp, it can't give much light.

5. *M*. Chia li mei yu an tien têng, shih tsai k'o hsi.

5. What a pity we haven't fitted electric light in the house.

6. *S*. Pu yao chin. Wo chiu tien i chih la chu.

6. Never mind, I will light a candle.

7. *M*. Yu yang huo mei yu.

7. Have you any matches?

VOCABULARY OF DIALOGUE No. 21

1. 毯   T'an.³ Carpet, rug.

2. 暗   An, ngan.⁴ Dark, secret.

3. 點   Tien.³ To ignite, to light, as lamps, fires, etc.

    燈   Têng.¹ Lamp.

4. 盞   Chan.³ Classifier of lamps.

    油   Yu.² Oil.

    亮   Liang.⁴ Bright, light.

5. 安   An, ngan.¹ ⁴ To fix, place.

    電   Tien.⁴ Electricity, lightning.

6. 要   Yao.⁴ Important. (Same word as for "want", etc.)

    緊   Chin.³ Important. (Same word as for "tight".)

    要緊   Yao-chin. Important.

    枝   Chih.¹ Classifier of candles, pens, etc., branch.

    蠟   La.⁴ Wax.

    燭   Chu.² Candle.

7. 洋火   Yang-huo. Matches (foreign fire).

8. *S.* Wo hsiang k'ou tai li yu i ho, k'o shih chao pu cho la.

8. I thought I had a box in my pocket, but I can't find it.

9. *M.* Na chiu mei yu fa tzu.

9. Then there is nothing we can do.

" Mei yu fa tzu "—a very common expression of despair, equal to " There is nothing we can do about it ".

10. *S.* Wo chiu pa ti t'an na tao wai pie'rh ch'ü, tou i tou.

10. I will take the carpet outside and shake it.

11. *M.* Hao, wo chiu kei ni pang mang, pa t'an tzu chüan ch'i lai. (*or*) (tieh ch'i lai).

11. Good, I will help you to roll up the carpet.

12. *S.* Hsien tsai t'ien ch'i liang, chia li ying tang shêng huo.

12. It is getting cool now, we ought to light fires in the house.

13. *M.* Yuan tzu li yu t'an (mei) mo yu.

13. Is there any coal in the yard ?

14. *S.* I tie'rh yeh mei yu, chin nien hai mei yu mai la.

14. None at all, we haven't bought any this year, yet.

" I tie'rh yeh mei yu ". " Yeh " in this position adds great strength to the negative.

15. *M.* Ch'u fang yu ch'ai huo mei yu.

15. Is there any firewood in the kitchen ?

16. *S.* Yu. Wo chiu fang tsai huo lu li ch'ü tien.

16. Yes. I will put some in the stove and light it.

17. *M.* Mei yu yang huo, tsên yang pan ni.

17. But how shall we manage without matches ?

8. 袋　　Tai.⁴ Bag, pouch.
　口袋　K'ou-tai. Pocket, bag, sack.
　找　　Chao.³ To look for, seek.

10. 抖　　Tou.³ To shake, shudder.

11. 捲　　Chüan.³ To roll up, a roll.
　疊　　Tieh.² To fold up, a fold.

12. 涼　　Liang.² Cool, chilly.
　應　　Ying.¹ Ought.
　應當　Ying-tang. Ought.
　生　　Shêng.¹ To produce, to light a fire.
13. 炭　　T'an.⁴ Coal.
　煤　　Mei.² Coal.

15. 柴　　Ch'ai.² Firewood, fuel.
　柴火　Ch'ai-huo. Firewood.
16. 爐　　Lu. Lou.² Stove, brazier.

18. *S.* Wo shang ko pi jên chia ch'ü, chieh ch'ü.

18. I will go to our next-door neighbours and borrow from them.

" Ko pi jên chia "—the people on the other side of the partition or wall, so neighbours, close ones.

19. *M.* K'uai ch'ü pa. Wo shên shang chüeh tê lêng. I hui lai chiu shêng huo pa.

19. Go without delay. I feel cold. Light the fire as soon as you come back.

" I hui lai, chiu . . ."—" as soon as you come back, then . . .".

20. *S.* T'ai yang k'uai hsia ch'ü ti shih hou, jên jên tou chüeh tê lêng.

20. Just before sun-down everybody feels cold.

21. *M.* Ni k'an na kuei tzu li mien yu jung t'an, na ch'u liang ch'uang lai.

21. In the cupboard (wardrobe) there you will find some blankets. Take out a couple.

22. *S.* Hsien shêng t'ang i t'ang; to kai shang i tie'rh. Tsai to ho k'ai shui, ch'u i tie'rh han. Kuo liang t'ien chiu hao la.

22. Lie down sir with some extra covers. Then drink lots of hot water to induce perspiration. (And you will be all right again in a few days (lit. two days).

23. *M.* K'ai k'ai na ko ch'ou t'i. Li pie'rh yu fa han yao. Wo ch'ih san liang k'o. Tsai pa têng mieh la, wo yao shui chiao.

23. Open that drawer. There is some medicine in it to induce perspiration. I will take two or three tablets. Then put out the lamp, I want to sleep.

18. 隔　　　　Ko.² Partition.
　　壁　　　　Pi.⁴ Screen, partition wall.
　　隔壁人家Ko-pi-jên-chia. Neighbours.

19. 覺　　　　Chüeh. Chiao.² Feel, be conscious of.
　　冷　　　　Lêng.³ Cold.

20. 陽　　　　Yang.² The sun, male principle, south.

21. 櫃　　　　Kuei.⁴ Wardrobe, cupboard.
　　牀　　　　Ch'uang.² Bed, classifier of blankets, etc.
　　絨　　　　Jung.² Wool, woollen.
　　絨　毯　　Jung-t'an. Blanket, rug.
22. 躺　　　　T'ang.³ To recline, lie down.
　　汗　　　　Han.⁴ Perspiration.
　　出　汗　　Ch'u-han. To perspire.
　　顆　　　　K'o.¹ Classifier of pills, seeds, pearls, etc.

23. 抽　　　　Ch'ou.¹ To draw out.
　　屜　　　　T'i.⁴ Drawer, in a table, etc.
　　抽　屜　　Ch'ou-t'i. Drawer.
　　滅　　　　Mieh.⁴ To put out, as a lamp, candle, etc.
　　藥　　　　Yao.⁴ Yo.⁴ Medicine.
　　葯　　　　Ditto　　　Ditto.
　　睡　　　　Shui.⁴ To sleep.

DIALOGUE No. 22

Discussion between Master (*M*) and Servant (*S*) on some personal needs such as Washing, Waking, Wages, etc.

1. *M.* Na jê shui lai, wo yao hsi lien.

1. Bring me some hot water to wash my face.

2. *S.* Hsien shêng pu yao hsi tsao ma.

2. Don't you want to have a bath?

3. *M.* K'ung p'a jê shui pu kou hsi tsao.

3. I am afraid there will not be enough hot water for a bath.

4. *S.* Yeh kou la. Shui hên jê, t'ien tien lêng shui, chiu pu ta li.

4. Just about enough. The water is very hot, and if a little cold is added, it should be about enough.

"Yeh", we saw in the last dialogue, strengthens the negative it precedes; here we see how it modifies the sense of a positive expression; *e.g.*, "enough", just enough, no surplus.

5. *M.* K'o shih wo yeh tê kua lien, yung lêng shui pu hsing.

5. But I must shave as well, and cold water won't do for that.

6. *S.* Hsien shêng k'o la ma. Wo pa i pei liang k'ai shui, na tao lou shang ch'ü la.

6. Are you thirsty sir. I have taken a glass of cold boiled water upstairs.

The "la" at the end of the sentence marks the whole as being in the past tense.

VOCABULARY OF DIALOGUE No. 22

1. 熱   Jê.[4] Hot.
   洗   Hsi.[3] To wash.
   臉   Lien.[3] The face, countenance.
2. 澡   Tsao.[3] To bathe.
   洗澡   Hsi-tsao. To take a bath.

4. 添   T'ien.[1] To add to, increase.

5. 刮   Kua.[1] To scrape, to shave.
   刮臉   Kua-lien. To shave the face.

6. 凉開水 Liang-k'ai-shui. Cold boiled water.

7. *M.* Ming t'ien wo yao
tsao tsao ti ch'i
lai. Ni wu tien
chung lai chiao
wo.

7. I want to get up very
early to-morrow
Come and call me a
five o'clock.

The duplication of the adverb " tsao " intensifies the meaning a
" very early ".

8. *S.* Wo k'an hsien shêng
lei la, hai shih
tsao tien shui ti
hao.

8. I can see that you ar
tired sir. You wil
do well to get to bee
a little early.

9. *M.* Wo ming t'ien ch'i
lai ti shih hou,
yao kei wo sung
wên shui hsi shou.

9. Bring me some warn
water to wash m
hands when I get u
to-morrow.

10. *M.* (*cont.*). Tso t'ien
ni pa ch'uang mei
yu p'u hao, wo
mei yu shui hao
chiao.

10. You did not make th
bed properly yester
day. I did not slee
very well.

11. *S.* Tui pu ch'i hsien
shêng. Tso t'ien
shih ch'ing t'ai
to, mang pu kuo
lai.

11. I am sorry sir. Ther
was too much t
do yesterday, an
I couldn't overtak
the work.

" Tui pu ch'i "—match not rise, I have not done what the circum
stances called for; apologies !
" Mang pu kuo lai "—busy not get round, too much to do.

12. *M.* Yao shih ni shih
ch'ing t'ai to, kan
pu kuo lai ti shih
hou, wo chiu kai
kei ni chao i ko
pang mang ti.

12. If you have too muc
to do, and cannot d
everything, I mus
get someone to hel

8. 累　　　Lei.⁴ Fatigued, tired.
　 睡　　　Shui.⁴ To sleep, slumber.
　 睡覺　　Shui-chiao. To sleep.

9. 溫　　　Wên.¹ Warm, mild, to warm up.
　 手　　　Shou.³ Hand, hands.

10. 鋪　　　P'u.¹ To spread, or make a bed.

11. 對不起 Tui-pu-ch'i. To offend, apologise.

13. *S.* Chiao hsien shêng fei hsin. Pu kuo hai yu i chien shih ch'ing ho hsien shêng shuo.

13. Many thanks (lit. I have caused you to expend thought) But there is another matter on which I must speak to you.

" Chiao . . . fei hsin "—cause . . . expend heart; thank you !

14. *M.* Shih shih mo shih ch'ing, ni shuo pa.

14. Tell me what it is.

15. *S.* Hsien tsai ch'êng li t'ou shêng huo ch'êng tu t'ai kao, kuo jih tzu hên nan.

15. The standard of living in the city is so high that I find it difficult to live.

" Shêng huo "—life, living, conditions of life.
" Kuo jih tzu "—to pass the days; " living " in the sense of " to get a living ".
" Chêng tu "—standard. " Piao chun " is also used.

16. *M.* Ni i ko yüeh chêng to shao ch'ien.

16. How much do you earn a month ?

17. *S.* Pa k'uai ch'ien i ko yüeh, pu kou yung.

17. Eight dollars. It isn' enough.

18. *M.* Na mo, wo chiu kei ni chia san k'uai ch'ien i ko yüeh, hsing pu hsing.

18. Then I will give you a rise of three dollar a month. Will that do ?

19. *S.* Mien ch'iang. Hsieh hsieh.

19. I must make it do Thanks.

5. 城   Ch'êng.² The city.

活   Huo.² Living, livelihood, lively.

生活   Shêng-huo. One's life, livelihood, etc.

程   Ch'êng.² Capacity.

度   Tu.⁴ Standard.

程度   Ch'êng-tu. Capacity, standard.

生活程度 Shêng - huo - ch'êng - tu. The standard of
          living.

日   Jih.⁴ Day, the sun.

過日子 Kuo-jih-tzu. To live, to pass one's days.

難   Nan.² Difficult.

6. 掙   Chêng.⁴ To earn.

9. 强   Chi'ang. Make an effort.

DIALOGUE No. 23

The Week's Work in the House

Master or Mistress, *M*.   Servant, *S*.

1. *M*. Wo chiu pa ni t'ien   1. I will now tell yo
   t'ien, ying tang   about each day'
   pan ti shih, shuo   chores. On Monday
   kei ni t'ing.   you must do th
   Mei li pai i yao hsi   washing (laundry).
   i fu.

" T'ien t'ien "—day by day. " Mei t'ien " is also in common us
Notice " mei li pai ". " i, êrh, san, etc.", for the days of the wee
which begins with Monday. Sunday is " Li pai jih ", or " t'ien
or " Hsing ch'i jih " (" t'ien ").

2. *S*. Pa pu kan ching ti   2. Couldn't we send th
   i fu, sung tao hsi   dirty linen to th
   i tien ch'ü, hsing   laundry ?
   pu hsing.

3. *M*. Chiao hsi i tien hsi   3. To send the dirty line
   i fu, pu shang   to the laundry
   suan. Kan ching   uneconomical. F
   ti i fu sung hui   when the clean ga
   lai ti shih hou,   ments come bac
   ch'üan shih k'u   they are full of hole
   lung.

4. *S*. Na mo, chiao ts'ai   4. Then you have to g
   fêng pu i pu.   the tailor to pat
                            them.

5. *M*. Shih ti. Ni k'an   5. That is so. Look
   chê i chien han   this shirt, torn in t
   shan, ch'ê ti ti   many places alt
   fang t'ai to.   gether.

VOCABULARY OF DIALOGUE No. 23

1. 天天   T'ien-t'ien. Daily, every day.
   禮   Li.³ Worship, rite, ceremony.
   拜   Pai.⁴ Worship, revere.
   禮拜   Li-pai. Worship, the week, days of the week.
   每   Mei.³ Each, every.
   衣服   I¹-fu. Clothes.

2. 店   Tien.⁴ An inn, used of laundries.

3. 窟   K'u.¹ Hole, cave.
   窿   Lung.³ Hole, cave.

4. 補   Pu.³ To patch, a patch, repair, tonic.

5. 衫   Shan.¹ Shirt.
   汗衫   Han-shan. Shirt, vest.
   擇   Ch'ê.³ To tear, rend.

6. *S.* Hsi i tien ti kung jên, pu chia hsiao hsin, pu ju chia li hsi ti hao.

6. The workmen in th laundry don't tak special care, (so) w had better wash a home.

" Chia hsiao hsin "—add a little heart, pay careful attention; fo the " little heart " is intended to denote concentration.

7. *M.* Mei li pai êrh, yao shou shih chia li ti fang wu, lou shang ho lou hsia.

7. Every Tuesday yo must do all th rooms in the house upstairs and down.

8. *S.* Shou shih k'o fang ho hsi tsao fang, shih wo ti shih; shou shih fan t'ing ho ch'u fang, shih ch'u tzu ti shih, shih pu shih.

8. To clear up the guest room and the bath room is my job, bu the dining-room an the kitchen are th cook's responsibility aren't they?

" Ch'u tzu " more definitely means cook than " ta shih (ssu) fu " as " ch'u " is kitchen.

9. *M.* Ling wai hai yu shu fang ho ts'ê so, chê hsieh kuei shui pan ni.

9. In addition there ar the study and th W.C. To whom ar we to look for doin these?

" Ts'ê so "—w.c.; also " mao fang " or " mao ssu ".
" Kuei shui pan "—revert who do?

10. *S.* P'ing ch'ang chê hsieh tou shih k'an mên ti huo shih ma fu kan ti.

10. Normally these ar the responsibility o the gateman or th groom.

11. *M.* Wu lun shui kan, chia li tsung tê yao kan ching, chêng ch'i.

11. No matter who do the work, the hous must be kept clea and tidy.

" Wu lun "—not discuss, so, no matter.

6. 小心　　Hsiao-hsin.　Take care, cautious.

8. 廳　　　T'ing.[1]　Hall, court, room.

9. 厠　　　Ts'ê.[4]　Ssu.[4]　Private, closet.
　　所　　So.[3]　A place.
　　厠所　Ts'ê-so.　W.C.
　　歸　　Kuei.[1]　Revert to, to belong to.

10. 平　　　P'ing.[2]　Level, constant, ordinary.
　　常　　Ch'ang.[2]　Usual, ordinary, constant.
　　平常　P'ing-ch'ang.　Usual, ordinary.
　　看門的　K'an-mên-ti.　Gatekeeper.
　　馬夫　Ma-fu.　Groom.

12. *S.* T'ing hsien shêng ti fên fu.

12. **Your orders shall be obeyed.**

" T'ing "—hear, in the sense of obey; " fên fu "—orders.

13. *M.* Mei li pai liu yao ts'a yin tzu ho po li ch'i chü; ch'üan fang tzu ti ti t'an yao tou i tou, huo cho kua tsai yüan tzu li tan i tan.

13. **Every Saturday you should polish the silver and glass ware. Take up the carpets from all rooms and shake them, or hang them in the yard and beat them.**

14. *S.* Chê yang tso, hui ch'ên hên ta, chiao lin chü pu hsi huan.

14. **But that will cause a lot of dust, and the neighbours won't like it.**

" Chiao . . . pu hsi huan " (" chiao " makes the verb passive)—will be displeased.

15. *M.* Na pu hsiang kan, chia li tê chiang chiu wei shêng.

15. **That doesn't matter, we must observe hygiene in the home.**

" Pu hsiang kan "—not his concern, so does not matter.
" Chiang chiu " 4 means to be particular about.
Another " chiang 1 chiu 4 " means to put up with something which is not quite as one would like it. (See Dialogue 27, sentence 21.)

16. *S.* Ko jên yao chiang chiu ko jên ti wei shêng, tan shih k'o pu yao fang

16. **Every man ought to be particular about hygiene as far as he himself is concerned ;**

12. 吩   Fên.¹ Command, order.
    咐   Fu.⁴ Command, order.

13. 擦   Ts'a.¹ To rub, polish.
    銀   Yin.² Silver, money.
    玻   Po.¹ Glass.
    璃   Li.² Glassware.
    器   Ch'i.⁴ Vessel, utensil.
    撣   Tan.³, ⁴. To dust, beat.
    挂   Kua.⁴ Hang up.

14. 灰   Hui.¹ Ashes.
    塵   Ch'ên.² Dust, small particles.
    鄰   Lin.² Neighbouring, neighbour.
    居   Chü.¹ Dwell.
    鄰 居   Lin-chü. Neighbours.
    喜   Hsi.³ Pleasure, joy.
    歡   Huan.¹ Pleased, rejoice.
    喜 歡   Hsi-huan. To be pleased, rejoice.

15. 相   Hsiang.¹ Mutual.
    干   Kan.¹ Concern.
    不 相 干   Pu - hsiang - kan. **Of no concern, of no moment.**
    講   Chiang.³ To be particular, explain.
    究   Chiu.⁴ To analyse, examine, be particular about.
    講 究   Chiang-chiu. To be concerned or particular about.
    衛   Wei.⁴ To guard, protect.
    衛 生   Wei-shêng. Hygiene.

16. 妨   **Fang.¹** Hinder, obstruct.
    各   Ko.⁴ Each, every.

ai jên chia ti wei shêng.

but surely he must not make it more difficult (hinder) for others to observ hygiene.

" Jên chia "—others, other people.

17. *M.* Ni shuo ti yu li. Hsien tsai pu yao to shuo hua, kan ni ti ch'ü pa.

17. There is reason in what you say. But now less of this chatter, get on with your job.

" Kan ni ti "—mind your own business !

18. *S.* Hsien shêng kei wo i k'uai kan ching ti ma pu, wo chiu ch'ü mo cho tzu, i tzu, ching tzu, i ch'ieh ti chia chü.

18. If you will provide me with a clean duster, I will dust the table, chairs, mirror, and all the rest of the furniture.

19. *M.* Hao. Yeh pu yao wang la, mo chia chü ti shih hou, yao pa ch'uang hu k'ai k'ai, huan huan k'ung ch'i.

19. Good. And don't forget to open the windows when you are dusting, to change the air.

20. *S.* T'ien ch'i hao ti shih hou, k'o i chê yang pan; kua fêng hsia yü ti shih hou, k'ung p'a pu hsing.

20. In fine weather that can be done; but when it is windy or wet, I fear that would be inadvisable.

16. 碍   Ai⁴. Stand in the way, hinder.
　　妨碍   Fang-ai. Hindrance, obstruct.

17. 幹你的   Kan-ni-ti. Mind your own business.

18. 麻   Ma.² Hemp.
　　麻布   Ma-pu. Duster.
　　抹   Mo.³ To dust, polish, rub with the hand.
　　鏡   Ching.⁴ Mirror.
　　傢   Chia.¹ Tools, furniture.
　　具   Chü.⁴ Implements.
　　傢具   Chia-chü. Utensils, furniture.
　　切   Ch'ieh.⁴ All, everything.
　　一切   I-ch'ieh. Everything, all.

19. 換   Huan.⁴ To change, exchange.
　　空   K'ung.¹ Empty, vast, air.
　　氣   Ch'i.⁴ Atmosphere, air.
　　空氣   K'ung-ch'i. Air, fresh air.

20. 風   Fêng.¹ The wind.
　　颳   Kua.¹ To blow.
　　括風   Kua-fêng. Windy.
　　雨   Yü.³ Rain.
　　下雨   Hsia-yü. To rain, it is raining.

DIALOGUE No. 24

Talking Accounts with the Cook

Mistress, *M.*   Cook, *C.*

1. *M.* (*to cook*). Ta ssu fu lai suan chang.

1. Come and reckon accounts.

2. *C.* T'ai t'ai shao wei têng i têng, wo na chang pu ho ch'ien pi.

2. Just a moment, while I fetch the account book and pencil.

3. *M.* Chê ko (pên) li pai ni mai la shêm-mo tung-hsi, man man ti shuo pa.

3. What have you bought this week? Tell me slowly.

4. *C.* Chê ko li pai wo mai la yang jou, pai ts'ai, ti tan, hung lo po, chi tan, hua shêng.

4. I have bought this week mutton, cabbage, potatoes, carrots, eggs and peanuts.

" Hsing-ch'i " is the secular designation of the week, and is used also for the individual days of the week, with the numeral " i, êrh san, etc.," attached. The other common term for week is " li-pai " which lit. means worship, and was introduced by the Christian missionaries. The older Chinese designation of the days of the week consisted of names of planets.

5. *M.* Mu yu mai niu jou, ya tzu, yeh chi ma.

5. Haven't you bought any beef, ducks or pheasants?

VOCABULARY OF DIALOGUE No. 24

2. 簿   Pu.⁴ Account-book, note-book.
   帳簿   Chang-pu. Account-book.
   鉛   Ch'ien.¹ Lead, black-lead.
   鉛筆   Ch'ien-pi. Pencil.
3. 本   Pên.³ This, native, one's own.

4. 星   Hsing.¹ Star.
   期   Ch'i.² Date, period of time.
   星期   Hsing-ch'i. Week.
   白   Pai.² ⁴ White.
   白菜   Pai-ts'ai. Cabbage.
   地   Ti.⁴ The earth.
   蛋   Tan.⁴ Egg, egg-like.
   地蛋   Ti-tan. Potatoes.
   紅   Hung.² Red.
   蘿   Lo.² Carrots.
   蔔   Po.¹ Carrots.
   雞蛋   Chi-tan. Eggs, egg.
   花   Hua.¹ Flower.
   花生   Hua-shêng. Peanuts.

5. 牛肉   Niu-jou. Beef.
   鴨   Ya ¹ (tzu). Duck.
   野   Yeh.³ Wild, rustic.

6. *C.* Chê chi t'ien shih ch'ang shang mei yu chê hsieh tung hsi. Hou t'ien kan chi, yeh hsü yu mai ti.

6. There are none in the market these days. But the day after to-morrow is market day. There may be some then.

7. *M.* To jih mei yu ch'ih pai ts'ai hua, pu shih mei yu ni.

7. We have not eaten cauliflower for a long time. Surely there are some to be had?

8. *C.* Yu shih yu, k'o shih chia ch'ien t'ai ta, wo pu kan mai.

8. There are some, but the price is too high, I dare not buy.

9. *M.* Ta kai yin wei pu shih shih hou. Liu hsin, chia lo ti shih hou chiu mai.

9. Probably that is because it is not the season. Watch out, and when the price comes down, buy.

" Liu hsin "—take care.
" Chia lo "—falling prices. " Chia chang " is rising prices.

10. *C.* T'ai t'ai hsi huan ch'ih shêng ts'ai ma. Hsien tsai yu to yu p'ien i.

10. Do you like salads? They are plentiful and cheap just now.

" Yu to yu p'ien i ". " Yu . . . yu "—both . . . and.

11. *M.* Hsi huan ch'ih, k'o shih tê hsiao hsin, shêng ts'ai tsung tê hsien yung k'ai shui, hsi kuo, ts'ai kan ch'ih.

11. Yes, but you must be careful, salads should be washed in boiled water before one dare eat them.

" Ts'ai " in such phrases means " then " in a logical sense of sequence. Something must first be done, and " then " something else *can* happen.

6. 市   Shih.[4]   Market.
   場   Ch'ang.[2] Open place, square, market.
   市場   Shih-ch'ang. Market.
   集   Chi.[2] The fair.
   趕集   Kan-chi. To go to the fair, hold a fair.

7. 白荣花 Pai-ts'ai-hua. Cauliflower.

9. 時候   Shih-hou. Time, season.
   留   Liu.[2] To keep, hold.
   留心   Liu-hsin. Observe, notice, give attention
           to.
   落   Lo. Lao.[4] To come down, to fall, as
           prices, leaves.

10. 生   Shêng.[1] Raw, as opposed to cooked.
    生荣   Shêng-ts'ai. Salads, raw vegetables.
    又   Yu.[4] Both, again.

12. *C*. Chin t'ien wo shên shang pu shu-fu, fa shao, k'ung p'a shang la fêng la.

12. I am not very well to-day, I am feverish. I fear I have caught cold.

" Shang fêng ", wounded by the wind, so means catch cold. Other expressions for this are " chao liang ", or " shou fêng ".

13. *M*. Wo ch'ing tai-fu (i shêng) lai k'an i k'an, hao pu hao.

13. I will call a doctor to see what is the matter, shall I ?

" Tai fu ", a common designation of doctor; others are " I shêng ", " k'an ping ti hsien shêng ".

14. *C*. Pu yao ch'ing hsi i, ch'ing Chung kuo hsien shêng, kei wo k'ai fang tzu, chiu hsing.

14. Don't ask a western doctor. I will ask a Chinese doctor to write out a prescription.

15. *M*. K'o shih chang hai mei yu suan, t'ung kung hua la to shao ch'ien.

15. But we haven't taken the account yet. How much have you spent altogether ?

16. *C*. T'ung kung hua la shih i k'uai wu mao liu.

16. I have spent altogether eleven dollars and fifty-six cents.

17. *M*. K'ung p'a chê ko chang suan ts'o la, ni tsai suan suan.

17. I fear you have made a mistake in this account, try again.

18. *C*. Wo k'an mei yu suan ts'o. Wo hai shêng hsia liang k'uai ch'i.

18. I think it is right. I have a balance of two dollars seventy.

19. *M*. K'ung p'a ni nao ching pu ch'ing ch'u, wo k'an ni hai hsia ch'ien chiu mao.

19. I think your brain must not be quite clear, I think you are short ninety cents.

12. 舒服　　Shu-fu. Comfortable, happy, contented.
　　 燒　　 Shao.[1] Hot, feverish, heat.
　　 發燒　 Fa-shao. To be hot, have a fever.
　　 傷　　 Shang.[1] To injure, to catch (cold), be
　　　　　　　 injured.

13. 大　　　Ta.[4] Great, big.
　　 大夫　 Tai.[4] Doctor.
　　 醫　　 I.[1] To heal, cure.
　　 醫生　 I-shêng. Doctor.

14. 西醫　　Hsi-i. Western doctor.
　　 中國先生 Chung-kuo-hsien-shêng. Chinese doctor.
　　 方　　　Fang [1] (tzu). Prescription.
　　 開方子　K'ai-fang-tzu. Write a prescription, to
　　　　　　　 prescribe.

18. 剩　　　Shêng.[4] Remainder, left over.

19. 欠　　　Ch'ien.[4] To be short, to owe.
　　 腦　　 Nao.[3] The brain.
　　 腦經　 Nao-ching. Brain.

20. *C.* Ych hsü t'ai t'ai   20. Perhaps you are right.
    suan ti tui. Wo   My head is a little
    ti nao tzu chiu   bit fuzzy.
    shih hun i tie'rh.

20. 昏   Hun.[1]   Confused.

DIALOGUE No. 25

Travelling by Road

Between two friends, *A* and *B*

1. *A*. Ming t'ien wo yao ch'u mên.
1. To-morrow I intend to travel.

2. *B*. Hsien shêng shang na-êrh ch'ü.
2. Where are you thinking of going?

3. *A*. Ta suan shang P'u T'ien Ch'ih ch'ü, k'an i ko p'êng yu.
3. I plan to go to P'u T'ien Ch'ih, to look up one of my friends.

Note " k'an " in the sense of " call on " a person. Sometimes the expression " k'an-wang " is used, the " wang " being the word for expect, hope, etc., and so you get the idea of " going to inquire about ", much as we say " I am going to ' look up ' my friend ".

4. *B*. Hao, wo yüan i p'ei nin ch'ü, hsing pu hsing.
4. Good, I would like to accompany you — may I?

" P'ei " means to accompany, but is only used of " equals " in the social scale. A servant cannot use it to his master. If it were a servant speaking he would say " Wo ken hsien-shêng ch'ü ", *i.e.*, I will follow you.

5. *A*. Tan shih ni yao tai ni tzu chi tsai lu shang ch'ih ti tung hsi.
5. All right, provided you carry your own road rations. (Lit. but you ought to carry . . .)

6. *B*. Na pu ch'êng wên t'i, hsien-shêng chi tien chung ch'i shên.
6. That presents no difficulty, what time shall you start?

7. *A*. Tsai ch'ing tsao, t'ai yang kang shang lai ti shih hou, tung shên.
7. Very early, as soon as the sun rises, we will start.

VOCABULARY OF DIALOGUE No. 25

3. 打算   Ta-suan. To plan, propose, think of doing.
   普   P'u.³ Universal.
   池   Ch'ih.² Pool, pond.
   普天池 P'u-t'ien-ch'ih. The name of a place.

4. 陪   P'ei.² To accompany, act as companion, etc.

6. 題   T'i.² To mention, subject of discourse.
   問題   Wên-t'i. A question.
   不成問題 Pu-ch'êng-wên-t'i. That makes no question.
7. 太陽   T'ai-yang. The sun.
   剛   Kang.¹ Just now, just then.
   動身   Tung-shên. To move, start on a journey.
   起身   Ch'i-shên. To move, start on a journey.

8. *B*. Hsien shêng tso chiao ch'ê, hai shih ch'i shêng k'ou ni.

8. Are you going by cart (Peking cart) or riding?

Note the difference between " ch'i " and " tso ". The former means to ride astride, so is applicable to bicycle or horse riding. " Tso " is used of travelling by any vehicle which permits of " sitting " in the ordinary way.

9. *A*. Yeh pu tso chiao ch'ê, yeh pu ch'i ma, wo-mên pu hsing pa.

9. Neither by cart nor by horse, we will walk.

" Yeh pu . . . yeh pu "—neither . . . nor.

10. *B*. Na t'ai fei shih, tsêm-mo pu tso ch'i ch'ê ni.

10. But that is difficult, why don't you go by auto?

11. *A*. Tso kung kung ch'i ch'ê, pu shu fu, lu tao pu p'ing, tien p'o ti li-hai.

11. To go by omnibus is not comfortable, the road is rough and one gets badly jolted.

" Li hai " is a very common adverb indicating an extreme condition, much as we use " terribly " in colloquial speech.

12. *B*. P'u Tien Ch'ih li chê li to ma yüan.

12. How far is Pu Tien Ch'ih from here?

13. *A*. Ta yüeh shih wu li lu.

13. Probably about fifteen li.

" Ta yüeh " (yo) is generally used, of statements about figures, measurements, etc., as is " ta lüeh " (whereas " ta kai " may be applied to any condition where vague probability or generalities are implied). But this is not a hard and fast distinction.

14. *B*. Na tao pu yüan, pu hsing yeh k'o i.

14. That is not very far for sure, walking is possible.

8. 轎 Chiao.⁴ A sedan chair.

 轎車 Chiao-ch'ê. A mule-cart, Peking cart.

 騎 Ch'i.² To ride astride.

 牲 Shêng.¹ An animal, cattle.

 牲口 Shêng-k'ou. Animals in general, horses, mules, donkeys, camels, etc.

9. 步 Pu.⁴ A step, pace, on foot.

 步行 Pu-hsing. To walk, go on foot.

0. 費 Fei.⁴ To spend, waste.

 費事 Fei-shih. To spend oneself on something, difficult.

 汽車 Ch'i-ch'ê. Motor car (lit. vapour car).

1. 公 Kung.¹ Public, general, official.

 公共汽車 Kung-kung-ch'i-ch'ê. The omnibus.

 顛 Tien.¹ Upset, jolting, bumpy.

 簸 Po.⁴ Winnow. Po³. Used of the jolting movement.

 厲 Li.⁴ Sharp, severe, oppress.

 害 Hai.⁴ Hurt, injure.

 厲害 Li-hai. Extreme, terribly.

3. 約 Yüeh.¹ Agree, pledge, about.

 大約 Ta-yüeh. Roughly, about, of measurements.

15. *A.* K'o-i shih k'o-i, tan
    shih pi hsü tai i
    ko lêng jê shui
    p'ing tzu, chuang
    man liao k'ai shui
    ch'ü ho.

15. No, there is nothing
    against walking it,
    but it is necessary
    to carry a thermos
    flask full of boiled
    water to drink.

Note " k'o shih k'o-i ", where the verb " k'o-i " is duplicated with
the idea of modifying the strength of it. Here " it is just possible "
to walk, but there are conditions attached to walking it.

16. *B.* Na ko wo tao wang
    pu liao, hai yu
    shêm-mo kai tai
    ti ni.

16. That I shan't forget,
    ought one to take
    anything else?

" Pu liao " following a verb indicates impossibility of the verbal
action being carried into effect. It differs from " pu te ", used in
this way, in that the latter usually carries with it a sense of " oughtness " or " fitness ".

17. *A.* Yeh tai i ko yü san
    huo yü i, fu t'ien
    k'ên hsia yü.

17. Bring either an um-
    brella or a raincoat,
    in the heat it is likely
    to rain.

" K'ên " means willing, and so in colloquial speech tends to be
used in the sense of " prone to "; " disposed to ", etc.

18. *B.* Hsien-shêng yü liao
    tê hao, wo chao
    pan chiu shih la.

18. You exercise good fore-
    thought, I will carry
    out your orders (a
    politely humorous
    expression).

19. *A.* Wo - mên i ching
    p'ao la shih lai li
    lu, wo-mên tsai
    lü kuan t'ing i
    hui'êrh, hao pu
    hao.

19. We have walked about
    ten li, shall we stop
    at an inn for a while?

15. 必須   Pi-hsü.   Necessary, must.

17. 傘   San.³   Umbrella, parasol.

雨傘   Yü-san.   Umbrella.

雨衣   Yü-i.   Raincoat.

伏   Fu.²   The dog-days, great heat.

伏天   Fu-t'ien.   The height of summer.

肯   K'ên.³   Willing, prone to.

18 料   Liao.⁴   To calculate.

預料   Yü-liao.   Foresee, foresight.

照   Chao.⁴   According to, shine, photograph.

照辦   Chao-pan.   To act according to instructions.

9. 跑   P'ao.³   To run, also to walk (long distances).

旅   Lü.³   Travel, journey.

舘   Kuan.³   Hostel, hotel, etc.

旅舘   Lü-kuan.   Hotel, hostel.

停   T'ing.²   To halt, stop.

一會兒   I-hui-rh.   A while, a short time.

20. *B.* Chê t'iao lu shang ti lü tien pu tsêm-mo hao, tao pu ju tso tsai lu p'ang, hsieh i hui'êrh.

20. The inns on this stretch of road are not very good, let's sit by the roadside and rest awhile.

" Pu tsên-mo (tsêm-mo) hao ". The "tsêm-mo" has the sense of " very ", " much ", although its basic meaning is " how, why, what? ", etc.

21. *A.* T'ung i, wo - mên yeh k'o i ho i k'ou shui, ch'ih chi k'uai ping kan.

21. Agreed, we can also have a drink of water and munch a few biscuits.

" T'ung i ", lit. same meaning, so agreed.
" Ping kan ". Note how " kan ", dry, comes *after* the noun. So in " p'u-t'ao-kan ", which means raisins, lit. grapes dried.

22. *B.* Ai ! lao-hsien shêng tao P'u T'ien Ch'ih hai yu chi li lu.

22. Ai ! you old friend (teacher), how far is it to P'u T'ien Ch'ih?

" Lao ", old, an epithet of respect when addressed to strangers.

23. *A.* Pu yüan, hai yu wu liu li lu.

23. Not far, there is still about five or six li.

24. *B.* Ch'ien mie'rh ti lu hao tsou pu hao tsou.

24. Is the road good ahead ?

25. *A.* Hao tsou, pu kuo ts'un tzu wai pie'rh yu chi ko ni k'êng chiu shih la.

25. Good going, there are a few puddles outside the village, but that is all.

26. *B.* Ts'un tzu li pie'rh, yu fan kuan mei yu.

26. Is there a restaurant inside the village ?

20. 條   T'iao.² Length, classifier of long things.
    店   Tien.⁴ Inn.
    旁   P'ang.² Side.

21. 餅   Ping.³ Biscuit, cake.
    餅乾   Ping-kan. Biscuits.
    同   T'ung.² Together, with.

25. 村   Ts'un.¹ Village.
    坑   K'êng.¹ Pit-hollow.

26. 飯館   Fan-kuan. Eating-house, restaurant.

27. *A*. Mei yu hao ti, mai ti yeh pu kuo shih chia ch'ang pien fan.

27. Nothing very good they sell just ordin ary everyday food.

" Chia ch'ang pien fan ", frequently written up on the outside wal of a wayside inn (lit. home ordinary ready food).

28. *B*. Fan kuan, hao chao pu hao chao ni.

28. Is the restaurant eas to find?

29. *A*. Hao chao, i chin ts'un mên, tsai lu tung ti chiu shih la.

29. Easy to find, as soo as you enter the vil lage gate, it is on th east side of the road

" I chin . . . chiu "; the " i " has the sense of " as soon as " whe coupled with a verb followed by " chiu ".

30. *B*. Lao chia, lao chia.

30. Thanks, sorry to hav detained you.

" Lao chia ". " Lao " means to trouble, and " chia " mean chariot, which again is used as an appellation of honour. So " la chia " means " I have troubled you Sir ". It can therefore b appropriately used for the equivalent of our " Sorry to have trouble you ".

31. *A*. Mu yu shêm-mo, li tang ti.

31. That's nothing, th usual courtesy.

27. 家常便飯 Chia-ch'ang-pien-fan.   Everyday food, always ready.

DIALOGUE No. 26

Travelling by Train

Between two friends, *A* and *B*

1. *A*. Chê ko ch'ê shih
   wang Peiching
   k'ai ti ch'ê pu
   shih.

1. Is this the train for
   Peking?

2. *B*. Pu shih, chê shih
   wang Hankou
   k'ai ti ch'ê.

2. No, it is the train for
   Hankow.

3. *A*. Wang Peiching k'ai
   ti huo ch'ê, shih
   tsai na i ko yüeh
   t'ai ni.

3. On which platform is
   the train for Peking?

" Yüeh t'ai ", lit. moon terrace. I will hazard a guess that the
term arose from the fact that at some station or other in the early
days of railways in China the platform was of the crescent form, and
so the term " moon " came to be applied to all station platforms
whatever their form.

4. *B*. Shih ti san hao yüeh
   t'ai.

4. Platform No. 3.

5. *A*. Hsien-shêng yao ta
   na i têng ti p'iao.

5. Which class ticket do
   you want?

" Ta " is used instead of " mai ", to buy, for a number of things
including tickets.

6. *B*. Chê i t'ang shih
   k'uai ch'ê, hai
   shih man ch'ê ni.

6. Is this train express or
   slow?

Note that " t'ang " is a classifier of trains. It also means a
particular journey of a train.

7. *A*. Shih man ch'ê, k'o
   shih t'ou êrh têng
   tou yu.

7. It is slow, but it has
   both first and second
   class coaches.

VOCABULARY OF DIALOGUE No. 26

3. 火車   Huo-ch'ê.   Train (lit. fire-cart).
   月台   Yüeh-t'ai.   Platform.

4. 號   Hao.⁴   Number, designation.

5. 打   Ta.³   To book, as a ticket.
   票   P'iao.⁴   Ticket, voucher.

6. 趟   T'ang.⁴   Time, turn, track, classifier of
           trains.

8. *B.* Kua ti fan (ts'an) ch'ê mei yu.

8. Is there a restaurant car on it?

" Kua "—to hook on, a more descriptive expression than the neutral " yu "—is there?

9. *A.* Mei yu fan (ts'an) ch'ê, k'o shih yu ch'u fang.

9. No restaurant car, but a kitchen car.

10. *B.* Ch'ê shang nêng mai shêm-mo fan.

10. What food can one buy on the train?

11. *A.* Nêng mai niu ju p'ai, chi tzu t'ang, ch'ao chi tan têng têng.

11. Beef-steak, egg soup, omelette, etc.

" Têng, têng "—kinds, kinds, a good equivalent of etc.

12. *B.* K'o i, chao chiao fu kei wo pan tung hsi.

12. Good, get a porter to carry my luggage (things).

" K'u li ", lit. bitter strength—an apt description of a coolie's life is sometimes used. There are several suggested derivations of the word, in Hindi, Tamil and Turkish languages.

13. *A.* Pan hsing li yu i ting ti chia ch'ien ma.

13. Is there a fixed price for carrying baggage?

14. *B.* Liang ko t'ung tzu i chien shih ting chia, ling wai hai tê kei chi ko chiu ch'ien.

14. Two coppers a piece is the fixed price, but you will have to give a few coppers as a pourboire.

15. *A.* Na mo wo-mên shang ch'ê pa.

15. Well, let's get aboard the train.

16. *B.* I lu p'ing an.

16. A peaceful journey to you.

" I lu "—I, one, in the sense of " the whole ", a common use of the word.

8. 挂   Kua.⁴ To hook up, used of connecting
          coaches.

   餐   Ts'an.¹ To dine, a meal.

11. 排   P'ai.² Chop, steak, row, rank.
    牛肉排 Niu-ju-p'ai. Beef-steak.
    炒   Ch'ao.³ Fry, roast.
    炒雞蛋 Ch'ao-chi-tan. Scrambled eggs, omelette.

12. 脚   Chiao.³ Foot, leg, used for porters.
    脚夫   Chiao-fu. Porter, coolie.
    搬   Pan.¹ To move, carry from one place to
          another.

13. 行李   Hsing-li. Baggage.

14. 銅   T'ung.² Copper, copper coin, with " tzu ".
    酒錢   Chiu-ch'ien. Wine money, a tip.

16. 平   P'ing.² Peaceful, level, calm.
    安   An.¹ Peace.
    平安   P'ing-an. Peace, a Christian greeting.

17. *A.* T'i wo wên hou chia 17. My respectful inquiries
　　li pie'rh ti jên.　　　　　to your family.

" Wên hou " is used when sending inquiries or respects by means
of another.

18. *B.* Huo ch'ê shih chi 18. What time does the
　　tien chung tao　　　　train arrive in Pek-
　　Peiching.　　　　　　ing?

19. *A.* Na tê k'an lu shang 19. That all depends on
　　t'ung pu t'ung.　　　　whether the line is
　　　　　　　　　　　　clear.

" K'an " is look, see, etc., and so readily acquires the sense of
" it depends ".

20. *B.* Chê chi t'ien huo 20. These days there are
　　ch'ê hên to.　　　　　a good many goods-
　　　　　　　　　　　　trains on the line.

" Huo " is goods, and is in the fourth tone, thus distinguishing it
from " huo ", fire, in the third tone, which means the ordinary train.

21. *A.* K'o jên yeh shih pu 21. Passengers are numer-
　　shao.　　　　　　　　ous too.

" K'o " means traveller as well as guest.

22. *B.* K'an kuang ching, 22. It looks from the cir-
　　shih chü hsiang　　　cumstances as though
　　yao pien kêng.　　　　there is going to be a
　　　　　　　　　　　　change in the situa-
　　　　　　　　　　　　tion.

" K'an " here means it looks, it seems, etc.

23. *A.* Pu ts'o, yün ti tui 23. True, lots of troops are
　　wu, yeh shih to　　　being transported.
　　la.

17. 替   T'i.⁴ Instead of, for.
    問候   Wên-hou. To inquire after one's well-being.

19. 通   T'ung.¹ To pass through, clear, way, con-
            nection.

22. 光   Kuang.¹ Light.
    景   Ching.³ Circumstances, prospect.
    光景   Kuang-ching. Circumstances.
    局   Chü.² Position, plan.
    時局   Shih-chü. The situation.
    像   Hsiang.⁴ Like, image.
    變   Pien.⁴ To change, alter.
    更   Kêng.¹ Alter, change, more, etc.
    變更   Pien-kêng. To change.
23. 運   Yün.⁴ To transport, move, revolve, luck.
    隊   Tui.⁴ A company, as of soldiers.
    伍   Wu.³ Rank of five, military.
    隊伍   Tui-wu. Soldiers, military.

24. *B.* Hsien-shêng t'ing ti shêm-mo hsiao hsi (hsin wên).

24. What news have you heard?

25. *A.* Mei yu shih mo k'o k'ao ti hsiao hsi, pu kuo yao yen, tao pu shao.

25. I have no reliable news, but the air is full of rumours.

26. *B.* P'an wang tsai pu yao ta chan; lao pai hsing shih k'u chi la.

26. I hope there is not going to be fighting again; the country folk are in bitter straits.

27. *A.* Chün fa , pu kuan na hsieh, chih ta suan k'uo ch'ung tzu chi ti ti p'an.

27. The militarists pay no regard to that, they are solely concerned with the enlarging of their spheres of influence.

24. 消   Hsiao.[1] To disperse, used with the next for news.

    息   Hsi.[2] Breathe, interest, news.

    消息   Hsiao-hsi. News, information.

    新聞   Hsin-wen. News (lit. new hearing).

25   靠   K'ao.[4] Rely, reliable, dependable, trust.

    可靠   K'o-k'ao. Dependable, trustworthy.

    謠言   Yao.[3] Lies, false.

    謠言   Yao-ycn. Lies, rumours.

26. 盼   P'an.[4] Look for, hope.

    望   Wang.[4] Expect, look for, look at someone.

    盼望   P'an-wang. Hope, expect.

    戰   Chan.[4] Fight, war, alarmed.

    打戰   Ta-chan. To wage war.

    老百姓   Lao-pai-hsing. The common people (hundred surnames).

    極   Chi.[2] The extreme limit, sign of superlative.

    苦極了   K'u-chi-la. Severe suffering, in terrible plight.

27. 軍   Chün.[1] Army, military, forces.

    閥   Fa.[2] Rank, class.

    軍閥   Chün-fa. The militarists, military party.

    管   Kuan.[8] Control, concern, heed.

    不管   Pu-kuan. To be unconcerned, pay no heed.

    只   Chih.[3] Only, solely.

    擴   K'uo.[4] Expand, extend.

    充   Ch'ung.[1] To fill.

    擴充   K'uo-ch'ung. To expand and fill, aggrandisement.

    地盤   Ti-p'an. Sphere of influence, territory (lit. earth-plate).

28. *B.* Ai ya, ts'ai kuo ti shih T'ung Hsien, hai yu liang ko ch'ê chan, chiu tao la Peiching.

28. I say, the station we have just passed is T'ung Hsien, there are only two more stations before we arrive at Peking.

' Liang chan " is another way of expressing this.

29. *A.* Kên hsien-shêng t'an hua, shih chien pu chüeh tê kuo ti na mo k'uai.

29. The time has passed quickly. I have not noticed (the time) as we talked together.

80. *B.* Ling kuo chiao pu shao.

30. I have learned a lot from you.

31. *A.* Na êrh ti hua ni.

31. Nonsense.

28. 縣   Hsien.⁴ District of administration, county town.

  站 Chan.⁴ Station, post.

  車站 Ch'ê-chan. Railway station.

29. 談   T'an.² To talk, gossip.

  時間 Shih-chien. Time, duration.

DIALOGUE No. 27

Travelling by Steamer and Train

Between two friends, *A* and *B*

1. *A*. Chi tien chung k'ai ch'uan.

   1. At what hour does the steamer start?

2. *B*. T'ing shuo liu tien chung k'ai ch'uan.

   2. I hear (lit. have heard said) that it leaves at six o'clock.

3. *A*. Hsien tsai chi tien chung.

   3. What time is it now?

4. *B*. San tien pan chung.

   4. Half past three.

5. *A*. Na mo, shih hou hai tsao.

   5. Then it is still early.

" Shih-hou hai tsao ", lit. the time is still early.

6. *B*. Pu ts'o, tan shih k'ai ch'uan i ch'ien, wo yu hsieh shih ch'ing kan.

   6. Correct, but before the steamer sails I have a few things to do.

Note the position of " i ch'ien ", before. Like " i hou ", after, it always follows the phrase which it qualifies.

7. *A*. Ni ta la ch'uan p'iao mei yu.

   7. Have you booked your ticket for the boat?

8. *B*. Ta la p'iao, pu kuo hsing li hai mei yu shou shih hao la.

   8. I have bought my ticket, but my baggage is not yet ready.

Note " hao " in the sense of ready: " fan hao la mei yu "—is the food ready?

VOCABULARY OF DIALOGUE No. 27

1. 船　　　Ch'uan.[2]　Boat, ship.
　　開船　　K'ai-ch'uan.　The staiting of a steamer, depart.

9. *A.* Na mo yang, ni hsin
li tzu jan yu i
tie'rh chao chi.

9. In that case you are
naturally a bit anx-
ious.

You could say "ni chao chi", but "hsin li", in your heart, is more figurative.

10. *B.* Shih tê. Hsing
k'uei yu chi ko
p'êng yu pang
mang

10. Just so, but fortunately
I have a few friends
to help.

11. *A.* Hao. Hsien shêng
kan k'uai ch'ü
pan pa. Wo pu
tsai tan wu ni ti
kung fu.

11. Good. Hurry up and
get the job done. I
will not hinder you
any longer.

"Tan wu kung fu", lit. obstruct or prevent work, so hinder or delay anyone.

12. *B.* Tsa mên ch'uan
shang tsai chien.

12. Then we'll meet again
on the boat.

13. *A.* Tsai chien.

13. Till then, good-bye.

14. *B.* Hsien shêng yün
ch'uan pu yün
ch'uan.

14. Do you suffer from sea-
sickness?

15. *A.* T'ou chi t'ien, wo
chüeh tê pu hên
shu fu, tan shih
ch'uan shang
kuan la, chiu pu
chüeh tê tsên
yang.

15. During the first few
days I feel a little
bit uncomfortable,
but after one has got
accustomed to the
boat, I don't feel it
very much.

"Kuan la"—to be accustomed to, get used to, a very useful phrase.

16. *B.* Hsien shêng tao kuo
wai kuo mo yu.

16. Have you travelled
abroad?

17. *A.* Ying Kuo, Fa Kuo,
Mei Kuo, wo tou
tao kuo.

17. I have been in England,
France and America.

9. 急   Chi.² Haste, urgent.
   着   Cho. Chao.² Attain to.
   着急 Cho-chi. To be bothered, in haste.

10. 幸   Hsing.⁴ Felicitous, fortunate.
   虧   K'uei.¹ Lucky, luckily.
   幸虧 Hsing-k'uei. Fortunately.

11. 趕快 Kan-k'uai. Quickly, speedily.

14. 暈   Yün.⁴ Dizzy.
   暈船 Yün-ch'uan. To be seasick, mal-de-mer.

15. 慣   Kuan.⁴ To be accustomed to.

17. 法國 Fa⁴-kuo.² France.
   美   Mei.³ Beautiful, admirable.
   美國 Mei-kuo. U.S.A., America.

18. *B*. Hsien shêng hui shuo Fa Kuo hua ma.

18. Can you speak French ?

19. *A*. Hui shuo chi chü t'ung ch'ang ti hua.

19. I can speak just a few sentences on every-day affairs.

20. *B*. Fu na pie'rh ti shui t'u pu fu.

20. Did the climate over there suit you ?

" Fu . . . shui t'u pu fu ", lit. agree . . . water earth not agree. Does the climate agree with you ?

21. *A*. Chiang chiu pa.

21. Just so-so.

22. *B*. Na pie'rh ti t'ien ch'i, tsê mo yang.

22. What is the weather like over there ?

23. *A*. Hsia t'ien pu hsiang Chung Kuo jê, tung t'ien pu hsiang Chung Kuo lêng.

23. It is not so hot as in China during the Summer, and not quite so cold in the Winter.

" Pu hsiang "—not like, not as.

24. *B*. Hsien shêng yeh ch'ih tê kuan Fa Kuo fan ma.

24. And did you get used to French food ?

25. *A*. Fa Kuo fan mei yu Chung Kuo fan ti tzu wei ; pu kuo ch'ih shang chi t'ien, yeh chiu tui fu.

25. French food is not so tasty as Chinese, but after trying it for a few days, it is not too bad.

Note this way of expressing comparison : " mei yu . . . (ti) tzu wei ", lit. has not Chinese food's flavour.

" Tui fu ", without any other qualifying word, means " just satis-factory ", nothing to enthuse about.

26. *B*. Ai ya, chin t'ien kua ta fêng, ch'uan shang pu ta wên tang.

26. My ! what a wind is blowing to-day. It is not very steady aboard.

20. 服水土　Fu-shui-t'u.　To find the climate agreeable (lit. agree-water-earth).

21. 將就　Chiang[1]-chiu.[4]　Can put up with it.　(See Note after sentence 15, Dialogue 23.)

23. 夏　Hsia.[4]　Summer (usually followed by " t'ien ").

　　冬　Tung.[1]　Winter (usually followed by " t'ien ").

25. 滋　Tzu.[1]　Rich, in sense of flavour.
　　味　Wei.[4]　Taste, flavour.
　　滋味　Tzu-wei.　Flavour, taste.

26. 穩　Wên.[3]　Steady, firm, secure, stable.
　　穩當　Wên-tang.　Steady, firm.

27. *A.* **Nik'an,** po lang tsên yang ti fan t'êng ch'i lai, ch'uan yao pai tê li hai.

27. Look at those waves, what a height they are ! the boat is very unsteady.

28. *B.* Pieh p'a. Chih shêng hsia san t'ien ti hai lu, ch'uan chiu tao la ma t'ou.

28. Don't be afraid. Only three more days of the sea, and the boat will put in at the port.

" Pieh " is short for " pu yao "—do not !

29. *A.* P'an wang. Yüeh tsao yüeh hao.

29. Let's hope so. The earlier the better.

30. *B.* Fang hsin pa.

30. Don't worry !

" Fang hsin ", lit. let go your heart, heart's ease.

27. 海　　Hai.³　Sea.
　　波　　Po.¹　Waves of the sea.
　　浪　　Lang.⁴　Waves of the sea.
　　翻　　Fan.¹　To turn over.
　　騰　　T'êng.²　To rise up, mount.
　　翻騰　　Fan-t'êng.　To mount, as waves.
　　搖　　Yao.²　To roll, as a ship, shake.
　　擺　　Pai.³　To swing, as a ship, shake.
　　搖擺　　Yao-pai.　The rock and swing of a boat.
28. 碼　　Ma.³　Docks, jetty.
　　碼頭　　Ma-t'ou.　The docks, harbour.

9

DIALOGUE No. 28

Some Common Idioms

This lesson is an exercise in the use of the compound verb with
" pu " in between to represent " inability " to carry out the action
or function of the principal verb.

The " possibility " of doing so is represented in one of two ways,
viz.: —

Sentence 1. Kan shang la. I can catch up. . . .
      Kan tê shang. do. do.
So with all the rest.

1. T'a p'ao ti t'ai k'uai,
wo kan pu shang.

1. He runs too quickly, I
can't catch up with
him (kan pu shang
is also used of one's
inability to compete
with anybody in any
sphere).

2. Chê ko chuan ch'iang
mei yu fêng 'erh, lo
ssu, chuan tsuan pu
chin ch'ü.

2. This brick wall has no
cracks, I can't get a
screw in.

3. Chê ko shui hu i ching
ch'êng man, tsai yeh
chuang pu chin la.

3. This water jug is al-
ready full of water,
I can't pour any
more in.

4. Wo ti shih ch'ing t'ai
to, pan pu tao la
(mang pu kuo lai).

4. I have too many things
to do, I can't manage
them.

5. Ni yao chi tê su yü
shuo ti hao, mang

5. You should remember
the proverb which

VOCABULARY OF DIALOGUE No. 28

2. 墻　　Ch'iang.² Wall.
　　磚　　Chuan.¹ Brick.
　　縫　　Fêng.² A crack, split.
　　螺　　Le, lo.² A screw.
　　螺絲釘 Lo-ssu-ting. A screw.
　　轉　　Chuan.³ Revolve, to turn.
　　鑽　　Tsuan.¹, ³ To bore; awl, Tsuan.⁴ Gimlet.
3. 壺　　Hu.² Pot, kettle.
　　盛　　Ch'êng.² To contain. Used with " man ",
　　　　　　full, to fill.

5. 俗　　Su.² Common, vulgar.
　　俗語　Su-yü. Proverb, common saying.

chê pu hui, hui chê pu mang.

well says, " The busy man is unable, the able man is never busy."

6. Chê ko t'ung tzu chuang ti t'ai chin, wo na pu ch'u lai.

6. This bucket is too tightly packed, I can't pull anything out.

7. Chin t'ien wo tai ti tung-hsi t'ai to, mai pu ch'u ch'ü.

7. I have brought too many things to-day, I can't sell them all.

8. Chê i k'uai mu t'ou t'ai ying, ting tzu yeh ta pu chin ch'ü.

8. This piece of wood is too hard, I can't knock a nail in.

9. Hsin li mien ti i ssu to, k'o shih shuo pu ch'u lai.

9. I have many ideas tucked away in my mind (lit. heart), but I can't express them.

10. Chung-kuo jên yu chü su hua shuo, Ch'a hu chu chi tan tao pu ch'u lai, chiu shih chê ko i ssu.

10. The Chinese have a common saying, " If you boil an egg in a teapot, you can't pour it out ", which expresses this idea.

PROVERBS.

Here, in sentence 10, we have an instance of the use of the proverb. Others are scattered through the dialogues, and a number of them have been collated in Dialogue 38. The Chinese love to use proverbs; their everyday speech is full of them. Proverbs represent the concentrated wisdom of the ages, and form a most fascinating and fruitful study of Chinese philosophy.

11. Wo ti êrh to lung la, t'a shuo hua, wo t'ing pu ch'u lai.

11. I am a little deaf, I can't hear what he says.

8. 硬   Ying.⁴ Hard.

10. 倒   Tao.⁴ Pour, pour out.

11. 耳   Êrh.³ Ear.
    朵   To.³   Ear, pendant, classifier of pendent
                     things.
    耳朵   Êrh-to. Ear.
    聾   Lung.² Deaf, to be deaf.

12. T'a ti yen ching hsia liao, t'a shêm-mo yeh k'an pu chien.

12. He is blind, he cannot see anything.

13. T'a shih chin shih yen, k'an pu ta ch'ing ch'u.

13. He is short-sighted, he cannot see clearly.

14. T'a shih ko ya pa, hua yeh pu hui shuo, jên chia shuo hua, t'a yeh t'ing pu chien.

14. He is a deaf mute, he cannot speak himself, and when others speak he cannot hear them.

15. Yao shih hsia liao yen, shêm-mo yeh k'an pu chien.

15. If a man is blind he cannot see anything at all.

16. T'a ti ko pei fa ma, ni mo t'a, t'a yeh pu chüeh tê.

16. His arm is benumbed, if you touch him he can't feel it.

17. T'a shih la chih chüeh.

17. He lost consciousness.

18. Chê i chien i shang t'ai tsang, wo hsi pu kan ching.

18. This garment is too filthy, I can't wash it clean.

19. To shih i tzu, ta ta ti shih chin, chiu k'o i hsi kan ching la.

19. Use more soap, and exert more strength, then it can be washed clean.

12. 眼   Yen.³ Eye.
    睛   Ching.¹ Eye, iris, pupil.
    瞎   Hsia.¹ Blind.

14. 啞   Ya.³ Dumb.
    吧   Pa.¹ Dumb.
    啞吧   Ya-pa. Deaf mute.

16. 摩   Mo.² To feel.
    胳   Ko.¹ Arm.
    臂   Pei.⁴ Arm.
    麻   Ma.² Numb.
17. 失   Shih.¹ To lose.
    失覺   Shih-chüeh. To become unconscious.
18. 裳   Shang.² Clothes.
19. 胰   I.² Soap.
    勁   Chin, ching.⁴ Strength.

DIALOGUE No. 29

Clothing and Personal Matters

Between two students, *A* and *B*

1. *A*. T'ien lêng, wo-mên ch'uan mien p'ao huo wai t'ao.
1. In the cold weather, we wear our cotton wool gown or an overcoat.

2. *B*. Ni mên pu ch'uan p'i ngao ma.
2. Don't you wear your fur gown?

3. *A*. P'i ngao tao ch'uan pu ch'i.
3. We can't afford to wear furs.

" Ch'uan pu ch'i "—cannot afford to wear, lit. wear not rise (to).

4. *B*. Nien ch'ing ti jên, hsi huan yang chuang.
4. The younger generation prefer foreign style.

" Nien ch'ing ti jên " *or* " Ch'ing nien jên ".

5. *A*. Na shih tzu jan ti.
5. That is natural.

6. *B*. Hsia t'ien to ch'uan sha pu, ch'ou tzu.
6. In the summer most people wear gauze or single silk gowns.

7. *A*. Tung t'ien ch'uan p'i hsieh, hsia t'ien ch'uan pu hsieh.
7. In the winter we wear leather shoes, in the summer cloth shoes.

8. *B*. Tai ti shih ts'ao mao, huo chê yang mao.
8. We wear straw hats or a sun helmet.

" Tai ", to wear, is used for anything worn on the head.

9. *A*. Nü jên ti i shang mo têng i tie'rh ts'ai hao.
9. The womenfolk like modern clothes.

VOCABULARY OF DIALOGUE No. 29

1. 棉　　Mien.[2]　Cotton, cotton wool.
   袍　　P'ao.[2]　Long gown.
   套　　T'ao.[4]　Cover, overcoat, wrapper.
   外套　Wai-t'ao.　Overcoat.
2. 襖　　Ao.　Ngao.[3]　Outer gown, lined coat.
   皮襖　P'i-ao.　Leather or fur coat.

4. 年輕　Nien-ch'ing.　Young, youthful.
   裝　　Chuang.[1]　Style, appearance, feign, attire.

6. 紗　　Sha.[1]　Gauze.

8. 戴　　Tai.[4]　To wear or carry on the head.
   遮　　Chê.[1]　To cover, screen.
   遮陽帽　Chê-yang-mao.　Sun helmet.
9. 摩登　Mo-têng.　Modern (transliteration).

10. *B.* Hsiu tzu, kua tzu, tu shih tuan ti.

10. Sleeves and gown are both short.

11. *A.* Wa tzu, hsien tsai shih hên ch'ang.

11. Stockings are very long now.

12. *B.* Hsüeh shêng yu ch'uan hsi chuang ti shih hao.

12. Students have a personal liking for western garb.

13. *A.* Li fa, yeh shih yang chuang ti to.

13. Haircutting is also foreign style for the most part.

14. *B.* Pien tzu shih lao pu chien liao.

14. The queue is scarcely ever seen.

" Lao pu chien "—seldom or rarely seen. " Ch'ing i pu chien " is also used.

15. *A.* Shu i shu t'ou fa.

15. Comb your hair.

16. *B.* Shua i shua t'ou fa ho ya ch'ih.

16. Brush your hair and teeth.

17. *A.* I fu yao ch'i chêng, kua tzu yao k'ou hao.

17. Keep your clothing tidy, and your coat buttoned.

18. *B.* Chih chia yao hsiu chêng; shou, lien, yao pao ch'ih kan ching.

18. Your finger nails must be kept in good order, and one's hands and face should be kept clean.

19. *B.* Ch'u mên, yao tai hsi lien p'ên, ts'a lien pu, ho shou chüan, yeh pu yao wang la tai ya shua.

19. When you travel you should take with you a washing basin, face cloth and towel and don't forget your toothbrush.

1. 韈　　Wa⁴ (tzu).　Stockings, socks.

2. 嗜　　Shih.⁴　Fond of, addicted to.
   好　　Hao.⁴　Like, fond of.
   嗜好　Shih-hao.　A liking for, addicted to

3. 理　　Li.³　To arrange, dress.
   髮　　Fa.³　The hair of the head.
   理髮　Li-fa.　Haircut.

4. 辮　　Pien⁴ (tzu).　The queue, plait.
   老不見　Lao - pu - chien.　Rare, scarcely seen (lit. long time not see).

5. 梳　　Shu.¹　Comb, to comb.
   頭髮　T'ou-fa.　Hair of the head.

6. 刷　　Shua¹ (tzu).　To brush, a brush.
   牙　　Ya.²　Teeth.
   齒　　Ch'ih.³　Teeth.

7. 扣　　K'ou⁴ (tzu).　To button, button.

8. 指　　Chih.³　The fingers, toes, to point.
   甲　　Chia.³　Nails of fingers or toes, sheath.
   指甲　Chih-chia.　Finger or toe nails.
   保　　Pao.³　To guard, protect, preserve.
   持　　Ch'ih.²　To preserve, hold, grasp.
   保持　Pao-ch'ih.　Keep, preserve.

9. 出門　Ch'u-mên.　To travel (lit. go out of the door).
   盆　　P'ên.²　A basin, bowl, bath.
   洗臉盆　Hsi-lien-p'ên.　A washhand basin.
   絹　　Chüan.⁴　Napkin, handkerchief, towel.

20. *A.* Tsao ch'i, tsao shui,
     mei t'ien yün
     tung, shih pao
     ch'ih k'ang chien
     ti hao fang fa.

20. Early to rise and early
     to bed, with exercise
     every day, is an ex-
     cellent rule of health.

21. *B.* Pa tzu chi so hsüeh
     ti chiao kei pieh
     jên, yeh shih
     chang chih shih
     ti fa tzu.

21. Teach others what you
     yourself learn, is also
     a method of extend-
     ing one's knowledge.

" So hsüeh ti ", an illustration of " so " as a relative pronoun;
that which one has learned.
" Pieh jên "—others. You will also hear " t'a (often read t'o)
jên " for this.

22. *A.* Ni p'êng chien
     ch'iung k'u jên
     yao t'i hsü t'a
     mên.

22. When you meet with
     the poor you should
     sympathise with
     them.

23. *B.* Jên mei yu fan ch'ih
     kai chou chi t'a
     mên.

23. When they have no
     food, then relieve
     them.

24. *A.* Yao fan ti wei pi
     jan shih ch'iung.

24. Beggars are not of ne-
     cessity poor.

" Wei pi jan "—not necessarily, a little bookish, but often used
The common colloquial form is " pu pi ".

25. *B.* Hai tzu mên yao
     chiao hsün t'a-
     mên shou kuei
     chü.

25. Teach children to be
     polite.

" Shou kuei chü ", lit. observe the rules (of conduct). " Kuei "
is a pair of compasses, and " chü " the carpenter's square, and so
you get the idea of things that are clearly defined, such as rules,
regulations, etc.

20. 運動   Yün-tung. Exercise, of physical character, movement, a movement.

康   K'ang.[1] Well, hale, hearty, peace.

健   Chien.[4] Sturdy, strong.

康健   K'ang-chien. Healthy, strong, well.

方法   Fang-fa. Method, way of doing things.

21. 知識   Chih-shih. Knowledge.

22. 窮   Ch'iung.[2] Poor, poverty-stricken.

窮苦   Ch'iung-k'u. Very poor, pitiable.

體   T'i.[3] Sympathise, respect, limbs, body.

恤   Hsü.[4] Pity, sympathise.

23. 賙   Chou.[1] To be charitable, help, assist.

濟   Chi.[4] To save, help, deliver.

24. 未   Wei.[4] Not yet.

未必然   Wei-pi-jan. Not necessarily (lit. not-yet-must-be).

25. 訓   Hsün.[4] To teach, instruct.

教訓   Chiao-hsün. Instruction, to teach.

守   Shou.[3] To keep, observe.

規   Kuei.[1] Rule, custom, manners.

矩   Chü.[3] Rule, used with preceding for customs, manners, etc.

DIALOGUE No. 30

Learning Chinese: the Tones, Dialects, Writing, etc.

THE TONES.

Tones refer to the pitch or inflection of the voice when speaking in Chinese. The number of tones in Chinese varies from four in the Pekinese dialect to as many as twelve in some of the Cantonese dialects. The student is referred to the chapter on Tones for the main points arising out of a discussion on this subject.

Foreigner, *F.*   Chinese, *C.*

1. *F.* Chung Kuo hua nan hsüeh pu nan hsüeh ni.

1. Is Chinese difficult to learn?

2. *C.* Hsieh tzu pu nan, shuo hua pu yung i.

2. The writing is not difficult, but spoken language is not easy.

3. *F.* Shuo hua tsên yang pu yung i, nan ch'u tsai na'rh ni.

3. Why is it not easy to speak, just where does the difficulty lie?

4. *C.* Wai kuo jên shuo Chung Kuo hua, nan ch'u tsai ssu shêng ti to.

4. For the most part foreigners speaking Chinese experience difficulty in regard to the four tones.

5. *F.* Chê ssu shêng shih shih mo. *or* Shih mo chiao tso ssu shêng.

5. What are the four tones?

6. *C.* Ti i chiao shang p'ing, huo yin p'ing; ti êrh chiao hsia p'ing, huo

6. The first is called the "upper-even" tone, the second the "lower-even" tone,

VOCABULARY OF DIALOGUE No. 30

4. 聲   Shêng.[1]   Tone, voice, repute.

6. 賞   Shang.[3]   Name of second tone, reward, bestow.

yang p'ing; ti
san chiao shang
shêng; ti ssu
chiao ch'ü shêng.

the third the "ris-
ing" tone; and the
fourth the "reced-
ing" tone.

7. *F.* Wo t'ing shuo, shuo
Chung Kuo hua
yu wu shêng, tui
pu tui.

7. I have heard that there
are five tones in
Chinese, is that cor-
rect?

8. *C.* Yeh pu nêng shuo
pu tui, yin wei
yu ti ti fang, t'a
mên chia shang i
ko ju shêng.

8. I can't say that that is
wrong, for in some
places they add an
"entering" tone.

"Yu ti ti fang"—some places. "Yu ti"—there are some. (See
12 below.)

9. *F.* Hsüeh Chung Kuo
hua, yung shih
mo fa tzu hao ni.

9. What method of learn-
ing Chinese can you
recommend? (lit.
"use what method
is a good one?")

10. *C.* Ch'ing i wei Chung
Kuo jên tang
hsien shêng, ni i
chü i chü ti kên
cho t'a nien.

10. Invite a Chinese to act
as your teacher, and
read after him sen-
tence by sentence.

Note "tang"—to act as, to be.
"I chü i chü ti"—sentence by sentence, a very common idiom.

11. *F.* Wo kên cho t'a nien
ti shih hou, chin
hsin ti hsiao fa
t'a ti k'ou yin,
tui pu tui.

11. And I suppose you
would recommend
me to do my utmost
to copy his pronun-
ciation as I follow
him in the reading

8. 入　　　Ju.⁴　Name of entering tone, to enter.

10. 當　　　Tang.¹　To represent, act as, be, regard as.

11. 效　　　Hsiao.⁴　To imitate, copy.
　　効法　　Hsiao-fa.　To imitate.
　　口音　　K'ou - yin.　Pronunciation (lit. mouth -
　　　　　　　　　　sound).

12. *C.* Tui la. Pu kuo shih
yu ti jên shuo
kuo yü, yeh yu
pu shao ti jên
shuo t'u hua.

12. Yes that is right. But
some speak the
National language,
while there are a
good many others
who speak local dia-
lects.

"Kuo yü", the National language, used on the radio, and now
rapidly becoming current throughout China, and destined gradually
to eliminate the confusion of dialects, which are numerous.
"T'u hua", the patois, or local dialect of the common people.

13. *F.* Wai kuo jên hai
shih hsüeh kuo
yü hao, shih pu
shih.

13. I suppose it is better for
foreigners to learn
the National lang-
uage, isn't it?

14. *C.* Pu ts'o. Hsien tsai
ko ch'u tou t'ung
hsing kuo yü.

14. Yes, the National language is now current
everywhere.

"Ko ch'u t'ung hsing"—current everywhere, lit. every place
through goes.

15. *F.* Ling chiao hsien
shêng, hsieh
Chung Kuo tzu,
shih yung na
yang ti pi hao.

15. May I ask what is
the best kind of pen
to use for writing
Chinese characters?

16. *C.* Hsieh Chung Kuo
tzu, hai shih yung
mao pi ti hao.

16. It is best to use the hair
brush for writing
Chinese.

17. *F.* Yung kang pi hsing
pu hsing.

17. Will a steel pen do?

18. *C.* Hsing shih hsing,
pu kuo mei yu
mao pi hao.

18. Yes, but it is not so
good as a hair brush.

"Hsing shih hsing", another instance of "qualifying" influence
on the verb by duplication of it, lit. doing will do, but.

12. 語   Yü.³ Words.

國語   Kuo-yü. The Chinese national language.

土話   T'u-hua. Dialects (lit. earth-words).

14. 各處通行 Ko-ch'u-t'ung-hsing.   Everywhere current,
universal.

19. *F.* Wo k'an chien kuo   19. I have seen some people
      yu jên yung ch'ien   using pencils (for
      pi.   this purpose).

" Yu jên "—some, short for " yu ti jen ". (See 8 and 12 above.)

20. *C.* Yu ti shih, pu   20. That is possible. But
      kuo wo hai shih   I must still exhort
      ch'üan ni, ts'ung   you to use the brush
      ch'i t'ou yao   from the start.
      yung mao pi.

" Yu ti shih ", yet another illustration of " yu ti ", meaning some,
lit. there are some (instances of this) affair, sort of thing.

21. *F.* Ling chiao, ling   21. Thanks for your ad-
      chiao.   vice.

" Ling chiao ", another way of expressing thanks, lit. I have
received instruction (from you).

20. 勸   Ch'üan.[4]   Exhort, encourage.
    起頭   Ch'i-t'ou.   The beginning, start.

DIALOGUE No. 31

Asking a Favour. Time Idioms

Two friends, *A* and *B*

1. *A*. Wo ch'ing hsien shêng fei hsin, t'i wo tso i chien shih.

1. I shall be very grateful if you will do something for me.

2. *B*. Pu k'o ch'i. Ni yao wo t'i ni tso shih mo.

2. Don't stand on ceremony. What do you want me to do for you?

3. *A*. Wo hsiang lai, mei yu hsiang hsien shêng ch'iu kuo shih mo.

3. Hitherto I have not asked you for any favours.

" Hsiang . . . ch'iu "—ask of . . . lit. appeal *towards* . . .
" Hsiang " has the meaning of " towards ".

4. *B*. Hsien tsai, ni chiu ching yao shih mo.

4. What really do you want me to do now?

5. *A*. P'an wang chiang lai hsien shêng t'i pa wo ti êrh tzu.

5. I hope that you will take a personal interest in my son's future.

6. *B*. T'a hsien tsai tso shih mo shih.

6. What does he do now?

7. *A*. Ts'ung ch'ien t'a tsai pan kung shih, tang shu chi.

7. He was a clerk in the office formerly.

VOCABULARY OF DIALOGUE No. 31

3. 向 來   Hsiang-lai. Hitherto, up to now.
   求   Ch'iu.² To implore.

4. 究   Chiu.⁴ Finally, after all, but, etc.
   竟   Ching.⁴ Really, finally.
   究 竟   Chiu-ching. Really, at bottom.
5. 將 來   Chiang-lai. In the future.
   提   T'i.² Mention, raise a matter.
   拔   Pa.² Raise, help up.
   提 拔   T'i-pa. Help along, promote, raise.
   兒 子   Erh-tzu. Son.

7. 從 前   Ts'ung-ch'ien. Formerly.
   室   Shih.⁴ Room, house, office, bureau.
   辦 公 室   Pan-kung-shih. Office, bureau (lit. transact
            public (affairs) room).
   書 記   Shu-chi. Secretarial assistant, clerk.

8. *B.* Wei shih mo t'a
yao ling wai chao
kung tso.

8. Why is he wanting to
find another job?

9. *A.* Ch'i ch'u ti shih
hou, t'a men tui
t'a hên hao, i hou
chiu chien chien
ti lêng tan ch'i
lai la.

9. They treated him very
well at first, but
gradually cooled off
(in their attitude to-
wards him).

10. *B.* T'a mên tui tai t'a
ti t'ai tu, kai
pien, pi ting yu
i ko yüan ku.

10. But there must be some
reason for their
change of attitude
towards him.

11. *A.* T'a mên i ch'ien tai
t'a hou, i hou tai
t'a po, mei yu
shih mo tao li.

11. (Yet) there is no sense
in their treating him
so well before and so
meanly afterwards.

12. *B.* Yeh hsü t'a mên
ching chi shang,
yu k'un nan pa.

12. Perhaps they are in
financial difficulties.

" Ching chi shang "—in the matter of economics. In Chinese the
tendency is to use " shang ", which literally means " on ", in expressions of this kind. We should say " in ".

13. *A.* Hsien shêng shuo ti
tui. So i t'a mên
chien shao la t'a
ti hsin shui.

13. That is just it (lit. what
you say is correct).
And so they have
reduced his salary.

" Hsin-shui "—salary, lit. firewood and water, the " fee " formerly
paid by pupils to their Chinese teacher, an honorarium.

14. *B.* T'a mên hai mei yu
ta fa t'a tsou pa.

14. I suppose they haven't
dismissed him yet?

8. 工作   Kung-tso. Work, task, labour.

9. 對   Tui.⁴ Treat, behave towards.
   漸   Chien.⁴ Gradually.
   漸漸的   Chien-chien-ti. Gradually.
   冷淡   Lêng-tan. Coolly, uninterested (cold-weak).

10. 待   Tai.⁴ To treat; to behave.
    態   T'ai.⁴ Behaviour, bearing, attitude.
    態 度   T'ai-tu. Attitude.
    改 變   Kai-pien. To change, alter.
    必 定   Pi-ting. Must, of necessity.
    緣 故   Yüan.² Cause, reason.
    故   Ku.⁴ Cause, reason.

11. 厚   Hou.⁴ Generous, thick.
    薄   Po, Pao.² Mean, stingy, thin.

12. 經濟   Ching-chi. Economics, financial circum-
                  stances.
    困   K'un.⁴ Straitened, distressed.
    困 難   K'un-nan. Special difficulties, straits.

13. 減   Chien.³ To reduce, diminish.
    薪   Hsin.¹ Fuel, firewood, used with the next.
    薪 水   Hsin-shui. Salary. See note.

15. *A.* Tao hsien tsai hai
mei yu. K'ung
p'a pu chiu, t'a
mên chiu i ting
pu yao t'a liao.

15. Not up to the present.
But my fear is that
before long they will
certainly dispense
with his services.

" Tao hsien tsai "—up to now, lit. arrive present. " Hsien tsai "
is present, of time.

16. *B.* Chi jan ju tz'u, wo
yeh pu nêng pu
pang mang.

16. In these circumstances
I cannot do other
than offer to help.

" Ju tz'u "—like this.
" Pu nêng pu . . .", an illustration of the common use of the
double negative to impart strong positive emphasis.

17. *A.* Ch'ien wan, ch'ing
hsien shêng fei
hsin.

17. I entreat you by all
means to exert your-
self (on our behalf).

" Ch'ien wan "—see Vocabulary.

18. *B.* Mei yu shih mo.
Chê shih li so tang
jan ti.

18. It is nothing. Quite a
natural obligation.

" Li so tang jan ti ", an ornate way of saying " li tang "—what
one ought to do.

19. *A.* T'a yao shih chiang
lai, chao tao i ko
hao shih ch'ing,
chên shih t'o
hsien shêng ti fu.

19. If he (the son) gets a
good post later on,
we shall be truly
obliged to you.

" T'o . . . fu ", a polite and circumlocutory phrase for thanks, lit.
I am indebted to your favour for . . .

20. *B.* Na'rh ti hua. Man
man tsou.

20. No no, not at all. Take
care (lit. go slowly)

15. 不久   Pu-chiu.   Before long, soon (not-long-time).
不要   Pu-yao.   Dismiss (not-want).

16. 既   Chi [4] (jan).   Since, seeing that.

17. 千萬   Ch'ien-wan.   By all means (lit. thousand-ten-thousand).

DIALOGUE No. 32

Between Chinese Official (*O*) and an English visitor (*E*) on local education, crops, public health, etc.

1. *E.* Hsien shêng hui shuo Ying kuo hua ma.

1. Can you speak English?

2. *O.* Hui i liang chü, t'ai pu kou yung. Hsien shêng hui chiang Chung kuo hua ma.

2. Just a few words, totally inadequate. Can you speak (intelligibly) in Chinese ?,

" I liang chü "—a few words, lit. one or two sentences. " I pan chü ", a sentence and a half, is also used.

" Ta pu kou yung ", *or* " t'ai pu kou yung ", a good instance of what is called " grammar by position " The " ta " *or* " t'ai ", being where it is in the sentence, has the meaning of " extremely ". If the sentence were " pu ta kou yung ", the " ta " would not have such emphatic significance. The latter sentence means " not quite enough for use ", which is very different from " entirely inadequate ".

3. *E.* Wo chêng tsai hsüeh ni, hai pu ta hui.

3. I am just learning, and can speak little as yet.

" Chêng tsai hsüeh ni "—I am studying it, with the sense of not having got very far, only just beginning, etc. The " ni " is practically equivalent to a full stop.

4. *O.* Hsien shêng hên chih tao pi kuo ti fêng su.

4. You understand (are well acquainted with) our manners and customs.

" Fêng su ", *or* " fêng t'u jên ch'ing—local (" t'u ") manners and feelings (" jên ch'ing "). It is important to " make allowances " in China for circumstances. That is what " jên ch'ing " implies. The Chinese, according to their Confucian ethical philosophy, never administer justice nor pronounce judgment strictly according to written law. They always consider a man's circumstances.

VOCABULARY OF DIALOGUE No. 32

3 正在   Chêng-tsai.   In process of doing something.

4. 風俗   Fêng-su.   Customs of the people.

5. *E.* Chih tao ti yu hsien,
wo lai ling chiao,
ling chiao.

5. In a limited way. I
have come to learn
from you.

6. *O.* Hsien shêng t'ai
ch'ien hsü, t'ai
k'o ch'i.

6. You are too humble-
minded, too court-
eous altogether.

7. *E.* Wo lai ta t'ing kuei
hsien jên min ti
ch'ing hsing.

7. I have come to inquire
about the people in
your district.

" Ta t'ing "—to inquire.

8. *O.* Hên hao. Hsien
shêng hsiang chih
tao na i fang mien
ti shih ch'ing.

8. Very good. On what
particular aspect of
their life would you
like information ?

9. *E.* Hsien t'an chiao yü
i fang mien.

9. Let us begin by dis-
cussing education.

10. *O.* Mei ko ts'un tzu yu
ch'u têng hsiao
hsüeh, ta i tien ti
chên tzu yu kao
têng hsiao hsüeh.
Hsien li yu chung
hsüeh.

10. In each village there
is a lower primary
school, and in each
of the bigger mar-
ket towns there is
a higher primary.
In the county town
there is a middle
school.

" Mei ko ", *or* " mei i ko "—each.

11. *E.* Hsüeh hsiao li, yeh
shou nü shêng
ma.

11. Are girls received in the
schools ?

12. *O.* Pu ts'o. Ko hsüeh
hsiao, tou shih
nan nü tsai i k'uai
êrh, shang hsüeh.

12. Yes, every school is
co-educational (lit.
male and female
students study to-
gether).

" Ko hsüeh hsiao "—every school.

5. 限　　　　Hsien.⁴ Limit, boundary, to fix.

6. 謙　　　　Ch'ien.¹ Humble, modest.
　 謙虛　　　Ch'ien-hsü. Modest, unassuming.

9. 育　　　　Yü.⁴ Rear, nurture.
　 教育　　　Chiao-yü. Education.
　 方面　　　Fang-mien. Aspect of a subject, side, aspect.

10. 初　　　　Ch'u.¹ The beginning, primary.
　 初等　　　Ch'u-têng. Primary grade.
　 鎮　　　　Chên ⁴ (tzu). Market town, mart, to guard, repress.
　 高等　　　Kao-têng. Higher grade, higher primary.
　 中學　　　Chung-hsüeh. Middle school.
　 校　　　　Hsiao.⁴ School.

11. 生　　　　Shêng.¹ Raw, unfamiliar, used for students.

13. *E.* Lao pai hsing tou
shih tzu ma.

13. What about the older
folk, are they literate?

14. *O.* Shih tzu ti pu to.
Chin nien yao t'i
ch'ang i ko shih
tzu yün tung.

14. Very few are literate.
We are promoting a
literacy campaign
this year.

" Yün tung "—a movement of any kind, campaign.

15. *E.* Chiao shih, shih tsai
na'rh pi yeh ti.

15. And your teachers,
where have they
graduated?

16. *O.* Chiao shih, shih pên
shêng shih fan
hsüeh hsiao pi
yeh ti to.

16. Most of the teachers
are graduates of the
provincial training
college.

Note the use of " pên " for " this ", " our ", " native ", etc.

17. *E.* Yeh yu nü chiao
shih ma.

17. And do you use women
teachers?

18. *O.* Yu shih yu, pu kuo
pu to.

18. Yes, but not many.

19. *E.* Chin nien chuang
chia tsêm-mo
yang.

19. How are the crops this
year?

20. *O.* Chin nien nien t'ou
hên fêng shêng,
pai hsing tou hên
p'ing ching.

20. The harvest is excellent
this year, and the
people generally are
contented (lit. quiet,
calm).

21. *E.* Chê pie'rh chung
ti shih shih mo
chuang chia to.

21. What kind of crops are
grown here mostly.

13. 識字　　Shih-tzu.　Literate, literacy (know-charac-
　　　　　　　ters).

14. 倡　　　Ch'ang.⁴　To lead.
　　提倡　　T'i-ch'ang.　To promote, lead, take the
　　　　　　　initiative.

15. 教師　　Chiao-shih.　Teacher.
　　畢　　　Pi.⁴　Finish, end.
　　業　　　Yeh.⁴　Course, occupation, profession.
　　畢業　　Pi-yeh.　Graduate from a course, school,
　　　　　　　college.
16. 範　　　Fan.⁴　Model, pattern.
　　師範學校Shih - fan - hsüeh - hsiao.　Normal training
　　　　　　　school.
　　省　　　Shêng.³　Province.

19. 莊　　　Chuang.¹　A farm, farmstead, the fields.
　　稼　　　Chia.⁴　Grain, crops, to sow.
　　莊稼　　Chuang-chia.　Crops, growing grain.
20. 年頭　　Nien-t'ou.　Harvest (year-head).
　　豐　　　Fêng.¹　Luxuriant, flourishing, abundant.
　　盛　　　Shêng.⁴　Abundant, flourishing.
　　靜　　　Ching.⁴　Placid, calm.
　　平靜　　P'ing-ching.　Quiet, undisturbed.

22. *O.* Mai tzu to. Pu kuo
　　　yeh yu hsiao mi,
　　　yu mai, mien hua,
　　　han yen.

22. Wheat in the main. But
　　　millet, oats, cotton
　　　and tobacco are also
　　　found.

23. *E.* Na mo, pai hsing
　　　na liang, pu fei
　　　shih.

23. In that case you have
　　　no difficulty in get-
　　　ting the people to
　　　pay their taxes?

" Pu fei shih "—not difficult, lit. not expend activity.
" Liang " originally means " grain ", but as taxes were usually
paid in grain the word came to have the meaning of taxes.

24. *O.* Yeh hên nan shuo,
　　　pu kuo pi pieh ti
　　　hsien fên ch'iang.

24. I can hardly say that.
　　　But (in that respect)
　　　we are better off
　　　than other districts.

25. *E.* Kuei ch'u jên min,
　　　yeh hên chiang
　　　chiu wei shêng
　　　ma.

25. And are the people of
　　　your area interested
　　　in public health?

" Chiang chiu " here means " to be particular about ". (See
Dial. 27, sen. 21.)

26. *O.* Pu ta chiang chiu,
　　　ch'ang ch'ang fa
　　　shêng shih chêng.

26. They are not very par-
　　　ticular. We have
　　　frequent outbreaks
　　　of (infectious) dis-
　　　eases.

27. *E.* Chê pie'rh yu t'u
　　　fei mei yu.

27. Are there any bandits
　　　about here?

28. *O.* Mei yu. Chê pie'rh
　　　ti ching ch'a, ho

28. No. The police and
　　　military officials loy-

22. 麥   Mai. Mo⁴ (tzu). Wheat.
　　油麥   Yu-mai. Oats.
　　米   Mi.³ Millet, the grains in general.
　　小米   Hsiao-mi. Millet.
　　棉   Mien.² Cotton.
　　花   Hua.¹ Flower.
　　棉花   Mien-hua. Cotton, in growth, or raw.
　　旱   Han.⁴ Dry, used with the next.
　　旱烟   Han-yen. Tobacco.
23. 納   Na.⁴ To pay, take, receive, used with the
　　　　　　next.
　　糧   Liang.² Taxes, rations, grains.
　　納糧   Na-liang. To pay taxes.

24. 縣分   Hsien-fên. Administrative division, county.

26. 時   Shih.² Time.
　　症   Chêng.⁴ Disease.
　　時症   Shih Cheng. Epidemic.

27. 匪   Fei.³ Worthless, wrong, bandits, rebels.
　　土匪   T'u-fei. Local banditti.
28. 警   Ching.³ Alarm, startle, watch.
　　察   Ch'a.² To examine, investigate.

chün kuan tou chin chih.

ally discharge the duties of their office here.

29. *E.* Wo hsiang kuei hsien pu k'uei shih mu fan hsien.

29. I consider you need not be diffident to regard your district as a model.

30. *O.* Kuo chiang, kuo chiang.

30. Flattery ! flattery !

" Kuo chiang ", lit. over-praise.

28. 警察　　Ching-ch'a.　The police.
　　　盡　　Chin.[4]　To fulfil, exhaust possibilities.
　　　職　　Chih.[2]　Public office, appointment.
　　　盡職　Chin-chih.　To fulfil the duties of one's
　　　　　　　　office.
29. 愧　　　K'uei.[4]　Be diffident about.
　　　模　　Mu.　Mo.[2]　Model, pattern.
　　　模範　Mu-fan.　Model, pattern.

DIALOGUE No. 33

Doctor and Patient

Doctor, *D*.　　Patient, *P*.

1. *P.* Ni yao shih yüan i, chiu k'o i i chih wo ti ping.

1. If you were willing to heal me, (I feel that) you *could* do so.

2. *D.* Sui jan wo yüan i, hai shih pu nêng chih ni ti ping.

2. I cannot heal you, although I am willing to do so.

" Sui jan . . . hai ". Note the construction, " sui jan ", although, . . . " hai ", yet.

Note the use of " jan " with " sui ", although, and " chi ", since, to complete the adverbial form. (See sentence 9 below.)

3. *P.* Ni chi shih pu nêng chih wo ti ping, ni kai chieh shao wo kei pieh ti tai fu.

3. Since you cannot heal me, you will surely (ought to) introduce me to some other doctor.

4. *D.* Wo yeh kei ni hsieh chieh shao hsin, yeh sung ni tao tai fu na li ch'ü.

4. I will give you a letter of introduction, and also take you to the doctor myself.

" Yeh . . . yeh "—both . . . and ". The alternative form, " ping ch'ieh ", is fairly common amongst educated people.

5. *P.* Chê yang tso, i ting tui wo hên yu i, k'o shih wo pu hsiang ch'ü.

5. That would certainly be of advantage to me, but all the same I am disinclined to go.

6. *D.* Wei shih mo ni pu hsiang ch'ü.

6. And why are you disinclined to go?

7. *P.* Yin wei wo pu jên shih t'a, ho t'a pu shu hsi.

7. Because I don't know him, I am not well acquainted with him.

VOCABULARY OF DIALOGUE No. 33

1. 治   Chih.⁴ To cure, treat (medically, etc.).
   病   Ping.⁴ Disease, illness, sick.

3. 該   Kai.¹ Ought, owe.
   介   Chieh.⁴ Introduce, announce.
   紹   Shao.⁴ Introduce, hand down.
   介紹   Chieh-shao. Introduce, as one friend to
                      another.

5. 益   I.² Benefit, advantage.

6. 爲什麼 Wei-shih-mo. Why?

7. 習   Hsi.² Versed in, familiar, practised.
   熟習   Shu-hsi. Intimate, well acquainted.

8. *D.* Ni tsung jan ho t'a
       pu shu, ni yeh
       k'o i fang hsin,
       yin wei wo chih
       tao t'a shih i ko
       hao tai fu, tan
       pao t'a nêng i
       chih ni.

8. Although you are not
   well acquainted with
   him, you need have
   no anxiety. For I
   know him to be a
   good doctor, and I
   am sure he can cure
   you.

" Tsung jan " is not as common as " sui jan " (see 2 above), but
it permits of a slightly different emphasis from it. " Tsung jan " is
used when you want to say " but supposing that be so ", " allowing
for that ", etc.

9. *P.* Ni chi jan chê yang
       ti ch'üan wo, wo
       chiu tsun ming
       chiu shih la.

9. Since you urge me to
   this extent, I am
   ready to do as you
   say.

10. *D.* Ni chê yang ti t'ing
        wo ch'üan, wo
        yeh hên kao
        hsing.

10. I am delighted that
    you should take my
    advice so readily.

11. *P.* Wo pu tê pu chao
        cho ni so shuo ti
        ch'ü tso.

11. I cannot do other than
    act as you suggest.

12. *D.* Ni yao hsiao hsin,
        pu yao pa wo kei
        ni ti hsin tiu la.

12. Take care not to lose
    the letter I have
    given you.

" Wo kei ni ti hsin "—the letter which I gave you.
The " so ", relative pronoun, is understood.

13. *P.* Pu p'a, wo pu hui
        tiu tiao ti.

13. Have no fear, it is out
    of the question for
    me to lose that.

" Hui " means able to, so the sense is " I *simply cannot* lose it "

14. *D.* Yao shih ni tieh
        tao la, chiu pu
        kan tan pao tsên
        yang.

14. But in the event of your
    falling one could not
    be sure about that.

8. 縱   Tsung⁴ (jan). Although, lax.
   放 心 Fang-hsin. Don't worry !
   因 爲 Yin-wei. Because, for, on account of.
   擔   Tan.¹ Undertake, carry, used with the
             next.
   擔 保 Tan-pao. Guarantee, stand surety for.

9. 遵   Tsun.¹ To accord with, follow, obey.

0. 聽我勸 T'ing-wo-ch'üan. Follow my advice.
   興   Hsing.¹ Elated, rejoice.
   高 興 Kao¹-hsing.⁴ Elated, highly pleased.

3. 掉   Tiao.⁴ To let fall, fall.
   丟 掉 Tiu-tiao. To let fall, lose.

4. 跌   Tieh.¹ To stumble, fall.
   跌 倒 Tieh-tao. To fall.

15. *P.* Hsin yao shih tiao hsia lai la, wo chiu kan k'uai pa t'a, shih ch'i lai.

15. If the letter were to fall I should pick it up again straight away.

16. *P.* (*cont.*) Tai fu lai tao chê li, huo cho wo tao t'a na li ch'ü, pu shih i yang ti ma.

16. Isn't it all the same whether the doctor comes here, or whether I go to him i

17. *D.* Pu i yang, yin wei t'a na li yu yao p'in ho yao pu.

17. Not at all, because h has medicines and dressings there.

18. *P.* K'o shih tai fu hai mei yu kei wo k'an mo, yeh mei yu yung wên tu piao, liang.

18. But, doctor, you have not yet taken my pulse, nor used the thermometer to take my temperature.

19. *D.* Ni yeh mei yu kao su wo, ni shên shang na'erh t'êng la. Wo k'an ni jê tu ping pu kao. Shên ch'u shê t'ou lai, k'an i k'an.

19. Neither have you told me where you feel the pain (lit. on your body where pain) I don't think your temperature is high But put out your tongue and let me see it.

20. *P.* T'êng shih tu tzu t'êng la, t'ou yeh t'êng la.

20. I have stomach ache also headache.

21. *D.* Ta hsiao pien tsêm-mo yang, t'ung pu t'ung.

21. What about your bowels and urine are they all right (lit. free not free).

22. *P.* Hsiao pien t'ung la, ta pien pu t'ung.

22. Urination is all right but my bowels are constipated.

15. 拾   Shih.[2]   To pick up.

17. 藥   Yüeh. Yao.[4]   Medicine, drugs.
    品   P'in.[3]   Sort, kind, class, character.
    藥品   Yüeh-p'in.   Medicines, as a whole.
    藥布   Yao-pu.   Bandages, lint, etc.
18. 脈   Mai.[4]   The pulse.
    看脈   K'an-mo.   To take the pulse.
    温度表   Wên-tu-piao.   Thermometer.

19. 疼   T'êng.[2]   Pain, to be in pain.
    伸   Shen.[1]   To extend, put out.

1. 大便   Ta-pien.   To pass a stool (big-convenience).
    小便   Hsiao-pien.   To urinate (little-convenience).

23. *D.* Na mo, wo k'ei ni
p'ei hsieh yao.
Ni pu yao ho
nung ch'a, ch'ang
ch'ang ho tan
ch'a pa.

23. Then I will make you
up a purge. And
don't drink strong
tea. Always take
weak tea.

Note the use of " nung " and " tan " to express strong and weak
of liquids. " Yen " is also used for " strong " of liquids.

24. *P.* Ch'ing tai fu kei wo
p'ei i fu wan yao
pa. Wo pu nêng
ch'ih yao fên.

24. And doctor, I should
like you to make me
up a dose of pills.
I can't take powders.

23. 濃 Neng. Nung.² Thick, strong, rich, of liquids.

   瀉 Hsieh.⁴ To purge, drain, diarrhœa.

24. 配 P'ei.⁴ To mix, make up, as medicines.

   副 Fu.⁴ A dose, classifier of medicine doses.

   丸 Wan.² Pill, pills.

   粉 Fên.³ Medicinal powder, flour, meal.

DIALOGUE No. 34

On Personal Characteristics and Relationships

Two friends, A and B

1. *A.* Chao hsien shêng ti p'i ch'i ju ho.

1. What sort of a man is Mr. Chao (lit. what is his temper like) ?

2. *B.* T'a shih i ko hsin p'ing, ch'i ho ti jên.

2. He is an even-tempered and kindly man.

3. *A.* T'ing shuo t'a ti t'ai t'ai ti p'i ch'i pu hao.

3. I hear that his wife is an ill-tempered woman.

4. *B.* Ni shuo ti tui, tan shih t'a ti chang fu, kei t'a li i ko hao pang yang.

4. That is true, but her husband gives (sets) her a good example.

5. *A.* I ko jên, yao shih pu jên ch'i, ch'ang ch'ang hui fa shêng ma fan.

5. If a person cannot control his temper, it is a constant source of trouble.

Note the use of " fa shêng " in the sense of create, produce, make, etc.

6. *B.* Pu kuo Chao hsien shêng shih ko hao jên, pu yüan i chia li pien fa shêng lo so.

6. But Mr. Chao is a good man, and is anxious that no trouble should arise in his home.

7. *A.* T'a mên chia li pien, ta kuo chia méi yu.

7. Have they ever come to blows at home ?

VOCABULARY OF DIALOGUE No. 34

1. 脾　　　P'i.² Spleen, stomach, disposition.
   脾氣　　P'i-ch'i. Disposition, temper.

4. 丈　　　Chang.⁴ Husband.
   丈夫　　Chang-fu. Husband.
   榜　　　Pang.³ Example, pattern.
   榜樣　　Pang-yang. Example, pattern.

5. 忍　　　Jên.³ Endure, repress, restrain.
   忍氣　　Jên-ch'i. Self-control, keep one's temper.
   痳　　　Ma.² Used with the next for trouble.
   煩　　　Fan.² Trouble, annoyance, annoy.

6. 囉　　　Lo.¹ Vexatious, annoyance.
   唆　　　So.¹ To incite, discord, mischief.

7. 架　　　Chia.⁴ Blows, squabble.
   打架　　Ta-chia. To come to blows, wrangle.

8. *B.* Mci yu, tan shih
yu ti shih hou,
mien pu liao ch'i
i tie'rh ch'ung t'u.

8. No, but at times it is
inevitable that they
should clash a little.

" Mien pu liao ", another illustration of the use of " pu liao ". to
express impossibility, impossible to avoid, unavoidable.

9. *A.* Yu ti shih hou, t'ing
chien t'a mên ta
shêng ch'ao tsui.

9. Sometimes I hear them
shouting and wrang-
ling.

10. *B.* 'Ai ya, chê shih chia
li mien ch'ang
chien ti shih.

10. Alas, this sort of thing
is common in home
life.

11. *A.* Hsien shêng k'an,
tsên yang nêng
pa chê chung shih
chien shao.

11. How do you think that
this sort of thing
might become less
frequent ?

" Nêng-kou "—can, able to—is often used as an alternative for
" nêng " alone.

12. *B.* I ko jên yao shih
chiao ao, ch'ang
ch'ang k'an pu
ch'i pieh jên.

12. If a man is proud he
is prone to despise
(look down upon)
others.

13. *A.* I ko jên yao shih
ch'ien pei, chiu
pu hui fa shêng
chê yang ti shih
ch'ing.

13. A humble-minded man
will never (lit. is un-
able to) cause this
kind of trouble.

14. *B.* T'a ti t'ai t'ai,
tsung hsi huan
t'an lun jên chia
ti ch'ang tuan.

14. His wife must take
pleasure in talking
about the faults and
failures of other
people.

8. 免不了 Mien-pu-liao. Unavoidable.
   衝　　　Ch'ung.[1] To clash, dash against, collide.
   突　　　T'u.[4] Rush against.
   衝突　　Ch'ung-t'u. Personal differences, quarrels.

9. 吵　　　Ch'ao.[3] Altercation, row, noise.
   嘴　　　Tsui.[3] Lips.
   吵嘴　　Ch'ao-tsui. Wrangle, quarrel.

11. 種　　　Chung.[3] Kind, sort.

12. 驕　　　Chiao.[1] Proud, arrogant.
    傲　　　Ao. Ngao.[4] Haughty, proud.
    驕傲　　Chiao-ao. Proud, haughty, arrogant.
    看不起　K'an-pu-ch'i. To despise, look down on
    　　　　　(look-not-rise).

    別人　　Pieh-jên. Others, other people.
13. 卑　　　Pei.[1] Low.
    謙卑　　Ch'ien-pei. Humble, modest.

14. 談論　　T'an-lun. Discuss, talk about.
    長短　　Ch'ang - tuan. Merits and shortcomings
    　　　　　(long-short).

15. *A.* Na mo, wo hsiang t'a ti chang fu ho t'a pu yung i ch'u.

15. In that case I imagine her husband must find it no easy task to get on with her.

" Ch'u " has a special meaning of " to live together ", " get on with one ".

16. *B.* Pu ts'o, tan shih t'a chin liang ti jên nai, pu jo t'a.

16. That is so, but her husband endeavours to be patient, doing his utmost not to provoke her.

17. *A.* Chao hsien shêng pi ting shih i ko ts'ung ming t'ung ta ti jên.

17. Then Mr. Chao must be a very intelligent and experienced man.

" Ts'ung ming t'ung ta "—an enlightened and perspicacious man.

18. *B.* Tui la, t'a shên t'ung Ju hsüeh.

18. That is so, he is well-versed in Confucian principles.

" Ju " is the classical name for Confucianism, sometimes spoken of as " Ju-chiao ", or as in the text, " Ju-hsüeh ".
" Shên t'ung "—deep and thorough.

15. 處　　　　Ch'u.³ To live with.
　　不容易處 Pu-yung-i-ch'u. Not easy to get on with.

16. 盡量的 Chin-liang-ti. Do one's utmost (to exhaust
　　　　　　　　one's capacity).
　　忍耐　 Jên²-nai.⁴ Be patient, put up with, endure.
　　惹　　 Jo.³ To provoke.

17. 聰　　 Ts'ung.¹ Intelligent, understanding, clever.
　　聰明　 Ts'ung-ming. Intelligent, clever.
　　通　　 T'ung.¹ Through, used with the next.
　　達　　 Ta.² Penetrate, inform.
　　通達　 T'ung-ta. Well informed, perspicacious.

18. 深　　 Shen.¹ Deep, profound, versed in.
　　儒　　 Ju.² Confucian, learned, scholarly.
　　儒學　 Ju-hsüeh. The Confucian teaching, Con-
　　　　　　　　fucianism.

DIALOGUE No. 35

Discussion between Master (*M*) and Servant (*S*) on scissors, the tailor, looking for someone, etc.

1. *M*. Na tao tzu lai, ko tiao chê i t'iao shêng tzu.

1. Bring a knife to cut this piece of string.

2. *S*. Chê t'iao shêng tzu t'ai ts'u, yung tao tzu ko pu tuan.

2. This piece of string is too thick for a knife to cut.

Note that " ts'u ", thick, and " hsi ", thin, are used of round long things like string, pillars, etc., while " hou ", thick, and " po ", thin, are used of flat objects.

3. *M*. Na mo, ling wai chao i t'iao pi chiao hsi ti shêng tzu, huo shih na chien tao lai, chiao i chiao.

3. In that case, either find a piece of finer string, or bring the scissors to cut it.

" Pi chiao . . . hsi ti "—comparatively fine, finer.

4. *S*. Ts'ai fêng pa chien tzu chieh ch'ü la.

4. The tailor has borrowed the scissors (and taken them away).

5. *M*. T'a chieh la wo mên ti chien tzu ch'ü tso shih mo.

5. What has he borrowed our scissors for?

Note " tso shih-mo " at the end of this sentence is equivalent to " why "? " He has borrowed our scissors . . . to do what? "

6. *S*. T'a shuo t'a tzu chi ti chien tzu t'ai tun, tê mo i mo.

6. He says his scissors are too blunt and in need of grinding.

VOCABULARY OF DIALOGUE No. 35

1. 割   Ko.[1] To cut.
 割掉   Ko-tiao. To cut off (cut-drop).
 繩   Shêng [3] (tzu). Rope, string, cord.
2. 斷   Tuan.[4] To cut off, break.
 割不斷 Ko-pu-tuan. Can't cut it.

3. 細   Hsi.[4] Fine, opposite of thick, or coarse.
 剪   Chien [3] (tzu). Scissors.
 剪刀   Chien-tao. Scissors.
 絞   Chiao.[3] To cut with scissors, twist, cross-
          wise.

6. 鈍   Tun.[4] Dull, blunt.
 磨   Mo.[2] To grind, rub, mill.

7. *M.* Ts'ai fêng shih pu shih hsien tsai kei wo mên tso i fu.

7. Isn't the tailor making some clothes for us at present?

Notice " shih pu shih " coming at the beginning of a compound question. It serves to emphasise the action as continuing in the present.

8. *S.* Shih ti. T'a shih tsai kei t'ai t'ai ts'ai tuan wai i, ho ch'ang p'ao.

8. He is making a coatee and coat for Madame.

9. *M.* Wo chih tao t'ai t'ai chi yü hsiang ch'uan tuan wai i, so i t'a chieh chien tao, yeh yu li yu.

9. I know that Madame is very urgently wanting to wear the coatee, and so he had some good reason for borrowing the scissors.

10. *S.* K'o shih yu i chien; k'ung p'a ts'ai fêng pa chien tao, liu ch'i lai la.

10. But there is just this point; suppose the tailor were to keep our scissors?

" K'o shih yu i chien ", used when interposing a qualification to views expressed.

11. *M.* Na suan pu liao shih mo, tsui yao chin ti shih yao t'a tsao tsao ti pa tuan wai i tso hao, chiao t'ai t'ai hsi huan.

11. That is of small moment. The most important thing is for him to get that coatee finished early, to please Madame.

12. *M.* (*cont.*) Ni tsêm-mo pu tsao kei wo shuo.

12. But why didn't you tell me before?

9. 於　　　Yü.² In, at, on, etc.
　 急於　　Chi-yü. Anxious about, in haste about.
　 由　　　Yu.² Reason, cause.
　 理由　　Li-yu. The reason why.

10. 留起來 Liu-ch'i-lai. To retain, keep.

11. 算不了 Suan-pu-liao. Of no importance or account.

13. *S.* Yin wei wo pu chih tao nin tsai na li.

13. Because I did not know where you were.

Note use of "nin", a polite form of "ni", the second personal pronoun.

14. *M.* Pu shih yin wei ni t'ai lan, mei yu yung hsin chao wo pa.

14. Isn't it (rather) because you are lazy, and have not tried to find me?

15. *S.* Pu shih ti, wo shih tsai chao pu cho hsien shêng.

15. No not that. I really could not find you.

16. *M.* Wo ping mei yu li k'ai chê ko ti fang, tsêm mo ni shuo chao pu cho wo ni.

16. But I haven't left this place, how can you say you couldn't find me?

17. *S.* Na tao ch'i kuai, wo tao ch'u chao nin, na'êrh yeh chao pu cho.

17. That really is strange. I looked everywhere for you, but couldn't find you.

" Na'êrh yeh . . . pu "—nowhere, not anywhere.

18. *M.* Pa liao. Kan ni ti ch'ü pa.

18. Enough of this. Get on with your job.

14. 用心   Yung-hsin.   To exert oneself, mentally (use
              heart).

15. 找不着   Chao-pu-cho.   Cannot find (seek not get).

16. 離開   Li-k'ai.   To depart, leave, take one's leave.

17. 奇   Ch'i.^{2} Strange, wonderful, rare.
    怪   Kuai.^{4} Extraordinary, unusual, strange,
              blame.
    到處   Tao-ch'u.   Everywhere.

18. 罷了   Pa^4-liao. To finish, that will do! say no
              more.

EXERCISE No. 36

Some Useful Idiomatic Phrases

1. **Pa** ni mên ti shu ta k'ai.

1. Open your books.

2. K'an ti chi chang ti chi chieh.

2. What chapter and verse shall we find? (lit. look at, with a view to reading).

3. Ni nien tao ti chi yeh.

3. To what page have you read?

4. **Mei** ko hsüeh shêng, tou yao nien ti êrh shih wu yeh ti, ti êrh chang, ti i chieh.

4. Each student must read chap. two, verse one, on page 25.

" Ko "—each, every, followed by " tou ", " tu "—all.

5. So yu ti hsien shêng tou yao tao hui.

5. All the teachers must come to the meeting.

" Tao hui "—come to the meeting—is really equal to our be present, attend.

6. Wo ho ni mên tsai i ch'i ti shih hou, ni mên yao chin liang ti fa piao ni mên ti i chien.

6. Express your opinions as far as you can, while I am here with you.

7. **T'a** ho wo mên t'ung hsing, tso wo mên ti ling tao.

7. He is going with us, to be our leader.

" Tso " has the same sense as " tang ", viz., to act as, to be.

8. Wo tsai chu wei mien ch'ien shuo chê yang ti hua, shih pu p'ei ti.

8. I am unworthy (not fit to) to say this kind of thing in your presence.

" Chu wei "—all (you) gentlemen. Used when addressing an audience

VOCABULARY OF EXERCISE No. 36

1. 打開   Ta-k'ai.   To open, as of books.

2. 章   Chang.[1]   Chapter, essay.
   節   Chieh.[2]   Verse, section.

3. 頁   Yeh.[4]   Page, leaf of a book.

5. 所有的 So-yu-ti.   All that there are.
   會   Hui.[4]   Meeting, conference, association.

6. 在一起 Tsai-i-ch'i.   Together.
   發表   Fa-piao.   To make known.
   意見   I-chien.   Opinions, ideas.

7. 導   Tao.[3]   To lead.
   領導   Ling-tao.   To lead, a leader.

8. 諸   Chu.[1]   All (precedes nouns).
   面前   Mien-ch'ien.   Presence, in front of.
   配   P'ei.[4]   Match, be worthy, be equal to.

9. Chang kuan tsai chün tui chung, tsou lai tsou ch'ü.

9. The officers go in and out amongst the troops.

10. T'a tsai lu p'ang kuan k'an.

10. He was looking on from the side of the road (an onlooker).

11. Na ko fang tzu chêng tsai tui mie'rh.

11. The house is exactly opposite.

12. Ling lu ti, tsai ch'ien mie'rh tsou.

12. The guide goes ahead.

13. Hu sung ti, tsai hou pie'rh tsou.

13. The escort goes behind.

14. P'êng yu mên ping p'ai ti, hsiang ch'ien tsou.

14. Friends advance shoulder to shoulder (side by side).

15. Ni chan tsai tang chung pa.

15. Stand in the middle.

16. Pu yao wang i k'uai êrh chi.

16. Don't crowd together.

17. Ta chia yao san k'ai.

17. Let all scatter.

"Ta chia", a common expression for "all", when referring to persons.

18. Hsiang li yüan i tie'rh ti hao.

18. It would be better if you moved apart a little.

19. Pi tz'u jang pu.

19. To make concessions on both sides (lit. mutually recede).

"Pi tz'u", lit. that, this, is the most usual expression for mutually.

20. Ta chia ch'ien chin pa.

20. Let all advance.

9. 長官　Chang-kuan. Officials, officers.
   軍隊　Chün-tui. Soldiers, military.

10. 旁　P'ang.² The side.
    觀　Kuan.¹ To look on, observe.

13. 護　Hu.⁴ To protect, guard.
    護送　Hu-sung. To escort, for protection.

14. 排　P'ai.² In rows, ranks, arrange, abreast.
    並排　Ping-p'ai. Shoulder to shoulder, in line.

15. 當中　Tang-chung. The midst, in the centre.

16. 擠　Chi.³ To crowd together, to press.

17. 散　San.⁴ To scatter, disperse.
    散開　San-k'ai. To scatter, disperse, apart.

19. 彼　Pi.³ That.
    此　Tz'u.³ This.
    彼此　Pi-tz'u. Mutual, mutually.
    讓　Jang.⁴ To concede, give way, yield.
    讓步　Jang-pu. To make concessions, yield (give step).

21. Chê chi nien t'a chin la pu.

21. He has made progress this last few years.

"Chin-pu", "t'ui-pu", lit. advance step, retard step, progress and retrogression.

22. T'a ti mei mei t'ui la pu.

22. His younger sister has retrogressed.

23. Kuan chang i chin lai, ta chia chiu chan ch'i lai, t'o mao chü kung.

23. As soon as the officials come in, let the whole group rise, doff hats and bow.

"I chin lài . . . chiu"—as soon as . . . come in . . . (you will do this or that).

"Chai" is a special term for taking off the hat or cap. But the usual expression for "taking off clothes", including caps and hats, is "t'o".

24. Hsiang tso hsiang yu, tou shih t'ing chiao shih ti ming ling.

24. As to whether we turn left or right it is the teacher's orders that must be obeyed.

25. I shih chu, san yao shu.

25. Clothes, food and shelter are the three important things.

26. Ch'uan tê nuan, ch'ih tê pao, shih jên jên so yao.

26. To be warmly clad and well fed is the desire of every man.

"Ch'ih tê pao"; cf. "ch'ih pao la"—I have eaten my fill—is not considered impolite as an expression of appreciation of a good meal.

21. 進步   Chin-pu. To advance, make progress.

22. 退   T'ui.⁴ To retreat, retire, move back.
    退步   T'ui-pu. Opposite of progress, to be retro-
            grade.
23. 脫   T'o.¹ To doff the hat, take off (clothes).
    鞠   Chü.² To bow, bend the body.
    躬   Kung.¹ The body, person.
    鞠躬   Chü-kung. To make a bow.

24. 左   Tso.³ Left.
    右   Yu.⁴ Right.
    命令   Ming-ling. Orders, commands.
25. 食   Shih.² Food.
    樞   Shu.¹ Cardinal, fundamental
26. 暖   Nuan.³ Warm, genial.
    飽   Pao.³ Replete, full.

DIALOGUE No. 37

Two friends, A and B, take a Walk in the Country

1. *A*. Chin t'ien kuo chieh, ko chi kuan fang chia, wo mên lü hsing hao pu hao.

1. To-day is a public holiday, all public offices are closed. What do you say to a ramble?

" Kuo "—to pass—used of special days and occasions; *e.g.*, " kuo nien " is to celebrate the (New) Year.

2. *B*. Hên hao, wo mên hsia hsiang ch'ü, i t'ung ch'ih yeh ts'an.

2. Very good, let us go into the country and have a picnic meal together.

" Hsia hsiang "; " hsia "—to go down (into the country).

3. *A*. Tsan ch'êng. P'an wang t'ien ch'i yao nuan ho.

3. Splendid (lit. approved). I hope it will be warm.

4. *B*. Chiu shih yin t'ien, yeh pu yao chin. Tsui k'o p'a ti chiu shih shan tien, ta lei.

4. Even if it is overcast it doesn't matter. What is most to be feared is thunder and lightning.

" Chiu shih . . . yeh "—even if . . . still, etc.
" K'o p'a ti ", one way of expressing the passive voice; what is to be feared.

5. *A*. K'o shih hsia t'ien pu hui hsia hsüeh ti.

5. (One thing about it and that is) It is Summer and it won't snow!

6. *B*. Pu ts'o, k'o shih nan pao pu hsia pao tzu.

6. True, but one can't be certain it won't hail.

VOCABULARY OF DIALOGUE No. 37

1. 節　　Chieh.[2] Feast, festival.
   機　　Chi.[1] Machine, organ of administration.
   關　　Kuan.[1] Public office, administrative department.
   機關　Chi-kuan. Public offices, associations, etc.
   假　　Chia.[4] Holiday.
   放假　Fang-chia. To close for holiday.
   旅行　Lü-hsing. To travel, go for a journey, picnic.
2 鄉　　Hsiang.[1] The country, countryside, rural.
   野　　Yeh.[3] Wild.
   餐　　Ts'an.[1] A meal.

3. 贊　　Tsan.[4] Praise, approve.
   成　　Ch'êng.[2] Approve.
   贊成　Tsan-ch'êng. To approve.
4. 陰　　Yin.[1] Dark, cloudy, overcast, the female principle.
   閃　　Shan.[3] Flash, lightning.
   閃電　Shan-tien. Lightning (flash electric).
   雷　　Lei.[2] Thunder.

5. 雪　　Hsüeh.[3] Snow.

6. 雹　　Pao[2] (tzu). Hailstones.
   難保　Nan[2]Pao[3]　Difficult to guarantee.

11

7. *A*. Tung t'ien hsia shu-ang, shan shang ti shu to ma hao k'an.

7. When there is frost in Winter, how beautiful the trees on the hills are !

8. *B*. Hao k'an shih hao k'an. Pu kuo ho kên hu li pie'rh, tou chieh la tung, hên pu fang pien.

8. Beautiful indeed. But when rivers and lakes are frozen up, it is very inconvenient.

" Hên pu "—extremely un-; cf. " pu hên ", not very, a difference of degree expressed by position of a word in the sentence.

9. *A*. K'o shih hsien tsai shih ch'iu t'ien, pu shih tung t'ien. Wo mên yu pu ta suan tso ch'uan, wo mên yao pu hsing.

9. But it is Autumn and not Winter. More-over we are not thinking of travelling by boat, we are going to walk.

10. *B*. Chin wan ti yüeh liang, ying kai shih yüan ti. T'ien ch'i ch'ing lang ti shih hou, hsing hsing yu kai to ma ti hao k'an.

10. It ought to be full moon to-night, and if the sky (weather) is clear, the stars ought also to be very beautiful.

11. *A*. Yao pu ch'i wu ts'ai hao. Hao pu hao wo mên hsien tsai chiu tsou pa.

11. It will be all right if there is no fog. What about making a start now ?

" Hao pu hao ", coming at the beginning of a query, means " What about . . . ? " " Do you approve ? ", etc.
" Chiu " here as often has the sense of " immediacy ".

12. *B*. K'o i. Ai ya. T'ien ch'i liang k'uai, ching chih yeh

12. Certainly. My ! the day is cool, the scenery fine, the flowers are

7. 霜　　Shuang.¹　Frost.
　 樹　　Shu.⁴　Tree.

8. 河　　Ho.²　River.
　 湖　　Hu.²　Lake.
　 凍　　Tung.⁴　To freeze.
　 方便　　Fang-pien.　Convenient.

9. 秋　　Ch'iu.¹　Autumn, harvest.

10. 月亮　　Yüeh-liang.　The moon.
　　 朗　　Lang.³　Clear, fine.
　　 圓　　Yuan.²　Round, circle.

11. 霧　　Wu.⁴　Mist.
　　 起霧　　Ch'i-wu.　To be misty, foggy.

12. 涼快　　Liang-k'uai.　Cool and invigorating.
　　 景　　Ching.³　Fine, prospect.

hao, hua tou k'ai la, tsai ts'ao ti shang mien tsou, to ma shu fu.

all in bloom, what a relief to be walking through the grassy meadows !

" To ma . . ."—how! when preceding an adjectival expression.

13. *A.* Ni k'an shan p'o shang ti miao, shan ting shang ti t'a, to ma hao k'an.

13. Just look at the temples on the hill slopes, and the pagoda on the hill top, how lovely !

14. *B.* Wo mên shang miao shang ch'ü, kên ho shang t'an i t'an.

14. Let's go up to the temple and have a chat with the bonzes (Buddhist priests).

15. *A.* Wo k'an chê tso miao shih Tao chiao, pu shih Fo chiao.

15. I think this is a Taoist temple, not Buddhist.

" Tso " is the classifier of temples, towers, houses, etc.

16. *B.* Na mei yu kuan hsi, tsa mên shang ch'ü tsai shuo pa.

16. That doesn't matter, let's go up and then we shall see.

17. *A.* Ai, chê hsieh ts'ang ying ho ma i, t'ao yen pu t'ao yen.

17. My ! but these flies and ants, what a nuisance they are !

" T'ao "—to beg, seek; " yen "—dislike. To ask for one's displeasure, so hateful, nuisance, etc.

18. *B.* Hsing k'uei chê li mei yu wên tzu. Wên tzu yao jên yao tê li hai.

18. Fortunately there are no mosquitoes here. They bite terribly.

12. 緻   Chih.⁴ Scenery, view.

    景緻   Ching-chih. Scenery, view.

    草地   Ts'ao-ti. The fields, on the grass, lawn.

13. 坡   P'o.¹ The slope of a hill.

    廟   Miao.⁴ Temple, fair.

    頂   Ting.³ Summit, top.

    塔   T'a.³ Pagoda, dagoba.

14. 和尙   Ho-shang.⁴ Buddhist priest.

15. 一座廟 I-tso-miao. A temple.

    道   Tao.⁴ Doctrine, principle, reason, way, etc.

    道教   Tao-chiao. Taoism, Taoist.

    佛   Fo.² Buddha.

    佛教   Fo-chiao. Buddhism.

17. 蒼   Ts'ang.¹ Fly, with the next.

    蠅   Ying.² Fly, with the preceding.

    螞蟻   Ma³-i.³ Ant.

    討   T'ao.³ To beg, seek.

    厭   Yen.⁴ Dislike.

    討厭   T'ao-yen. Annoying, vexing.

18. 咬   Yao.³ To bite.

19. *A*. Ai, k'an k'an lo t'o, lo tzu, mao lü, k'o to la.

19. I say ! look at this multitude of camels, mules and donkeys.

" K'o . . . to la ", the " k'o " for emphasis.

20. *B*. Tsung shih miao shang k'ai hsiang hui, k'o jên tao pu shao.

20. There must be a fair on at the temple, with this mass of visitors.

21. *A*. K'o pu shih ma. Yu jên pao hai tzu, yu jên pei cho hsing li, hai yu jen t'iao shui.

21. Quite so. Some are carrying their children, some have bundles on their backs, while others are carrying water (on their shoulders).

" K'o pu shih ma ", a very common phrase, expressing assent, agreement.

Note the different words used for " carry " according to the method of carrying. See Vocabulary.

22. *B*. Hên jê nao. Pi shih tsai ch'ang hsi.

22. Very gay and lively. There must be theatricals on.

" Jê nao " and " hung huo " are common terms for noise and bustle, associated with fairs, markets, etc.

23. *A*. Tsa mên shang miao shang ch'ü k'an k'an.

23. Come on, let's go up to the temple and see.

24. *B*. Ai, chieh kuang, chieh kuang.

24. Ai ! by your leave, make way.

25. *A*. K'an hsi yu shih mo hao ch'u.

25. What shall we gain by looking at theatricals ?

26. *B*. Huo ch'ü huo pu ch'ü, ni tê na ting chu i pa.

26. You had better make up your mind whether you are going or not.

" Huo . . . huo "—either . . . or.

19. 駱 Lo.⁴ Camel.
    駝 T'o.² Camel, with the preceding.
    驢 Lü.² Donkey.
    毛驢 Mao-lü. Donkey.
    騾 Lo ² (tzu). Mule.

20. 香 Hsiang.¹ Fragrant, incense.

21. 抱 Pao.⁴ To nurse, carry in the arms.
    孩 Hai ² (tzu). Child.
    背 Pei.² To carry on the back.
    挑 T'iao.¹ To carry on a pole on the shoulder.
    行李 Hsing-li. Baggage.

22. 鬧 Nao.⁴ Noise, bustle, disturb.
    熱鬧 Jê-nao. Bustling, hot and noisy.
    唱 Ch'ang.⁴ To sing.
    戲 Hsi.⁴ Theatricals, play on stage.
    唱戲 Ch'ang-hsi. Theatricals, to act, play on
          stage.

24. 借光 Chieh - kuang. By your leave! (borrow
          light).

25. 好處 Hao-ch'u. Benefit, advantage.

27. *A.* Pu ju ch'ên cho chê ko chi hui, ch'ü k'an i tz'u hsi pa.

27. Well, I suppose we had better take the opportunity to see a play.

" Tz'u "—a time, a turn. " T'ai " is the classifier of plays, lit. " stage ".

28. *B.* Wo k'an mei yu pieh ti pan fa. Jên chê yang ti yung chi, hsiang hui yeh hui pu ch'ü.

28. I fear (see) there is nothing else we can do. The crowd pressing on us as it is, even if we want to go back, we shan't be able to do so.

" *Pieh* mei yu pan fa " could also be used. Note this use of " pieh "—otherwise, apart from this, not have way of doing.
" Hsiang hui, etc.", a good illustration of " pictorial " expression, showing the working of the mind in the particular situation.

29. *A.* Hsing k'uei wo mên mei yu to k'ang tung hsi. Na li yu i ko jên ch'ien la i p'i ma, p'a ts'ai la jên.

29. Fortunately we have not brought much baggage with us (on a pole). There's a man leading a horse, I'm afraid it might trample on someone.

" K'ang "—carry on shoulder; see 21 above.
" Ch'ien "—to lead a horse—a special term for this action.

30. *B.* Wei hsien tê hên.

30. Very dangerous indeed.

Note " tê hên " following the adjective, again for emphasis.

27. 趁   Ch'ên.⁴   Avail of.
     機會   Chi-hui.   Opportunity.

28. 擁   Yung.¹   To crowd or press together.
     擠   Chi.³   To crowd together.

29. 扛   K'ang.²   To carry on shoulder.
     牽   Ch'ien.¹   To lead a horse by the bridle.
     匹   P'i.³, ⁵   Classifier of horses.
     踩   Ts'ai.⁴   To trample or step on.

30. 危險   Wei.²   Hsien.³   Dangerous.

EXERCISE No. 38

Common Proverbs

1. Tsai chia ch'ien jih hao.

   Tsai wai shih shih nan.

1. A thousand days at home is all right.

   But when you are away there are always difficulties.

"Shih² shih²"—always. The repetition of the noun indicates multiplication, even to universality; e.g., "t'ien t'ien" is every day.

2. Shou tê k'u chung k'u.
   Fang wei jên shang jên.

2. Extreme suffering makes one an outstanding man.

Note the parallelism here. "K'u chung k'u"—hardship in hardship; "jên shang jên"—man above man; both suggesting an extreme. "Fang", an alternative for "ts'ai"—"then" a logical sequence.

3. Chên chin tzu pu p'a huo lien.

3. True gold doesn't fear the refiners' fire.

4. Chung kua tê kua, chung tou tê tou.

4. You reap what you sow (lit. plant a melon and you reap a melon, plant beans and you get beans)

That which a man sows he shall also reap.

5. Ya tzu ch'ih huang lien, sui k'u pu nêng yen.

5. When a dumb man eats the "huang lien", he is unable to describe its bitterness.

To suffer in silence.
"Huang lien"—a bitter plant.

6. Lu yao chih ma li.

6. A long journey reveals the strength of a horse.

VOCABULARY OF EXERCISE No. 38

3. 金   Chin.[1] Gold, metal.
   煉   Lien.[4] To refine.
4. 瓜   Kua.[1] Melon.

黃 蓮   Huang lien.[2] A bitter plant.

遙   Yao.[2] Distant.

Jih chiu chien jêu hsin.

And you discern a man's heart after long acquaintance with him.

7. Ch'ui mao ch'iu tz'u.

7. Blowing the fur to find flaws (a faultfinder).

8. Pu p'a man, chih p'a chan.

8. It's well to keep going even if the going is slow. (Stagnation is to be dreaded.)

To keep going is important.

9. Yüan shui chiu pu liao chin huo.

9. A distant well (water) is of no avail to put out a fire which is near at hand.

Hope deferred maketh the heart sick.

10. Tso ching kuan t'ien.

10. Sitting in a well and looking at the sky (parochialism).

11. Ch'i hu nan hsia.

11. Once you are mounted on a tiger the difficulty is to get down.

You'll suffer for your rashness.

12. I ko jên chiao t'a liang chih ch'uan.

12. (Like) a man straddling two boats. (Hesitancy) " He who hesitates is lost ".

Hesitancy is dangerous.

13. Pu tao ho pien pu t'o hsieh.

13. Don't take your shoes off until you reach the river.

Meeting trouble halfway.

7. 吹　　Ch'ui.¹ To blow.
　 疵　　Tz'u.¹　A flaw, blemish.

9. 救　　Chiu.⁴　To save, deliver.

1. 虎　　Hu.³　Tiger.

2. 踏　　T'a.⁴　Step on, tread.
　 隻　　Chih.¹　Classifier of boats, shoes. etc.
　 脚　　Chiao.³　Straddle.

14. Ch'ien jên tsai shu, hou jên ch'êng liang.

14. Our forefathers planted trees, and their descendants avail themselves of the cool shade.

Our debt to our foretatners.

15. Shih niao tsai shu,

Pu ju i niao tsai shou.

15. Ten birds on the tree are not so good as one bird in the hand.

(One bird in the hand is worth ten on the tree.)

A bird in the hand is worth two in the bush.

16. Jên shih chiu ti hao. I fu shih hsin ti hao.

16. Old friends are best. New clothes are best.

17. Mou shih tsai jên. Ch'êng shih tsai t'ien.

17. Man proposes but God (Heaven) disposes.

18. Chin t'ien t'o la hsieh ho wa, pu chih ming t'ien ch'uan pu ch'uan.

18. We take off our shoes and socks to-day, but do not know whether we shall put them on to-morrow.

The uncertainty of life.

19. Hsia mao p'êng ssu lao shu.

19. A blind cat happens upon a dead rat.

Extraordinary luck.

20. Shan yu shan pao, o yu o pao.

20. Goodness brings a good reward, evil an evi recompense.

14. 栽   Tsai.[1]   To plant.
    乘   Ch'eng.[1]   Avail of.

15. 鳥   Niao.[3]   Bird.

17. 謀   Mou.[2]   To plan, devise.

9. 貓   Mao.[2][1]   Cat.
    死   Ssu.[3]   Dead, to die.
    鼠   Shu.[3]   Rat, mouse.
    老鼠   Lao-shu.   Rat, mouse.

0. 善   Shan.[4]   Good.
    惡   O.[4]   Evil.
    報   Pao.[4]   Report.

20. Shan o pu pao, shih
    hou wei tao.

If good and evil are
not requited, it is
(merely) because the
time has not yet
arrived.

21. Shan mên nan k'ai.
    Shan mên nan pi.

21. It is hard to prise open
the door of benevo-
lence, and equally
hard to shut it.

Used of charitable deeds. It is hard to get people to help you when
in need (from the standpoint of the needy). Once you have begun to
distribute alms, you will find it hard to stop (from the standpoint of
the benefactor); *i.e.*, there will always be a crowd of beggars round
you if you give to one.

20. 報   Pao.[4] Report, reward.

21. 閉   Pi.[4] To close.

DIALOGUE No. 39

In the City

Two friends, *A* and *B*, who meet a third friend, *C*

1. *A.* Tui mie'rh, na tso shih t'ou tsao ti fang tzu, shih shih mo.

1. What is that stone building opposite?

" Shih t'ou tsao ti "—made or built of stone.

2. *B.* Ni wên ti shih cha ch'i kan ti na ko fang tzu ma.

2. Are you asking about that building with the flag-pole?

3. *A.* Shih ti. Kua kuo ch'i ti na ko fang tzu.

3. Yes, the building with the national flag flying.

4. *B.* Ai. Na shih " Ai Kuo Tien Ying Yüan ". Ni yao k'an tien ying ma.

4. Oh, that is the " Patriotic Cinema Theatre ". Do you want to see the films?

5. *A.* Ch'êng li ti yin hang, chi tien chung kuan mên.

5. What time do the banks in the city close?

" Kuan mên ". The difference between " kuan " and " shang " should be noted. " Kuan " is used of doors on hinges; " shang " of shutters.

6. *B.* Yin hang san tien chung kuan mên, ch'ien p'u i chih k'ai tao chiu tien chung.

6. The big banks close at three, but the cash shops keep open until nine o'clock.

VOCABULARY OF DIALOGUE No. 39

1. 石   Shih² (t'ou). Stone.
   造   Tsao.⁴ To build, made.

2. 插   Ch'a.¹ To stick in.
   旗   Ch'i.² Flag, banner.
   桿   Kan.³ Staff, pole.

4. 影   Ying.³ Shadow, image.
   電影   Tien - ying. The cinema film (electric-shadow).
   愛國   Ai-kuo. Patriotic.

5. 行   Hang.² A store, shop, etc.
   銀行   Yin-hang. A bank.

6. 鋪   P'u.⁴ A shop.
   錢鋪   Ch'ien-p'u. A Chinese cash shop.

7. *A.* Wo chê li yu i
  chang hui p'iao
  (chih p'iao) yao
  huan ch'êng hsien
  ch'ien, ts'ai nêng
  k'an tien ying.

7. I have a cheque here
 which I must cash
 before I can go to
 the pictures.

" Huan ch'êng "—change it to become . . .
" Ts'ai "—change your money first and " *then* " you will be able.
The " ts'ai " of logical sequence.

8. *B.* Ch'ien tien yeh kei
  ni huan, yeh pu
  k'ou ch'ien.

8. The cash shops will
 change it for you,
 and charge no dis-
 count.

9. *A.* Na mo, wo mên
  hsien shang yu
  chêng chü, wo
  yao ta tien pao
  kei wo nei jên.

9. Then let us go to the
 post office first. I
 want to send a tele-
 gram to my wife.

" Nei jên ", used in referring to one's own wife, but not to the wife
of another man. " Chia li ti " is a common synonym, *i.e.*, " the
one in my home ".
" Kei " often means " to ".

10. *B.* Yu chêng chü, li
  chê'rh yüan ya.
  Hai shih tien pao
  chü pi chiao chin.

10. The post office is quite
 far from here. The
 telegraph office is
 nearer.

11. *A.* Pu kuo wo i ting
  yao pa chê liang
  fêng kua hao hsin,
  chi kei wo kung
  ssu ti ta pan.

11. But I must first send
 these two registered
 letters to the mana-
 ger of my firm.

" Ta pan "—the big boss. Others in order of seniority are " erh
pan ", second boss, " san pan ", third boss, and so on.

12. *B.* I fêng kua hao hsin,
  t'ieh to shao yu
  p'iao.

12. How many stamps must
 one put on a regis-
 tered letter ?

7. 滙　　　Hui.⁴ To exchange money.
　　滙票　Hui-p'iao. Bank cheque, draft, etc.
　　支票　Chih-p'iao. Bank cheque, draft, etc.

8. 扣　　　K'ou.⁴ To deduct, discount.

9. 郵　　　Yu.² To convey, postal service.
　　政　　Chêng.⁴ Government, administration.
　　郵政局　Yu-chêng-chü. The post office.
　　報　　Pao.⁴ Report, announce, inform.
　　電報　Tien-pao. Telegram.
　　打電報　Ta-tien-pao. To send a telegram.
　　內　　Nei.⁴ Inside, within.
　　內人　Nei-jen. Wife, my wife.

11. 挂號　Kua-hao. To register, letters, parcels, etc.
　　一封信　I-feng-hsin. A letter.
　　司　　Ssu.¹ Manage, board, company.
　　公司　Kung-ssu. A public company.
　　大班　Ta-pan. Manager, chief.
　　寄　　Chi.⁴ To send.

12. 貼　　T'ieh.¹ To stick on, as stamps.
　　郵票　Yu-p'iao. Postage stamps.

13. *A.* Na wo pu hsiao tê.
Wo mên shang
chü tzu li ch'ü,
wên i wên.

13. That I don't know.
But we will go to the
office to inquire.

14. *B.* Hao. Ai, kuo lai
ti chiu shih i
ko t'ung hsiang.
Hao ya, hsiang
pu tao tsai chê li
p'êng chien ni. Ni
mang shêm-mo.

14. Good. Hello, here's
a fellow - townsman
coming along. Hello!
I did not expect to
come across you
here. What's your
hurry?

"Hsiang pu tao", used of anything that *unexpectedly* happens.
"Ni mang shêm-mo"—you hurry what? What is your hurry?

15. *C.* Ai, liao pu tê. Wo
ti tsu fu pei ch'i
ch'ê pan tao la.
Shou la chung
shang. Wo hsien
tsai shang i yüan
k'an t'a ch'ü.

15. Ah, terrible! My
grandfather has been
knocked down by a
motor car. He has
sustained severe in-
juries, and I am just
going to the hospital
to see him.

"Liao pu tê"—terrible—may be applied to propitious as well as
unpropitious events, but more generally it is used of the latter.
"Pei", the normal passive sign; translated "by".

16. *B.* K'o hsi, k'o hsi. Pu
kan liu lan ni, t'i
wo wên hou ling
tsu pa.

16. I am sorry (what a
pity). I mustn't de-
tain you. Greetings
to your grandfather
(lit. inquiries on my
behalf to . . .).

17. *C.* Hsieh hsieh. Tsai
chien.

17. Thank you. Goodbye.

18. *B.* Tsa mên tao kuan
tzu li, ch'ih tung
hsi pa. Wo tu
tzu o la.

18. Let's go along to a
restaurant, and have
something to eat. I
am hungry (lit. my
stomach is hungry).

14. 同鄉　　T'ung-hsiang.　Fellow-villager, townsman.
　　想不到　Hsiang-pu-tao.　Unexpected (think not
　　　　　　　arrive).

15. 了不得　Liao-pu-tê.　Expression of emotion, elation,
　　　　　　　grief.
　　祖　　　Tsu.³　Ancestors.
　　受傷　　Shou-shang.　To receive an injury.
　　醫院　　I-yüan.　Hospital.
　　被　　　Pei.⁴　By (sign of passive).

16. 留攔　　Liu-lan.　To detain.
　　令祖　　Ling-tsu.　Your grandfather.

18. 肚　　　Tu⁴ (tzu).　Stomach, belly.
　　餓　　　O.⁴　Hungry.

19. *A.* K'o i. Wo pu hsiang ch'ih shih mo tung hsi. K'o shih wo tsui kan la. Wo yao ho i pei p'i chiu.

19. All right. I don't feel like eating anything. But I am thirsty (my lips are dry). I shall have a glass of beer.

20. *B.* Ai, chê ko kuan tzu pu ts'o, hai yu yin yo tui t'ing.

20. Ah, this is a very good restaurant, and there is a band to listen to.

21. *A.* Na pu shih yin yo tui, pu kuo shih liu shêng chi ti hsiang shêng.

21. That isn't a band, it is only a gramophone('s noise).

22. *B.* Wo k'an shih wu hsien tien kuang po ti yin yo.

22. I think it is the wireless broadcasting music.

23. *A.* K'o pu shih ma. Wo t'ing shuo chê'rh ch'a pu to mei wan shang tou yu t'iao wu. Ni hui t'iao wu pu hui.

23. Of course it is. I hear that almost every evening there is dancing here. Can you dance?

24. *B.* Hui shih hui. Wo chin t'ien t'ai lei la, pu hsiang t'iao wu.

24. Yes I can, but I am tired to-day and don't feel like dancing.

25. *A.* Na mo, wo mên chiu ch'ü k'an tien ying pa. I mien hsiu hsi, i mien chang chih shih.

25. Then let's go to the pictures. On the one hand we can take a rest and on the other increase our knowledge.

" I mien . . . i mien "—on the one hand . . . and on the other.

19. 嘴乾   Tsui-kan. Thirsty (lips dry).
    啤   P'i² (chiu). Beer.

20. 樂   Yo. Yüeh.⁴ Music.
    音樂   Yin-yo. Music.
    音樂隊   Yin-yo-tui. Band.
21. 留聲機   Liu-shêng-chi. Gramophone (retain-voice-machine).
    響聲   Hsiang³-shêng. Noise, sound.

22. 無線電   Wu-hsien-tien. Wireless (no-wire-electric).
    廣   Kuang.³ Wide, broadcast.
    播   Po.¹ To spread abroad.
    廣播電台   Kuang-po-tien-t'ai. A broadcasting station.

23. 跳   T'iəo.⁴ To dance, jump.
    舞   Wu.³ To posture, brandish, dance.

24. 累   Lei.⁴ Tired, fatigued.

25. 一面   I-mien. On the one hand.

26. *B.* Pu ts'o. Wo i wei
    na tao kêng yu
    hsing ch'ü (ch'ü
    wei).

26. Very good. I think
    that will be more
    interesting.

26. 趣　　Ch'ü.[4] Interesting, amusing.

興趣　　Hsing-ch'ü. Interesting, interest.

DIALOGUE No. 40

On War and Peace

Two friends, A and B

1. A. Wo chê i pei tzu ti kung fu, chiu p'êng tao la liang tz'u ti shih chieh ta chan.

1. I have experienced (lit. met with) two world wars in my lifetime.

2. B. Wei shih mo shih chieh shang pu nêng kou wei ch'ih ho p'ing ni.

2. How is it that peace cannot be organised on earth?

" Nêng i ", synonym for " nêng kou "—can, be able to.

3. A. Kên pên chiu shih yin wei kuo chia kên kuo chia, chung tsu kên chung tsu chih chien, fa hsien pu kung p'ing ti shih hsiang.

3. At bottom it is because between nations and races, certain injustices arise.

" Kên pên "—the root, source, etc., or
" Tao ti "—really, lit. arrive at bottom.
" Chih chien ". " Chih " the possessive goes better with " chien " than " ti ".
" Fa hsien ", lit. become evident, so reveal.

4. B. Ni ti i ssu shih shuo, pi hsien ch'ü hsiao i ch'ieh pu kung p'ing ti

4. Do you then mean, that in order to obtain a peaceful world, we must first eliminate

VOCABULARY OF DIALOGUE No. 40

1. 輩   Pei.⁴ Generation.

2. 維   Wei.² To maintain, organise.
   持   Ch'ih.² To organise, maintain.
   維持   Wei-ch'ih. To organise and keep going.

3. 之   Chih.¹ Like "ti", the sign of the pos-
         sessive, only with a slightly literary
         flavour.
   事項   Shih-hsiang. The details of affairs, affairs.
   族   Tsu.² A clan, tribe.
   間   Chien.¹ Between.

4. 取消   Ch'ü-hsiao. To cut out, eliminate.

shih, ts'ai nêng   everything that is
p'an wang tê tao,   unjust?
yu i ko ho p'ing
ti shih chieh ma.

" Ni ti i ssu shih shuo "—in exact terms your meaning is.
" Ts'ai "—of logical sequence. Cf. Dial. 39, sen. 7.

5. *A*. Shih chieh shang fa   5. The majority of wars
      shêng chan shih,   that arise on this
      to pan shih yin   earth are due to the
      wei wo kang ts'ai   reason I have just
      shuo kuo ti yüan   mentioned. But the
      ku. Pu kuo jên   fact that every man
      jên tou yu i ko   is selfish is something
      tzu ssu ti hsin.   that cannot be ig-
      Chê yeh pu k'o   nored.
      pu chu i ti.

" To i pan "—mainly, the majority.
" Pu k'o pu . . .", another example of the double negative for
emphasis.

6. *B*. Pu ts'o. Jên ti tzu   6. Quite right. The sel-
      ssu hsin, shih tsai   fish instincts of man
      nan yü ch'ü tiao.   are certainly hard to
                                  eradicate.

7. *A*. K'o shih hsien tsai   7. But the second Great
      ti, ti êrh tz'u ta   War is now over.
      chan i ching wan   Germany, Italy and
      la. Tê Kuo, I   Japan have all sur-
      Kuo, Jih Pên,   rendered.
      tou i ching t'ou
      hsiang la.

" Hsiang ", also read " chiang ", but not in the sense of surrender.

8. *B*. Ai ya. Chung Kuo   8. Ah! China has been
      ti k'ang Jih Pên   resisting Japanese
      ti ch'in lüeh, i   aggression for eight
      ching pa nien   years now.
      liao.

5. 私   Ssu.¹ Selfish, private.
  自私   Tzu-ssu. Selfish.
  原   Yuan.² Source.
  注   Chu.⁴ Fix.

6. 去掉   Ch'ü-tiao. To eliminate, get rid of.

7. 德國   Tê²-kuo. Germany.
  意國   I-kuo. Italy.
  日本   Jih-pen. Japan.
  投   T'ou.² To hand in, surrender.
  降   Hsiang.² To submit, surrender (with the
                preceding).

8. 抵   Ti.³ To resist.
  抗   K'ang.⁴ To resist, oppose (with the pre-
                ceding).
  侵   Ch'in.¹ To invade.

9. *A.* Liang pien ssu shang ti jên, tou fei ch'ang ti to la.

9. The killed and wounded on both sides are extremely (unusually) many.

10. *B.* Shih tsai pu shao. Fang tzu pei cha tan cha huai la ti, yeh shih hên to.

10. Very many indeed. And the number of buildings that have been destroyed by bombing is tremendous.

" Pei ", another instance of the Passive voice expressed in this way. See Dial. 39, sen. 15.

11. *A.* Mêng chün i ching chan shêng la, Tê Kuo ho Jih Pen i ching ta pai la. Ni hsiang chiang lai hai hui fa shêng chan shih ma.

11. Now that the Allies are victorious, and Germany and Japan have been defeated, do you think there will be another war?

" Chan shêng "—fight-win, get the victory.

12. *B.* Pu kan shuo i ting. Tan shih chê i tz'u chan chêng yung ti wu ch'i, fei ch'ang ti ts'an pao. Yeh hsü ko kuo tou shou la chê chung k'ung hsia (ho), tsai pu kan hsüan chan liao.

12. One cannot say for certain. But the weapons used during this war have been so cruel and terrifying, that perhaps as each nation has been so intimidated by the terror, no one will dare to proclaim war again.

" Chê i tz'u "—this, this instance of . . .
" Fei ch'ang ". " Fei " is not; " ch'ang " is usual, so extraordinary.
" Huo cho "—perhaps, possibly.

8. 略　　Lüeh.⁴　To plunder.
　　侵略　Ch'in²-lüeh.⁴　Aggression.

10. 被　　Pei.⁴ Sign of passive.
　　炸　　Cha.⁴　Smash, explode.
　　彈　　Tan.⁴　Bomb, bullet.
　　炸彈　Cha-tan.　Bomb.
　　壞　　Huai.⁴　Ruin, destroy, spoil.

11. 盟　　Mêng.²　Covenant, alliance.
　　盟軍　Mêng-chün.　The Allied Forces.
　　勝　　Shêng.⁴　Victory, conquer.
　　敗　　Pai.⁴　Defeat, spoil.

12. 武器　Wu³-ch'i.　Weapons.
　　殘　　Ts'an.²　Injure, cruel.
　　暴　　Pao.⁴　Violent, fierce, cruel.
　　恐　　K'ung.³　To terrify, fearsome.
　　嚇　　Hsia.⁴　Alarm, startle.
　　宣　　Hsüan.¹　To proclaim, make public.
　　宣戰　Hsüan-chan.　To declare war.
　　爭　　Chêng.¹　Wrangle, strive.

13. *A*. Wo hsiang hsin shih chê yang, ping ch'ieh chin nien liu shih to kuo, tsu chih la i ko lien ho hui, yao chin li ti wei ch'ih shih chieh ho p'ing.

13. I believe that it will be so. Moreover more than sixty nations have organised a League, with the idea of exerting every effort to maintain the peace of the world.

" Hsiang hsin "—to believe. The use of " hsiang " here is probably an instance of its reflective use, forming the middle voice form of the verb.

14. *B*. Ting hao. Tan shih wo k'an tsai pi yao shih, hai tê yung lien ho ti chün li, ju hai chün, lu chün, k'ung chün ti li liang, lai pang chu, hui i ts'ai neng yu mei man ti hsiao kuo.

14. Excellent. But I think that we shall have to use the united Forces, Navy, Army and Air Forces, in case of necessity, to help make it possible for this Assembly to function effectively.

" Lien ho ", *or* " lien pang "—connected or Allied States. Cf. **11**, where we have " mêng chün "—the covenanted or allied forces.

" Mei-man ". " Mei ' is good, excellent; " man " is full, satisfactory.

15. *A*. T'ung i la. Hsien tsai ti chêng chih chu i hên fu tsa. Yu min chu chu i, kung ch'an chu i, hai yu ch'i t'a ti ko ming ti ho shou chiu ti, ko chung chêng chih shang ti p'ai pieh.

15. Agreed. There exists at the present time a great variety of political theories. We have Democracy, Communism, and Progressive (revolutionary) and Conservative parties in Government circles.

" T'ung i "—same meaning, so agreed.

13. 信   Hsin.⁴ To believe.

相信   Hsiang-hsin. To believe, have faith.

組   Tsu.³ To organise, cord.

織   Chih.¹ To weave, but with the preceding means to organise.

且   Ch'ieh.³ Moreover, and.

聯   Lien.³ To connect, unite.

14. 海   Hai.³ The sea.

海軍   Hai-chün. The Navy.

陸軍   Lu⁴-chun. The Army.

空軍   K'ung-chün. The Air Force.

美滿   Mei-man. Complete, satisfactory.

效   Hsiao.⁴ Effect, effective.

效果   Hsiao-kuo. Result, effect.

會議   Hui⁴-I.⁴ Assembly.

助   Chu.⁴ Help, assist.

15. 治   Chih.⁴ To govern.

政治   Chêng-chih. Political, Government.

複   Fu.⁴ Double.

雜   Tsa.² Confused, complicated.

複雜   Fu-tsa. Complex, confused.

產   Ch'an.³ Property.

共產   Kung-ch'an. Communist (public or common property).

主義   Chu-i. -ism, idealogy.

其他   Ch'i-t'a. Others, other.

" Chu i ", equal to our -ism theory, idealogy, etc.; *e.g.*, " San Min Chu I ", the " Three People's Principles " of Sun Yat Sen.

" Fu-tsa ". " Fu " is double; " tsa " confused, so complex, complicated, many and varied.

" Ko-ming ", lit. change the decree, revolutionary.

16. *B.* Na tao pu yao chin. Pu p'a chêng chih shang ti tang p'ai to, chih p'a chung jên pu chu i chêng chih shang ti shih ch'ing.

16. But that is unimportant. We need not fear multiple political parties. What is to be feared is that the mass of the people pay no attention to politics.

" Tang p'ai "—parties, factions,

" Chia " is used to indicate a certain class or cross-section of people : " chêng-chih-chia "—politicians ; " wên-hsüeh-chia "—literary man, author (" wên " being letters, literature).

" Chu i " is a verb here, to pay attention or heed to. Cf 15 above.

15. 革 Ko.[2] To change, alter.

革命 Ko-ming. Revolutionary (change the decree).

守舊 Shou-chiu. Conservative (guard the old).

派 P'ai.[4] Party, separate, branch.

派別 P'ai-pieh. Parties.

16. 黨 Tang.[3] Party, association, faction.

衆人 Chung-jên. Everybody, the people.

CHINESE TEXT OF THE DIALOGUES

HINTS FOR THE STUDENT

As the aim of this book is to give the student a basic knowledge of both the written and spoken forms of the Chinese language, the forty dialogues have been prepared in Romanised and Chinese characters.

The student should use the Chinese characters from the very outset of his studies, and turn to the Romanised form only as a last resort.

Here are a few hints to aid the student in acquiring a mastery of the dialogues, *viz.* :—

1. Write out the sentences in the Chinese characters repeatedly.

2. Do not attempt to absorb too many sentences at any one session, especially at the beginning. Learn thoroughly what you do.

3. Constantly revise your past work.

4. As you write the sentences, repeat the separate sounds aloud. The actual hearing of the sounds is an additional aid to memory.

5. Frequently close the book and repeat the sentences without its aid.

6. Constantly compare your efforts at memorising with the text.

7. Vary the sentences by altering the pronouns, and the number and tense of the verbs.

8. Think of the " opposite " of adjectives, adverbs, etc., *e.g.*, " black " and " white "; " long " and " short "; " quickly " and " slowly ", etc., and make new sentences along this line.

9. As you have opportunity of conversing, use what you have learnt. Do not be afraid of making mistakes.

Listen attentively to the response especially if it is from a Chinese. This will often be preceded by a repetition of your question, probably in better " Chinese " !

10. Repeat the reply to yourself, and write down in a note-book anything that is new.

11. Finally, let me repeat advice given in the Introduction. Think of each sentence as a whole, as representing an " idea ", and do not be too anxious to analyse the sentence into its component parts. Ability to do this will come naturally as you acquire more of the language.

第一課

1 門口有人。　2 誰？　3 我。　4 是誰？　5 不知道。

6 我去看一看。　7 不用、我叫隆福去。　8 隆福。

9 哎。　10 來吧。　11 哎。　12 門口有人、你去看一看是誰。

13 哎。　14 先生貴姓？　15 我姓李、王先生在家嗎？

16 在家、請進來。　17 好。　18 李先生來了。　19 請進

來吧。　20 呀、李先生好哎。　21 好、王先生張先生都好哎。

22 好、好、請坐請坐。　23 謝謝。　24 泡茶。　25 說話、就來。

26 請李先生喝茶。　27 不敢當。　28 再坐一會兒。

29 對不住、有人等着、我得回去。　30 不送不送。

31 那兒的話。　32 再見、再見。

第二課

1 王先生來了。　2 請他進來。　3 王先生好呀？　4 好、太太喫過飯沒有？　5 喫了。先生喫了嗎？　6 還沒有喫。或偏過了。　7 請先生坐。　8 請太太先坐。　9 先生太客氣。或先生請坐。　10 不客氣、是理當的。　11 可以給先生泡茶。或沏茶。　12 哎、預備好了。　13 請先生喝茶。　14 謝謝。　15 中國話、我不大懂、　16 太太幾時到敝國來的？　17 我是上月才到貴國來的。　18 太太的中國話說得好。　19 過獎過獎。　20 眞的實在好　21 中國話容易學不容易學？　22 並不太難。　23 我願意把中國話學好。　24 我盡心的教你就是了。

第三課

1 這個是什麼。

2 那是一本書。

3 是什麼書。

4 是一本字典。

5 那個東西叫什麼。

6 那是一管鉛筆。

7 我們可以做什麼。

8 我們可以唸書。

9 我們可以唸什麼書。

10 我們可以唸這個讀本。

11 請先生唸、我聽。

12 那個法子不大好。

13 那麼、先生先唸、我就跟著唸、行不行。

14 行、這個法子很好。

15 要

16 理當理當。

17 現在

18 我們可以寫字。

19 好、我喜歡寫字。

20 會寫字不會。

21 不會、可是我願意學。

22 那麼、我就盡心的教你。

23 寫字用什麼東西。

24 我們用一管筆、一張紙、一塊墨、和一方硯台、再加上一點兒水、研墨。　25 我把這些東西拿來、我們就寫字。

26 好、我們寫字吧。

第四課

1 這個東西叫什麼。　2 那是一個茶盃（碗）。　3 茶盃和茶碗有什麼分別。　4 茶盃有把兒、茶碗沒有把兒。

5 那是什麼東西。　6 那是一個（把）茶壺。　7 茶壺和水壺一樣不一樣。　8 不一樣、茶壺是泡茶用的、水壺是燒水用的。

9 這些煙捲兒是誰的。　10 那些煙捲兒是我的。　11 有洋火（火柴）沒有。　12 有、你要不要。

13 不耍、我不喫（抽）煙。

14 這兩管筆是你的嗎。

15 這一管鋼筆是我的。

16 那一管呢？

17 那一管毛筆是不是你的呀？

18 不是我的、是我朋友的。

19 那一瓶墨水也是他的嗎。

20 不是他的、是先生的。

21 這些煙捲兒好不好？

22 不大好。

23 你在那兒買的？

24 在市場上買的。

25 在這裡有賣的沒有？

26 在這裡沒有賣的。

27 在那裡有賣的呢？

28 上大街上去、或者可以買。

29 咱們倆可以上街去買幾個吧。

30 好、咱們一塊兒去。

第五課

1 他來了沒有？ 2 他沒有來。 3 你來不來？ 4 我

們來不來？ 5 昨天他們來了麼？ 6 他們來了。 7 明天你

8 明天我們不來。 9 今天你去不去？

10 我去。 11 明天你回來不回來？ 12 明天不回來。

13 明天她回去不回去？ 14 是的、明天她回去。 15 你

上那裡去？ 16 我上街去。 17 我也去。 18 你去幹

什麼？ 19 我去買東西。 20 買什麼東西？ 21 買一頂

帽子和一雙鞋。 22 到過北京沒有？ 23 沒有到過。

24 起來、我們走吧。 25 等一等、得拿幾個錢。 26 那不

要緊、我帶得有錢。

看情形怎樣。

30 對了。

第六課

1
太太叫我吧。

2 是的、叫廚子和看門的(門房)來、我要
和你們說幾句話。

3 他們就來、哎、來了。

不用坐、我們站着的好。

4 坐下吧。

太太叫我們做什麼、我們照辦就是了。

5

6 今天我很忙、要大家幫忙。

7

的家具拿來、我要看一看。

8 先把喫飯

9
太太是叫我們把刀子、叉

子、調匙和勺子、都要拿來嗎?

10 是的、也要拿茶盃、碗

29 有的時候好、有的時候不好、是不是。

27 可是借人的錢不大好。

28 那要

碟子、和盤子。

11 這些東西拿來了，叫我們放在那裡呢。

12 把他們都放在桌子上。

13 太太今天晚上不是請客嗎？。

14 不是晚上請客，是今天下午請幾個人來喝茶。

15 那麼太太得叫厨房多烤麪包和點心。

16 黃油和菓子醬多不多？。

17 這些都夠十來個客人喫。

18 家具也夠十來個人用嗎？。

19 不大夠、要是刀子叉子不夠的時候、可以預備筷子叫他們使。

20 只怕有的人不會使筷子。

21 那倒沒有法子了。

第七課

1 先生好嗎？。

2 謝謝、先生你好。(P)承問承問。

3 先

生(您)喫了飯沒有。

4 喫了、先生(您)喫了嗎。還沒有喫

5 偏過了。(P)

6 貴姓。(P)

7 賤或敝姓王。(P)

我姓王。(C)

8 台甫。

9 草字清長。(P)

10 名字叫什麼或什麼名字。(C)

11 名叫清長或清長。(C)

12 名字叫什麼。

13 五十五或五十五歲。(C)

14 先生貴庚或先生貴甲子。(P)

大年紀或先生多大歲數。

15 先生高壽。

16 兄弟還小、虛度了五十五歲。(P)

17 先生貴國或貴國是那一國或貴國是那裡。

18 不敢當、敝國英國。(P)

19 先生是那裡來的。(C)

20 我是南京來的。

21 先生貴處或府上在那裡。(P)

22 不敢當、敝處北平。

23 北平離這裡多遠。

24 三百多里路。

25 先生往那裡去。

26 我上漢

27 閣下是走水路、還是走旱路來的呢。

28 我沒有走水路、也沒有走旱路，我是坐飛機來的。

29 走了幾天的工夫。

30 一共四天的工夫。

31 哎呀、非常的快。

第八課

1 家裡有幾個人。

2 統共六個。

3 父母還在嗎？或父母都在不在。

4 父親在，母親不在了。

5 令尊高壽。(P)

6 八十二歲。

7 令堂去世是多大年紀。(P)

8 五十六歲。

9 可惜可惜。

10 先生有寶眷沒有。(P)

11 還沒有成家。(P)

12 先生訂了婚沒有。

13 訂了。

14 先生結了婚嗎。(P)

15 結了婚了。

16 先生有幾個孩子？

17 四周

18 男的有幾個。（位（P）

19 兩個男的、兩個女的。

20 好福氣。

21 托福托福。(P)

22 先生令郎幾位。(P)

23 小犬兩個。(P)

24 令嬡有幾位。(P)

24a 小女兩個。

25 先生貴幹或先生有什麼差事或先生辦什麼公幹或先生幹什麼事？(C)

26 我是個商人或我做買賣。

27 先生奉了教沒有。(C)

28 在教。

29 是耶穌教、還是天主教呢。

30 我是耶穌教（或基督教）。

31 這裡有耶穌教堂或這裡有福音堂。

32 有牧師女教士在這裡嗎。

33 有女教士沒有牧師。

34 先生什麼時候到的中國。

35 我是三個月以前來的。

36 哎呀先生說的中國話真好。

37 過獎過獎

獎。我不過會講幾句。

38 再見再見。

第九課

A 數目字

1 一。

2 二。

3 三。

4 四。

5 五。

6 六。

7 七。

8 八。

9 九。

10 十。

11 兩個人。

12 兩本書。

13 十一。

14 十七。

15 二十。

16 八十。

17 一百。

18 六百。

19 九百。

20 一百一十(或一百一)。

21 一百一十二。

22 一百一十五。

23 一百七。

24 七百六十八。

25 這個數目字翻出來是

26 一百零五。

27 二百零九。

28 兩千

怎樣的唸呢?

或二千。

百零三。

四十二。

零零七。

42 八分之七。

數數吧。

一個。

幾。今天二十幾。

29 一千零八十九 或 一千八十九。

31 三千九百三。

34 三萬零五十六。

36 第一(頭一個。)

十五。

39 一半。

B 1 在地下有幾件東西。

3 束西夠數不夠數呢。

5 那麼、他們必需補上。

7 今天是星期(禮拜)三。

9 今天是初八。

32 一萬。

35 四萬零七個 或 四萬

37 第十八。

40 十分之一。

2 等一等我

4 我看少(差、短)着

6 今天是星期(禮拜)

8 今天初幾。今天十

10 頭一個月叫正

33 一萬一千

38 第一百三

41 四分之三。

30 三千九

月、末一個月（或第十二個月）叫臘月。

11 其餘那幾個月叫什麼？

12 二月、三月、四月、一直到十一月、都是一樣（都是照例的）。

13 可是十一月也叫冬月。 14 年底是什麼意思？

15 年底就是臘月最後幾天的意思。 16 過年是什麼意思？

17 過年就是新年頭一天的意思。

18 把這些玩藝兒分開給孩子玩。 19 把這些糖也分給他們。

20 可以每個人給他一份。 21 我已經分了兩次。

第十課

1 你身上帶了表沒有，

2 沒有、但是對面兒有鐘。

3 你看有幾點鐘。

4 我近視眼、看不清楚。

5 我看

見了、現在是（有）一點鐘。

6 哎、我約了一個朋友十二點半鐘見面、已經躭誤了。

7 也許他還在等你。

8 恐怕他等不到我、走了。

9 現在幾點鐘？

10 一點過一刻（或一點一刻）。

11 要是十二點一刻、我還可以趕得上。

12 要是十二點差一刻、那就更好。

13 現在幾點鐘。

14 一點二十五分、

15 那麼、再等十分鐘、就是兩點差二十五分、是不是。

16 不錯、不錯。

17 去年夏天你上那兒避暑去的？

18 去年我們那兒也沒有去、前年我們到嶗山去避暑的。

19 你從嶗山回來以後、做了什麼。

20 什麼也沒有做、我在家裡閒着。

21 從前

你不是愛打網球嗎。

22 那個時候、打網球、踢足球都是我喜歡的。

23 那麼、你後天來和我打網球好嗎。

24 大後天行不行。

25 不敢說因為前天我和一個朋友約好大後天和他打牌。

26 那麼、就是後天吧。

27 好、你帶兩個球拍子來。

第十一課

1 你有表沒有。

2 沒有、但是我家裡有一座鐘。

3 那個鐘對不對。

4 不對、那個鐘走得慢。

5 我的表走得快。

6 那麼、得把快慢改一改。

7 改了也沒有用。

8 怎樣沒有用呢。

9 我的表走的沒有準。

10 那麼、

你的表得修理。

11 不錯、可是不知道誰能替我修理。

12 我認得一個鐘表匠。

13 好、你拿我的表、叫他看看、好不好。

14 可以、不過今天上午我沒有工夫。

15 下午你有工夫沒有。

16 不一定、你把表給我、要是後半天有工夫、我就給你送去。

17 勞駕勞駕。

18 那沒有什麼。

19 今天晚上、我請幾個朋友喫飯、你能來不能來。

20 不敢當、我還有事。

21 你最好能來。我請你陪客。

22 喫飯要幾個鐘頭。

23 大概用兩個鐘頭。

24 喫了飯以後要打牌嗎。

25 隨便、我自己倒想下幾盤棋。

26 你們下棋、大家可以出去逛一逛。

27 那倒不行、女客

可以做針線、男客喫煙譚譚吧。　28 咱們不到半夜以前、

不會分手的。　29 十一**點**鐘以前回去就好。

第十二課

1 把窗戶關上。　2 恐怕關不上。　3 怎麼關不上。

4 有毛病。　5 有什麼毛病。　6 這幾天天氣發潮、叫

窗戶框子走了縫。　7 那麼得叫木匠來修理修理。

8 是的、我叫李司夫來看一看。　9 前門鎖上了沒有？

10 鎖上了或鎖不上那個鎖上了銹。　11 拿鑰匙來、試

一試。　12 最好先塗一點兒油。　13 你說的對、先塗一

點兒油吧。　14 把後門開開吧。　15 那個門我已經開了。

16 不要再關上。

17 要是把門敞開、恐怕小偸進來偸東西。

18 可不是嗎、不如把門關上。

19 這個瓶子的塞子、我取不出來。

20 那是因爲沒有合式的東西、得用一個螺絲轉。

21 把這個箱子（匣子、盒子、筒子）打開。

22 開這個箱子很費事。

23 怎樣費事呢。

24 釘子太多、全都上銹了。

25 那個好辦。你上王先生那裡去借他的鉗子。

26 要是王先生不在家、問誰去借呢？

27 他家裡總有用人、就向他借好了。

28 是的、我就去。

29 你經過園子的時候、看看水井蓋上了沒有。

30 我今天清早打完了水、就把井蓋上了。

31 你那幾個桶子都

盛(倒)滿了水嗎。

32　家裡所有的桶子、我都盛滿了水。

33　園子裡那個大水缸裝的是髒水、你倒出去了沒有。

34　我把那個髒水、完全倒出去了、一點兒也沒有留。

35　我把一件事情忘記了。

36　是什麼事情。

37　咱們

38　是甜的、可以用來煮飯泡茶。

井裡邊的水、是苦的、還是甜的呢。

第十三課

1　把這一張桌子搬到樓上去。

2　一個人搬不動、得叫幾個人來幫忙。

3　要幾個人幫忙。

4　至少要三個人。

5　雇三個人來抬桌子、經濟不上算。

6　可真不

上算、不如雇他們一天的工夫、還可以叫他們做別的事情。

7 那是自然的、還有什麼事叫他們做呢？　8 事情倒不

少、他們可以打掃院子、收拾廚房。　9 雇這種人、一天得

給多少工錢。　10 這樣的人都算小工、一天給他六毛錢

就行。　11 雇兩個人不夠嗎？　12 不夠、這個桌子很重、

兩個人抬不動。　13 那麼就雇三個人吧、他們幾點鐘上

工。　14 早上六點鐘上工、晚上六點鐘下工。　15 休息

幾個鐘頭？　16 中午他們要歇一個半鐘頭。　17 就這

樣的辦吧。　18 把這幾把椅子、搬到那邊去。　19 那邊

沒有空地、我想放在外頭好。　20 可是把椅子老丟

在外邊不大好、還不如拿到地**窖**子裡面去。　21 我想起

一個好法子了。　22 是什麼法子。　23 先把這一條長

桌子、搬到客房裡去。　24 是的、以後再做什麼呢。

25 再把這一條凳子掉過來、就有地方放這幾把椅子了。

26 是的、就這樣的辦吧。　27 先生得先讓我把桌子上的

東西搬走。　28 自然、再換一張乾淨的桌布。　29 晚上

請客不請客。　30 請四位客、所以要收拾飯廳。　31 大

師傅曉不曉得。　32 曉得、我昨天吩咐了他。　33 那麼、

我就好好兒的預備。　34 好、地毯要掃一掃、席子要翻過

來、器具要洗乾淨、端飯的時候要伶俐、什麼都要整整齊齊

的。

35 是的、聽先生的吩咐。

第十四課

1 這個東西有多重。　2 一石九斤半。　3 請你給我稱一稱這個包裹沒有過重吧。　4 過了重了。　5 究竟有多重？

6 八斤七兩八錢。　7 這個口袋裡有多少糧食。

8 有一石六斗七升。　9 再談一談尺寸吧。

10 那倒容易明白十分就是一寸、十寸就是一尺、十尺就是一丈。　11 可是有的時候、我聽人說、幾步幾步、這是什麼意思？

12 哎、是的、一步就是五尺。　13 那麼、兩步也是一丈、是不是。　14 不錯還得知道一百八十丈、就是一里。

15 那麼、三里就是差不多和一英里一樣遠。

16 差不多。

17 做一條褲子、得用多少材料？

18 那看材料的寬狹。

19 比方說、材料是二尺寬、用多少？

20 二尺寬的材料、得用一丈二尺的布。

21 一個人跑一小時（一點鐘）能跑多遠。

22 全世界最快的記錄、就是十英里。

23 哎喲、一個人想破了這個記錄、很費事。

24 不錯、不錯。

第 十 五 課

1 明天中午我要請三個客。

2 太太想喫什麼飯？

3 先預備幾個小碟子。

4 要肉湯不要？

5 要雞湯。

13

6 太太喫什麼肉？現在羊肉貴一點兒。

7 這幾天天氣

熱、喫涼菜也行、比如火腿、鷄片、牛舌頭等等。

8 再加

土豆、菠菜。

9 可是得把菜煮熟啦。

10 太太也要

喫甜的嗎？

11 是的、預備冰淇淋和點心吧。

12 要奶

餅和餅乾不要。

13 要末了還要喝咖啡。

14 太太不

要水果嗎？

15 買蘋果、梨、葡萄吧。

16 還要喝酒嗎？

17 黃酒就行、也要呂宋煙。

18 也許有一兩位客人是戒

酒的、最好先預備幾瓶汽水。

19 不錯

20 擺桌子得

找一個幫忙的。

21 你可以找老媽到厨房幫忙好了。

22 另外預備水煙袋、也許有人想抽水煙。

23 桌子上也

要擺糖、牛奶、鹽、胡椒麪、醋、醬油、和芥末吧。

24 牙籤

也不要忘了。

第十六課

1 街上有洋車（或黃包車）沒有。

2 有是有、不過不很多。

3 你趕快去給我雇一輛。

4 太太上那裡去。

5 我

要上李太太那裡去。

6 太太要雇來回車嗎。

7 雇

洋車是論里數還是論鐘點呢。

8 多半是論鐘點。

9 那麼、最好雇他三個鐘頭。

10 太太要我和他講價錢

嗎。

11 一個鐘頭應該給他多少錢。

12 我說不準、一

個鐘頭、大概該給他五毛錢。

13 我以爲五毛錢太多了

一點兒，你和他講價的時候、最好先少給他一點兒。

14 那不用說、我們做買賣、就是這樣。

中國商界、現在都是「言不二價」。

15 可是我聽說

定價、可是小買賣還是照舊講價。

去、價錢越少越好。

16 大商店多半都是

19 也不要躭誤工夫、快快的回來吧。

17 那麼、你快一點兒

18 那不用說、我盡力就是了。

能早回來、我就早回來。

20 我盡力的辦、

第十七課

1 趙小姐你認得不認得？

2 認是認得、可是不大熟識。

3 她多大歲數、你知道不知道？

4 不知道、我猜她是十

六歲上下。

不過母親早去世了。

5 她的父母都在世嗎？

6 她父親還在、

7 她早幾年去的世、你記得不記得。

8 不大清楚、我想她是五六年前去的世。

9 那麼、趙小姐是可憐的。

10 實在可憐。

11 她家裡一共幾個人。

12 通共八個人。

13 他弟兄幾位？

14 三個弟兄三個姊妹。

15 趙小姐是行幾。

16 她行二、她有一個哥哥、兩個兄弟、兩個妹妹。

17 那麼、照你的話、她也沒有姐姐、也沒有母親。

18 不錯、她早就擔負家裡邊兒的責任、也很懂家事。

19 趙小姐跟人訂了婚沒有？

20 不知道、我可以給你打聽。

21 我很喜歡託你替我辦這件事。

盼望我能辦得妥當不給你丟臉就是了。

23 咱們倆

24 是多年的老朋友你也很懂禮貌我看你不會叫我丟臉的。

豈敢豈敢、可是她親戚不少、不得罪一兩個人、是不容易

哪。 25 無論如何你不要說謊、要是你碰見什麼難處、恐

怕過不去的時候、你回來詳詳細細的告訴我、就得了。

26 你那樣的出主意、我很佩服、我不會對你失信的。

27 好、事情辦成了、我就好好兒的酬謝你。 28 別提那

個、我不過是盡力幫朋友的忙吧了。

第十八課

1 這個東西好。　2 但是這個比那個好。　3 所以我

們說這個更好。

4 據我看、這是最好的東西。

可以說是頂（挺）好。

5 也好。

7 這樣的布、不如那個好。

6 這個布不好、可是和那個一般更不好。

9 還有一個說法、就是這個比那個壞。

10 可是頭一個說法比第二個說法強。

8 也可以說這個和那一塊比一比。

12 要叫我比一比那一方面呢？

13 先比一比長短、再把布的好歹比一比、再比一比顏色、掉色不掉色。

11 拿這一塊布色不掉色。

14 這個布太貴、我買不起。

15 這個箱子太重、我挪不動。

16 就是我們倆想抬也抬不動。

17 這裡有根棍子、不過是太粗、我們拿不住。

18 我們

買的東西太多、一個小車裝不下。

兩個馬車也拉不動。

屋裡也放不下這些東西。

得下了。

23 不過站在椅子上、或是小台子上、就夠着了。

台子這麼高、也就行。

樣。

26 要是你比我先到家、可以和用人商量、怎麼辦怎麼好。

27 要是我比你晚到怎樣呢？

比你先到家、必是因爲你走錯了路。

誰辦就是了。

20 我們回到家的時候、恐怕一個

21 把他們堆起來、也許就裝

22 可是得小心、把東西堆起太高、恐怕夠不着。

25 可是也得看台子的寬狹怎

24 有

19 貨物實在太多、

29 那麼、誰先到、

28 要是我

第十九課

1 掌櫃的、恭喜發財。

2 托福、沒有什麼生意。

3 我要買綢子、有沒有。

4 有、先生要什麼樣兒的綢子、要好的還是要次一點兒的呢。

5 要好的、綢子是怎樣買的、是論尺、還是論斤。

6 綢子是論尺買的、茶是論斤、信封是論個買的。

7 領教領教、讓我看幾樣綢子吧。

8 這個綢子頂好、材料耐久、也不掉色。

9 多少錢一尺。

10 七毛錢一尺。

11 未免稍微貴了一點兒還有比這個賤一點兒的（便宜一點兒的）沒有。

12 有是有、可是別忘了「一分價錢一分貨」。

13 我雖是捨不得花那麼多的錢、不過這

個綢子的材料跟顏色都很好。給我量一丈五吧。

1 裁縫做好了、太太穿上身、一定是很好看的。

15 櫃上有多少人？

16 有二十多、都是懶的。

17 拿尺來量一量這個綢子。

18 你有沒有做蚊帳的材料。

19 有哪、上中下三等都有、太太喜歡那一種呢。

20 看看中等的吧、這個材料、也可以做簾子嗎。

21 分量輕了一點兒、再重一點兒的材料好。

22 我還要幾丈耐使一點兒的、做鋪蓋。

23 那倒好辦、我們也有很結實的布、做縛子很合式。

24 教我看看吧、可是你們快要關店門、不是嗎。

25 那沒關係、關了店門還得清算當天的賬

第二十課

1 要一雙鞋。　　2 請坐、要的是幾號。

3 大概是八號。　　4 先生要皮鞋、還是布鞋呢。

5 要皮鞋、穿布鞋不能擋泥水。　　6 不錯、可是在家裏閒着穿布鞋是很舒服的。

7 先把皮鞋拿來、試一試吧。　　8 這一雙、我看大小合式。

9 太緊、再試一雙大一點兒的。　　10 好、這雙正正式式舒服不舒服。

11 舒服、我就拿這一雙。　　12 在對面兒興隆記商店。

13 你能夠把這雙鞋送到我的家裏去嗎。　　14 行、先生府上在那兒。

15 上馬街四十六號。　　16 那不遠、我就打發一個夥計、給先生送去。

車費。

18 不必、給他幾個酒錢就得了。

17 叫他坐洋車、我給他開

第二十一課

1 你看一看這個地毯乾淨不乾淨？

看不大清楚。　3 把燈點上就看得清楚了。　2 這屋子太暗、我

燈裡沒有油、點不亮。　5 家裡沒有安電燈、實在可惜。　4 這一盞

6 不要緊、我就點一枝蠟燭。　7 有洋火沒有？　8 我

想口袋裡有一盒、可是找不着啦。　9 那就沒有法子。

10 我就把地毯拿到外邊兒去抖一抖。　11 好、我就給你

幫忙把毯子捲起來（或疊起來）。　12 現在天氣涼、家裡

應當生火。

13 院子裡有炭（煤）沒有。

沒有．今年還沒有買啦。

14 一點兒也

15 厨房有柴火沒有。

16 有、我就放在火爐裡去點。

17 沒有洋火怎樣辦呢。

18 我上隔壁人家去借去。

19 快去吧、我身上覺得冷、一

回來就生火吧。

20 太陽快下去的時候、人人都覺得冷。

21 你看那櫃子裡面有絨毯、拿出兩牀來。

22 先生躺一

23 開開那個抽屜、裏邊兒有發汗葯、我喫三兩顆、再把燈

躺多蓋上一點兒、再多喝開水、出一點兒汗、過兩天就好啦。

滅了、我要睡覺。

第二十二課

1 拿熱水來、我要洗臉。

2 先生不要洗澡嗎？

3 恐怕熱水不夠洗澡。

4 也夠了、水很熱、添點冷水就不大離。

5 可是我也得刮臉、用冷水不行。

6 先生早的起來、你五點鐘來叫我。

7 明天我要早點睡的好。

8 我看先生累了、還是渴了嗎？我把一盃涼開水拿到樓上去了。

9 我明天起來的時候要給我送溫水洗手。

10 昨天你把牀沒有鋪好、我沒有睡好覺。

11 對不起先生、昨天事情太多、忙不過來。

12 要是你的事情太多、幹不過來的時候、我就該給你找一個幫忙的。

13 叫先生費心、不過還有一件事情和先生說。　14 是什

麼事情、你說吧。　15 現在城裡頭生活程度太高、過日子

很難。　16 你一個月掙多少錢？　17 八塊錢一個月、不

夠用。　18 那麼、我就給你加三塊錢一個月、行不行。

19 勉強、謝謝。

第二十三課

1 我就把你天天應當辦的事說給你聽、每禮拜一、要洗衣

服。　2 把不乾淨的衣服送到洗衣店去、行不行？

3 敎洗衣店洗衣服、不上算、乾淨的衣服送回來的時候、全

是窟窿。　4 那麼、叫裁縫補一補。　5 是的、你看這

一件汗衫擰的地方太多。

6　洗衣店的工人不加小心、不如家裡洗的好。

7　每禮拜二要收拾家裡的房屋、樓上和樓下。

8　收拾客房和洗澡房、是我的事、收拾飯廳和廚房、是廚子的事、是不是？

9　另外還有書房和廁所、這三歸誰辦呢。

10　平常這些都是看門的或是馬夫幹的。

11　無論誰幹、家裡總得要乾淨整齊。

12　聽先生的吩咐。

13　每禮拜六要擦銀子和玻璃器具、全房子的地毯要抖一抖、或者挂在院子裡擤一擤。

14　這樣做、灰塵很大、叫鄰居不喜歡。

15　那不相干、家裡得講究衛生。

16　各人要講究各人的衛生、但是可不要妨碍人家生。

的衛生。

17 你說的有理、現在不要多說話、幹你的去吧。

18 先生給我一塊乾淨的抹布、我就去抹桌子、椅子、鏡子

19 好、也不要忘了抹傢具的時候、要把窗戶開開換換空氣。一切的傢具。

20 天氣好的時候、可以這樣辦、颳風下雨的時候、恐怕不行。

第二十四課

1 大司夫來算賬。

2 太太稍微等一等我拿賬簿和鉛筆。

3 這個禮拜、你買了什麼東西、慢慢的說吧。

4 這個禮拜、我買了羊肉、白菜、地蛋、紅蘿蔔、雞蛋花生。

5 沒有買牛肉、鴨子、野雞嗎？

6 這幾天市場上沒有這些東西、後天趕集、也許有賣的。

7 多日沒有喫白菜花、不是沒有呢。

8 有是有、可是

9 大概因為不是時候、留心

價錢太大、我不敢買。

價落的時候就買。

多又便宜。

10 太太喜歡喫生菜嗎？現在又

11 喜歡喫、可是得小心、生菜總得先用開

水洗過、才敢喫。

12 今天我身上不舒服、發燒、恐怕

傷了風了。

13 我請大夫（醫生）來看一看、好不好。

14 不要請西醫、請中國先生給我開方子就行。

15 可是

16 統共花了十一塊

17 恐怕這個賬算錯了、你再算算。

賬還沒有算、統共花了多少錢？

18 我看沒

五毛六。

第二十五課

1 明天我要出門。

2 先生上那兒去。

3 打算上普天池去看一個朋友。

4 好、我願意陪您去、行不行。

5 但是你要帶你自己在路上喫的東西。

6 那不成問題、

7 在清早太陽剛上來的時候動身。

8 先生坐轎車、還是騎牲口呢。

9 也不坐轎車、也不騎馬、我們步行吧。

10 那太費事、怎麼不坐汽車呢。

有算錯、我還剩下兩塊七。

20 也許太太算的對、我的腦子就是昏一點兒。

19 恐怕你腦經不清楚、我看你還下欠九毛。

11 坐公共汽車不舒服、路道不平、顛簸的厲害。

12 普天

池離這裡多麼遠？

13 大約十五里路。

14 那倒不遠、

步行也可以。

15 可是可以、但是必須帶一個冷熱水瓶子、

裝滿了開水去喝。

16 那個我倒忘不了、還有什麼該帶

的呢？

17 也帶一個雨傘或雨衣「伏天肯下雨」。

18 先

生預料得好、我照辦就是了。

19 我們已經跑了十來

里路、我們在旅館停一會兒好不好？

20 這條路上的旅

店不怎麼好、倒不如坐在路旁歇一會兒。

21 同意、我

們也可以喝一口水、喫幾塊餅乾。

22 哎、老先生、倒普

天池還有幾里路？

23 不遠、還有五六里路。

24 前面

第二十六課

1 這個車是往北京開的車不是？ 2 不是、這是往漢口開的車。 3 往北京開的火車、是在那一個月台呢？ 4 是第三號月台。 5 先生要打那一等的票？ 6 這一趟是快車還是慢車呢。 7 是慢車、可是頭二等都有。

25 好走、不過村子外邊兒有幾個泥坑就是了。 26 村子裡邊兒有飯館沒有。 27 沒有。 28 飯館好找不好找？ 29 好找、一進村門、在路東的就是了。 30 勞駕。

兒的路、好走不好走？

好的、賣的也不過是家常便飯。 31 沒有什麼、理當的。

勞駕。

8 挂的飯(餐)車沒有？

9 沒有飯(餐)車、可是有厨房。

10 車上能買什麼飯。

11 能買牛肉排、鷄子湯、炒鷄蛋等

等。

12 可以、找脚夫給我搬東西。

13 搬行李有一定

的價錢嗎？

14 兩個銅子一件、是定價、另外還得給幾個

酒錢。

15 那麼、我們上車吧。

16 一路平安。

17 替

我問候家裡邊兒的人。

18 火車是幾點鐘到北京？

19 那得看路上通不通。

20 這幾天貨車很多。

21 客

人也是不少。

22 看光景、時局像要變更。

23 不錯、運

的隊伍也是多啦。

24 先生聽的什麼消息(新聞)。

25 沒有什麼可靠的消息、不過謠言倒不少。

26 盼望再

不要打戰、老百姓是苦極了。

27 軍閥不管那些、只打算擴充自己的地盤。

站就到了北京。

28 哎喲、才過的是通縣、還有兩個車麼快。

29 跟先生談話、時間不覺得過的那麼快。

30 領過教不少。

31 那兒的話呢。

第二十七課

1 幾點鐘開船？

2 聽說六點鐘開船。

3 現在幾點鐘？

4 三點半鐘。

5 那麼、時候還早。

6 不錯？

7 你打了船票沒有。

但是開船以前、我有些事情幹。

8 打了票、不過行李還沒有收拾好啦。

9 那麼樣、你心裡自然有一點兒着急。

10 是的、幸虧有幾個朋友幫

忙。

11 好、先生趕快去辦吧、我不再躭誤您的工夫。

12 咱們船上再見。

13 再見。

14 先生暈船不暈船？

15 頭幾天、我覺得不很舒服、但是船上慣了、就不覺得怎樣。

16 先生到過外國沒有？

17 英國、法國、美國、我都到過。

18 先生會說法國話嗎。

19 會說幾句通常的話。

20 服那邊兒的水土不服。

21 將就吧。

22 那邊兒天氣怎麼樣。

23 夏天不像中國熱、冬天不像中國冷。

24 先生也喫得慣法國飯嗎。

25 法國飯沒有中國飯的滋味、不過噢上幾天、也就對付。

26 哎喲、今天刮大風、船上不大穩當。

27 你看波浪怎樣的翻騰

起來、船搖擺得厲害。

29 希望越早越好。

28 別怕、只賸下三天的海路、船就到了碼頭。

30 放心吧。

第二十八課

1 他跑的太快、我趕不上。

2 這個磚牆沒有縫兒、螺絲轉鑽不進去。

3 這個水壺已經盛滿、再也裝不進了。

4 我的事情太多、辦不到了(或忙不過來)。

5 你要記得俗語說的好、「忙者不會、會者不忙」。

6 這個桶子裝的太緊、我拿不出來。

7 今天我帶的東西太多、賣不出去。

8 這一塊木頭太硬、釘子也打不進去。

9 心裡面的意思多、可是說不出來。

10 中國人有句俗話說、

「茶壺煑鷄蛋、倒不出來」、就是這個意思。

11 我的耳朵聾了、他說話、我聽不出來。

12 他的眼睛瞎了、他什麼也看不見。

13 他是近視眼、看不大清楚。

14 他是

15 要是

16 他的胳臂發麻、你摩他他也不覺得。

17 他失了知覺。

18 這一件衣裳太髒、我洗不乾淨。

19 多使胰子、大大的使勁、就可以洗乾淨了。

個啞吧、話也不會說、人家說話、他也聽不見。

瞎了眼、什麼也看不見。

第二十九課

1 天冷、我們穿棉袍或外套。

2 你們不穿皮襖嗎。

3 皮襖倒穿不起。

4 年輕的人喜歡洋裝。

5 那是

自然的。

6 紗天多穿夏布、綢子。

7 冬天穿皮鞋、夏天穿布鞋。

8 戴的是草帽或遮陽帽。

9 女人的衣裳、摩登一點兒才好。

10 袖子、掛了、都是短的。

11 韈子現在是很長。

12 學生有穿西裝的嗜好。

13 理髮也是洋裝的多。

14 辮子是老不見了。

15 梳一梳頭髮。

16 刷一刷頭髮和牙齒。

17 衣服要齊整、掛子要扣好。

18 指甲要修整、手、臉要保持乾淨。

19 出門要帶洗臉盆、擦臉布、和手絹、也不要忘了帶牙刷。

20 早起早睡、每天運動、是保持康健的好方法。

21 把自己所學的敎給別人、也是長知識的法子。

22 你碰見窮

第三十課

1 中國話難學不難學呢。

2 寫字不難、說話不容易。

3 說話怎樣不容易，難處在那兒呢？

4 外國人說中國話、難處在四聲的多。

5 這四聲是什麼？或什麼叫做四聲？

6 第一叫上平（或陰平）、第二叫下平（或陽平）、第三叫上（賞）聲、第四叫去聲。

7 我聽說、說中國話有五聲、對不對。

8 也不能說不對、因為有的地方、他們加上一個入聲。

9 學中國話、用什麼法子好呢？

10 請一位中

國人當先生、你一句一句的跟著他唸。

時候、盡心的效法他的口音、對不對？

有的人說國語、也有不少的人說土話。

是學國語好、是不是？

15 領教先生、寫中國字是用那樣的筆好。

字、還是用毛筆的好。

行、不過沒有毛筆好。

的是、不過我還是勸你從起頭要用毛筆。

第三十一課

1 我請先生費心替我做一件事。

2 不客氣、你要我替

11 我跟著他唸的

12 對了、不過是

13 外國人還

14 不錯、現在各處都通行國語。

16 寫中國

17 用鋼筆行不行？

18 行是

19 我看見過有人用鉛筆。

20 有

21 領教領教。

你做什麼。

你究竟要什麼呢。

他現在做什麼事。

為什麼他要另外找工作？

很好、以後就漸漸的冷淡起來了。

度改變、必定有一個緣故。

他薄、沒有什麼道理。

先生說的對、所以他們減少了他的薪水。

沒有打發他走吧？

一定不要他了。

3 我向來沒有向先生求過什麼。

5 盼望將來先生提拔我的兒子。

7 從前他在辦公室當書記。

9 起初的時候、他們對他

10 他們對待他的態

11 他們以前待他厚、以後待

12 也許他們經濟上有困難吧。

14 他們還

15 到現在還沒有、恐怕不久他們就

16 既然如此、我也不能不幫忙。

4 現在

第三十二課

1 先生會說英國話嗎？

2 會一兩句、太不夠川、先生會講中國話嗎。

3 我正在學呢、還不大會

4 先生很知道敝國的風俗

5 知道的有限、我來領敎領敎。

6 先生太謙虛、太客氣。

7 我來打聽貴縣人民的情形。

8 很好、先生想知道那一方面的事情？

9 先談敎育一方面。

10 每個村子有初等小學、大一點的鎭子

17 千萬請先生費心。

18 沒有什麼、這是理所當然的。

19 他要是將來找到一個好事情、眞是托先生的福。

20 那兒的話、慢慢走。

有高等小學、縣裏有中學。　11 學校裏也收女生嗎。

12 不錯、各學校都是男女在一塊兒上學。　13 老百姓都

識字嗎。　14 識字的不多、今年要提倡一個識字運動。

15 教師是在那兒畢業的。　16 教師是本省師範學校畢

業的多。　17 也有女教師嗎。　18 有是有、不過不多。

19 今年莊稼怎麼樣。　20 今年年頭很豐盛、百姓都很平靜。

21 這邊兒種的是什麼莊稼多。　22 麥子多、不過也有小

米、油麥、棉花、旱烟。　23 那麼、百姓納糧不費事。　24 也

很難說、不過比別的縣分强。　25 貴處人民也很講究衛

生嗎。　26 不大講究、常常發生時症。　27 這邊兒有

第三十三課

1 你要是願意、就可以醫治我的病。

2 雖然我願意、還是不能治你的病。

3 你既是不能治我的病、你該介紹我給別的大夫。

4 我也給你寫介紹信、也送你到大夫那裡去。

5 這樣做、一定對我很有益、可是我不想去。

6 為什麼你不想去。

7 因為我不認識他、和他不熟那裡去。

8 你縱然和他不熟你也可以放心、因為我知道

習。

29 我想貴縣不愧是模範縣。

28 沒有、這邊兒的警察和軍官都盡職。

30 過獎過獎。

土匪沒有？

他是一個好大夫、擔保他能醫治你。

9 你既然這樣的

勸我、我就遵命就是了。

11 我不得不照着你所說的去做。

10 你這樣的聽我勸、我也很高

興。

不要把我給你的信丟了。

13 不怕、我不會丟掉的。

12 你要小心、

14 要是你跌倒了、就不敢擔保怎樣。

了、我就趕快把他拾起來。

15 信要是掉下來

到他那裏去、不是一樣的嗎？

16 大夫來到我這裏、或者我

有藥品、有藥布。

17 不一樣、因爲他那裏

有用溫度表量。

18 可是大夫還沒有給我看脈、也沒

19 你也沒有告訴我、你身上那兒疼

啦、我看你熱度並不高、伸出舌頭來看一看。

20 疼、是

肚子疼啦、頭也疼啦。

22 小便通啦、大便不通。

要喝濃茶、常常喝淡茶吧。

藥吧、我不能喫藥粉。

第三十四課

1 趙先生的脾氣如何。

2 他是一個心平氣和的人。

3 聽說他的太太的脾氣不好。

4 你說的對、但是她的丈夫給她立了一個好榜樣。

5 一個人要是不忍氣、常常會發生麻煩。

6 不過趙先生是個好人、不願意家裡邊發生囉唆。

7 他們家裡邊打過架沒有。

8 沒有、

21 大小便怎麼樣、通不通。

23 那麼、我給你配瀉藥、你不

24 請大夫給我配一副丸

但是有的時候、免不了起一點兒衝突。

見他們大聲吵嘴。

11 先生看怎樣能把這種事減少。

常常看不起別人。

10 哎喲、這是家裏面常見的事。

樣的事情。

15 那麼、我想她的丈夫和他不容易處。

14 他的太太總喜歡談論人家的長短。

13 一個人要是謙卑、就不會發生這

12 一個人要是驕傲、

他盡量的忍耐、不惹她。

17 趙先生必定是一個聰明

16 不錯、但是

通達的人。

18 對了、他深通儒學。

第三十五課

1 拿刀子來、割掉這一條繩子。

2 這條繩子太粗、用

刀子割不斷。

3 那麼、另外找一條比較細的繩子、或

是拿剪刀來絞一絞。

4 裁縫把剪子借去了。

借了我們的剪子去做什麼？

5 他

6 他說他自己的剪子太

鈍、得磨一磨。

7 裁縫是不是現在給我們做衣服？

8 是的、他是在給太太裁短外衣和長袍。

9 我知道太

太急於想穿短外衣、所以他借剪刀也有理由。

10 可是

有一件、恐怕裁縫把剪刀留起來了。

11 那算不了什

麼、最要緊的是要他早早的把短外衣做好、叫太太喜歡。

12 你怎麼不早給我說。

13 因為我不知道您在那裡。

14 不是因為你太懶、沒有用心找我吧。

15 不是的、我實

第三十六課

1 把你們的書打開。

2 看第幾章第幾節？

3 你唸到第幾頁？

4 每個學生、都要唸第二十五頁的第二章第一節。

5 所有的先生都要到會。

6 我和你們在一起的時候、你們要盡量的發表你們的意見。

7 他和我們同行、做我們的領導。

8 我在諸位面前說這樣的話、是不配的。

9 長官在軍隊中走來走去。

10 他在

16 我並沒有離開這個地方、怎麼你說找不着我呢。

17 那倒奇怪、我到處找您、那兒也找不着。

18 罷了、幹你的去吧。

在找不着先生。
找不着我呢。

路旁觀看。

面兒走。

向前走。

大家要散開。

讓步。

他的妹妹退了步。

脫帽鞠躬。

25 衣、食、住、三要 樞

第三十七課

11 那個房子正在對面兒。

13 護送的在後邊兒走。

15 你站在當中吧。

20 大家前進吧。

18 相離遠一點兒的好。

24 向左向右、都是聽教師的命令。

23 官長一進來、大家就站起來、

26 穿得暖、喫得飽、是人人所要。

12 領路的在前

14 朋友們並排的

16 不要往一塊兒擠。

21 這幾年他進了步。

19 彼此

1 今天過節、各機關放假、我們旅行、好不好？

2 很好、

我們下鄉去一同喫野餐。

3 贊成、盼望天氣要暖和。

4 就是陰天也不要緊、最可怕的就是閃電打雷。 5 可是夏天不會下雪的。

6 不錯、可是難保不下電子。

7 冬天下霜、山上的樹多麼好看。 8 好看是好看、不過河跟湖裡邊兒都結了凍、很不方便。

9 可是現在是秋天、不是冬天、我們又不打算坐船、我們要步行。

10 今晚的月亮、應該是圓的、天氣清朗的時候、星星又該多麼的好看。

11 要不起霧才好、好不好我們現在就走吧。

12 可以、哎喲、天氣涼快、景緻也好、花都開了、在草地上面走、多麼舒服。

13 你看山坡上的廟、山頂上的塔、多麼

好看。

14 我們上廟上去跟和尚談一談。

15 我看這座廟是道教、不是佛教。

16 那沒有關係、咱們上去再說吧。

17 哎、這些蒼蠅和螞蟻、討厭不討厭！

18 幸虧這裡沒有蚊子、蚊子咬人咬得厲害。

19 哎、看看駱駝、騾子、毛驢可多啦。

20 總是廟上開香會、客人倒不少。

21 可不是嗎、有人抱孩子、有人背着行李、還有人挑水。

22 很熱鬧、必是在唱戲。

23 咱們上廟上去看看。

24 哎、借光借光。

25 看戲有什麼好處。？

26 或去或不去、你得拿定主意。

27 不如趁着這個機會、去看一次戲吧。

28 我看沒有別的辦法、人這樣的擁擠、想可也回不去。

一匹馬、怕踩了人。

29 幸虧我們、沒有多扛東西、那裡有人牽了

30 危險得很。

第三十八課

1 在家千日好、在外時時難。

2 受得苦中苦、方為人上人。

3 真金子不怕火煉。

4 種瓜得瓜、種荳得荳。

5 啞子喫黃連雖苦不能言。

6 路遙知馬力、日久見人心。

7 吹毛求疵。

8 不怕慢、只怕站。

9 遠水救不了近火。

10 坐井觀天。

11 騎虎難下。

12 一個人腳踏兩隻船。

13 不到河邊不脫鞋。

14 前人栽樹、後人乘涼。

15 十鳥在樹不如一鳥在手。

16 人是舊的好、衣

服、是新的好。

17　謀事在人、成事在天。

18　今天脫了

鞋和襪、不知明天穿不穿。

19　瞎貓碰死老鼠。

20　善有善報、惡有惡報、善惡不報、時候未到。

21　善門

難開、善門難閉。

第三十九課

1　對面兒那座石頭造的房子是什麼。

2　你問的是挿

旗桿的那個房子嗎。

3　是的、挂國旗的那個房子。

4　哎、那是愛國電影院、你要看電影嗎。

5　城裡的銀行

幾點鐘關門。

6　銀行三點鐘關門、錢舖一直開到九點

鐘。

7　我這裡有一張匯票（支票）要兌成現錢、才能看電影。

8 那麼我們錢店也給你換、也不扣錢

9 先上郵政局、我要打電報給我內人。

10 郵政局離這兒遠呀、還是電報局比較近。

11 不過我一定要把這兩封挂號信、寄給我公司的大班。

12 一封挂號信、貼多少郵票？

13 那我不曉得、我們上局子裡去問一問。

14 好、哎、過來的就是一個同鄉、好呀、想不到在這兒碰見你、你忙什麼？

15 哎、了不得、我的祖父給汽車絆倒了、受了重傷、我現在上醫院看他去。

16 可惜可惜、不敢留攔你、替我問候令祖吧。

17 謝謝、再見。

18 咱們到館子裡喫東西吧、我肚子餓了、

19 可以、我不想喫什

麼東西、可是我嘴乾了、我要喝一盃啤酒。 20 哎、這個館子不錯、還有音樂隊聽。 21 那不是音樂隊、不過是留聲機的響聲。 22 我看是無線電廣播的音樂。 23 可不是嗎、我聽說這兒差不多每晚上都有跳舞、你會跳舞不會。? 24 會是會、我今天太累了、不想跳舞。 25 那麼、我們就去看電影吧、一面休息、一面長知識。 26 不錯、我以為那倒更有興趣、(趣味)。

第四十課

1 我這一輩子的工夫、就碰到了兩次的世界大戰。 2 為什麼世界上不能夠維持和平呢， 3 根本就是因為國家跟國家、種族跟種族之間、發現不公平的事項。

4 你的意思是說必先取消一切不公平的事、才能盼望得到一個和平的世界嗎。

5 世界上發生戰事、多半是因爲我剛才說過的原故、不過人人都有一個自私的心、這也不可不注意的。

6 不錯、人的自私心實在難於去掉。

7 可是現在的第二次大戰已經完了、德國、意國、日本、都已經投降了。

8 哎喲、中國抵抗日本的侵略、已經八年了。

9 兩邊死傷的人、都非常的多啦。

10 實在不少、房子被炸彈炸壞了的、也是很多。

11 盟軍已經戰勝了、德國和日本、已經打敗了、你想將來還會發生戰事嗎、

12 不敢說一定、但是這一次戰爭用的武器、非常的殘暴、也

許各國都受了這種恐嚇、再不敢宣戰了。　13 我相信是

這樣、並且今年六十多國、組織了一個聯合會、要盡力的維

持世界和平。　14 頂好、但是我看在必要時、還得用聯

合的軍力、如海軍、陸軍、空軍的力量來幫助、會議才能有

美滿的效果。　15 同意啦、現在的政治主義很複雜、有

民主主義、共產主義、還有其他的革命的和守舊的各種

政治上的派別。　16 那倒不要緊、不怕政治上的黨派

多只怕衆人不注意政治上的事情。

GRAMMAR

GRAMMAR NOTES

1. The Article.

The INDEFINITE article, *i.e.*, a, or an, is expressed by the numerical adjective " I " (one), followed by a " classifier ", which varies according to the noun it precedes, or which may be understood. (See 8, below.)

The most frequently used " classifier " is " ko " 個 which may be translated " piece ", *e.g.*, " I ko jên ", a man.

Other " classifiers " in common use are given in a separate paragraph below. (See 8.)

The DEFINITE article, *i.e.*, the, appears only in relative clauses, and then, as in all other cases, its place is taken by the distinguishing adjectives " chê ko " 這 個 This, and " na ko " 那 個 That. *E.g.*, The man whom I mentioned is " Wo so shuo ti *na ko* jên ". This man is " Chê ko jên ". That man is " Na ko jên ".

2. Distinguishing Adjectives.

We have already pointed out that " chê ko " means " this " and " na ko " means " that ". If the plurals " these " and " those " are required, they are formed by the addition of " hsieh " 些 to " chê " and " na " respectively, *e.g.*, These men, " Chê hsieh jên ". Those men, " Na hsieh jên ".

If you wish to distinguish definitely this group of men from another, you say " Chê i hsieh jên ", 這 一 些 人 This group of men, *or* " Na i hsieh jên ", 那 一 些 人 That group of men.

3. Personal Pronouns.

The personal pronouns are as follows: " Wo ", 我 I, me. " Ni ", 你 You. " T'a ", 他 He, she, it.

The plural of these is formed by the addition of " mên ", 們 : " Wo-mên ", 我們 We, us. " Ni-mên ", 你們 You. " T'a-mên ", 他們 They, them.

Formerly there was no distinction of gender in these pronouns, but more recently the distinction is sometimes made by writing the character " nü " 女 at the left-hand side of the characters, especially for " ni " 妳 and " t'a " 她 to express the feminine gender.

4. The Possessive Sign.

The most commonly used mark of the possessive is " ti " 的, which is added to the pronoun or noun which it qualifies, e.g., " Wo ti mao tzu ", My hat. " Ni-mên ti tung-hsi ", Your (pl.) things. " Na ko jên ti shu ", That man's book.

There is another mark of the possessive " chih " 之 but this has a somewhat literary flavour, and is only occasionally used in common speech. It is used in exactly the same way as " ti ".

Frequently the possessive is expressed in other ways, one of the more common being to use the distinguishing adjectives " chê ko ", " na ko ", etc., after the personal pronouns, e.g., " Wo chê ko tung hsi ", This thing of mine. " T'a na hsieh yen chüan'rh ", Those cigarettes of his.

5. Interrogative Pronouns.

Who? is " Shui ", 誰. Whose? is " Shui ti ", 誰的 e.g., Who is that? " Na ko jên shih shui ". Whose are those things? " Na hsieh tung hsi shih shui ti ".

Which? is expressed by " Na ko ", the " na " being in the third tone, e.g., " Na³ ko shih ni ti ", Which is yours?

When you wish to distinguish one of two things, or one of more, you should say " Na³ i ko shih ni ti ", Which one is yours?

What? is usually expressed by " Shih mo ", which is the popular form of " shên mo ", *e.g.*, What is this? is " Chê ko shih shih mo ".

6. Nouns.

Nouns are not divided artificially into different genders as in French or other Continental languages. But unless the gender is self-evident from the word itself, there are words for male and female of persons and animals, which are préfixed to the noun. *E.g.*, " Ni yu chi ko hai tzu ", How many children (no sex indicated) have you? " Wo yu san ko nan hai tzu ", I have three boys (" nan " meaning male). " Ni yu nü hai mei yu ", Have you any girls? ("nü " being female).

Note that " nan ", male, and " nü ", female, are applied only to persons. The words to distinguish the sex of animals are " mu ", 牡 male, and " p'in ", 牝 female.

Usually the plural of nouns is indicated by the plural form of the distinguishing adjective which precedes them, *e.g.*, " Na hsieh jên shang na³ erh ch'ü ", Where are those men going?

But " mên ", the sign of the plural with personal pronouns, is sometimes applied to nouns denoting persons, rarely, if ever, to " things ". *E.g.*, you can say " nan jên mên ", males, " nü-jên mên ", females, " hai-tzu mên ", children, but you cannot say " kou mên ", dogs.

Abstract Nouns are formed chiefly in two ways, as follows : —

(1) By joining together two adjectives of exactly opposite meaning; *e.g.*, " Ta-hsiao " (big-little) is size, " Ch'ang-tuan " (long-short) is length. " Yüan-chin " (far-near) is distance. " Kuei-chien " (dear-cheap) is price.

(2) By the addition of the word " ch'u " 處, meaning state or condition, to adjectives, *e.g.*, " hao ch'u "

benefit, advantage, " hai ch'u ", harm, injury, " yung ch'u ", use, usefulness, " nan ch'u ", difficulty, etc.

7. **Cases of Nouns and Pronouns** are usually distinguished by the position of the word in the sentence; *e.g.*, " Wo ai ni " is I love you, and " Ni ai wo " is You love me, as far as the Nominative and Objective or Accusative Cases are concerned.

It should, however, be noted that the Objective Case often precedes the verb of which it is the object. In such instances the object of the verbal action is usually prefixed by " pa ", or " na ", to take, *e.g.*, " Pa chê ko tung hsi, fang tsai chê li ", which means Put this thing here.

Many illustrations of this are given in the Dialogues.

The Dative Case is usually expressed by the words " kei ", give, " t'i ", instead of, or " wei ", for, *e.g.*, " Kei wo tso chê ko ", Do this *for* me. " Wo pu nêng pa wo ti shu sung kei t'a ", I cannot present my book *to* him. " Ni t'i wo wên hou ni chia li pie'rh ti jên ", Inquire about the well-being of your family *for* me.

8. **Classifiers.**

This is a class of words, as has been indicated above, which is used with nouns, to help to distinguish them one from the other. Quite a number will be found in the Dialogues. Examples are given below:—

1. Ko, 個 Piece, the most common, used almost for anything.
2. Ting, 頂 Used with caps, hats, etc.
3. Kuan, 管 Used with slender long things, like pipes, pencils, etc.
4. Chan, 盞 Used with lamps, wine cups, etc.
5. Pa, 把 Used with teapots, teacups, etc.
6. Tso, 座 Used with hills, temples, towers, etc.
7. T'ou, 頭 Used with animals.

8. Chien, 件　Used with affairs, details.
9. K'o, 顆　Used of small round things, like pearls, beads, etc.
10. Ts'êng, 層　Used of layers, strata, anything piled up, in tiers, etc.
11. Chang, 張　Used with tables.

There are many others, which will be found in any good dictionary. The student should exercise care in using the right classifier with nouns, as this is a mark of a good speaker.

10. Adjectives of Quality.

A whole Dialogue has been given to the subject of adjectives and their degrees of comparison. (See Dialogue 18.) There is therefore no need to go into any detail in this section. Note however that the adjectives are very simple, and do not change whatever their position in the sentence might be. You may say " Chê ko jên hao ", This man is good, or " Chê shih i ko hao jên ", This is a good man. " Ti " 的 is sometimes used when the adjective is in the predicative position, *e.g.*, " Na' ko tung hsi shih ko hao ti ", That is a good thing.

11. Adverbs of Manner are formed from adjectives usually by the duplication of the adjective and the addition of " ti ", 的, *e.g.*, " Hao hao ti ", Well. " Man man ti ", Slowly. " Wan wan ch'üan ch'üan ti ", Completely.

Adverbs of Place and Time have been fully illustrated in the Dialogues and do not call for special consideration here.

Adverbs of Approximation, nearly, about, etc., are usually formed by a phrase like " Ch'a pu to ", " Ch'a pu li ", " Pu ch'a shih mo ", " Ch'a pu to shao ", " Ta kai ", " Ta yüeh ", " Ta lüeh ". Words like

" generally " by " Ta kai shuo ", " Lüeh lüeh ti shuo ". Other expressions like " shang hsia ", up, down, or " tso yu ", left, right, are used for approximate figures.

12. The Auxiliary Verbs " to be " and " to have ".

The verb " to be " is represented by the one word " shih " 是 and is the same for all persons and numbers. Changes in TENSE or MOOD are expressed by additional words or phrases of temporal, conditional or imperative significance.

Likewise the verb " to have " is represented by the one word " yu " 有 and remains the same for all persons and numbers, the tenses and moods being expressed by additional words or phrases.

13. The Regular Verb.

Taking the verb " to come " 來 as an example, the following concise paradigm applies to all, *viz.*: —

Number and Person. No change, the differences being expressed by the pronouns or adjectives which accompany the verb.

Tense.

The Present Tense is the simple form of the verb, *e.g.*, " Wo lai ", I come, or I am coming.

The Past or Perfect Tense. " Wo lai liao " (la), or " Wo lai kuo ", I came, or I have come.

N.B.—While these two enclitics " liao " (la) and " kuo " are both used in most parts of China as indicated, you should use " kuo " and not " liao " (la) when you wish to refer to the distant past of completed action, *e.g.*, Have you ever been to Peking? or Did you ever go to Peking? is " Ni ch'ü *kuo* Pei-ching mei yu ".

The Future Tense is formed by preceding the verb with a word of future significance, like " chiang ", 將

" yao ", 要 " chiu " 就 etc.; *e.g.*, " T'a chiang lai ",
" T'a yao lai ", " T'a chiu lai ", or by two of these
words in combination; *e.g.*, " T'a chiu yao lai ", " T'a
chiang yao lai ", etc. There are other ways of expressing
the relative immediacy of a person's coming; *e.g.*, " T'a
li k'o chiu lai ", He is coming immediately, or, as in
Dialogue No. 1, " Shuo hua chiu lai ", As you speak he
comes, etc.

Compound Tenses like the Pluperfect, Future Perfect,
can also be expressed, chiefly by the addition of phrases
of Past or Future Past significance, to the verb; *e.g.*,
" T'a mei yu lai i ch'ien, wo i ching tsou la ", I had
gone before he arrived (Pluperfect). " Kan hsia li pai
êrh wo shih i ching tsou la ", I shall have gone by next
Tuesday (Future Perfect).

Present Participle. This is by adding the word " cho "
著 to the verb, and frequently by adding a phrase of
time; *e.g.*, " Kên *cho* t'a yu san ko jên ", Accompanying
him were three men. " T'a lai *cho* ti shih hou ", At
the time of his coming.

Moods.

The *Indicative* Mood has been adequately dealt with
above.

The *Imperative* Mood is the same as the indicative,
with or without additional words implying command,
exhortation, etc.; *e.g.*, " Lai " or " Lai pa " is Come !
" Wo mên tsou pa ", Let us go ! " Chiao t'a ch'ü ",
Tell him to go.

The *Infinitive* Mood is the same as the Indicative,
usually of course accompanied by some main verb; *e.g.*,
" Wo yüan i ch'ü ", I am willing *to go.*

The *Conditional* Mood again is as the Indicative,
usually preceded by a word or phrase implying Condition,
such as doubt, fear, probability, uncertainty, etc.; *e.g.*,
" Jo shih t'a ch'ing ni, ni chiu ying tang ch'ü ", *If* he

invites you, you ought to go. "Yao shih", 要是 If.
"T'ang jo", 倘若 Supposing. "Huo cho", 或者
Perhaps. "Yeh hsü", 也許 Perhaps. "K'ung p'a",
恐怕 I fear, lest. "Pu i ting", 不一定 Uncertain.
"Pu kan shuo", 不敢說 Cannot say, are a few instances
of the possibilities of the language to express the Conditional or Subjunctive Mood.

Other Auxiliary Verbs like "lai", 來, "ch'u", 出
"tao", 到, "liao", 了, "shang", 上, "hsia", 下
"chao", 着, "tiao", 掉, are all found in the text, in
combination with main verbs.

The student will note particularly the frequent refer-
ences in the Dialogue Notes to the way in which these
auxiliaries express possibility or impossibility of the
completion of the action of the main verb.

Note further that "tê", 得, when used as an auxiliary,
carries with it a sense of "oughtness", "fitness", etc.

The Passive Voice. This is most commonly expressed
by the words "chiao", written either 叫 or 教, but
chiefly 叫; by "pei", 被, or "shou", 受, and less
frequently "ai", 挨.

Examples are as follows:—

1. Na hsieh tung hsi pei   Those things were burned
   huo shao la.   by fire.

2. Wo ti mao tzu chiao   My hat was blown off by
   fêng kua la.   the wind.

3. Yeh su shou jên ti ling   Jesus was insulted by men.
   ju.

4. Na t'iao kou ai liao ta.   That dog was beaten.

14. Negatives and Prohibitions.

The principal Negatives are "pu", 不 and "mu", 沒
also pronounced "mei" or "mo". The student will
be helped by knowing that "pu" is usually used with
"shih", to be, while "mu" is used with "yu". The

common uses of these negative particles are illustrated below : —

1. Chê ko shih ni ti pu shih.   Is this yours or not?
2. Pu shih wo ti.   It is not mine.
3. Ni yu shu mei yu.   Have you a book?
4. Yu.   Mei yu.   Yes! No!
5. T'a lai pu lai.   Is he coming?
6. T'a pu lai.   No, he is not.
7. T'a ch'ü la mei yu.   Has he gone?
8. T'a hai mei yu ch'ü.   No, he has not gone yet.

Note that " ma " is often used for " mei yu " in questions; *e.g.*, " T'a lai la ma (mei yu) ", Has he come? " Ni yu i p'i ma ma (mei yu) ", Have you a horse?

The ordinary way of expressing *Prohibition* is to use a phrase like " Pu yao ", 不要, Do not, often shortened into " Pieh ", 別, or " Pu k'o ", 不可, " Pu kai ", 不該 or very strongly, " Ch'ien wan pu k'o ", 千萬不可; *e.g.*, " Ni pu yao kao su t'a ", Don't tell him. " Pieh tsou ", Don't go! " Chê ko hua, ni ch'ien wan pu k'o ho t'a shuo ", On no account must you tell him this, etc.

15. Either . . . or. Neither . . . nor.

The most common way of expressing these alternatives is as follows:— 或 . . . 或. 也不 . . . 也不.

" Ni *huo* ch'ü *huo* pu ch'ü, tê na ting chu i ", You must make up your mind either to go or not (whether to go or not).

" Wo *yeh pu* yao chan, *yeh pu* yao tso ", I neither want to stand nor sit. Note that sometimes the first " yeh " is omitted, but the sense is the same.

The above are the main grammatical points in the Chinese language which will form a guide to the beginner in understanding and framing sentences. This section by no means exhausts all the rules which a careful speaker of Chinese consciously or unconsciously observes. The language is so flexible and free that rules may or may not be observed. Practically everything that has been said above, or in the Notes which accompany the Dialogues, on the subject of Grammar, is open to modification. But the student will at least have observed from what has been written that there *is* such a thing as Chinese Grammar !

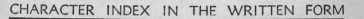

CHARACTER INDEX IN THE WRITTEN FORM

CHARACTER INDEX IN THE WRITTEN FORM

The 1,200 odd characters included in the Dialogues are reproduced in this Section, in the written form, with the Romanised equivalent, tone mark, and main meanings alongside.

Chinese characters, when written, differ in several respects from the printed forms. It is therefore useful for the student, at the very beginning of his studies, to become acquainted with the written forms.

In the Vocabularies accompanying the Dialogues and Exercises the printed form of the characters is used. By comparing these with the written equivalents the student will readily discern the differences and be ready to tackle a simple Chinese letter.

I strongly recommend the student to learn to write the Chinese characters in the form in which they are found in this Section. I think the effort will be found to be worth while, not only in the greater interest and pleasure which will result, but also in the help to memory which writing the characters affords.

The following hints will guide and help the student in this branch of the study. As is well known, the writing of Chinese characters is an art, just as much as the painting of pictures. So Chinese writers use the brush (mao pi), as only by that means can the artistic possibilities of the characters appear. But nowadays large numbers of the younger generation of Chinese students use fountain pens. Students of this book who have artistic gifts should get accustomed to using the brush. But probably the great majority will be content to use the fountain pen. Get one with a soft nib, which will allow of gradation of thick and thin in the strokes, and also permit of a flowing free-hand style. Even a good lead pencil of the right quality can serve quite well in the early stages, until the student has mastered the form and proportion of the characters.

If you use the brush you will of course use Chinese ink, rubbed with water on a slab.

First copy the characters just as they are in the index by placing a piece of tracing or other transparent paper over them. This will give you good style from the start. To write accurately and nicely it is important to write the different strokes of each character in the proper order. There are rules to guide the student in this respect, to which as usual there are some exceptions.

Chinese teachers habitually say that all the strokes required to form any character are found in the character " yung ", which means " Eternal ", and which is written

永

However, as W. Simon points out in his book " How to Study and Write Chinese Characters ",* at least fifteen different strokes, some of which are slight variants of others in the group, are readily discernible. These fifteen strokes, as given by Simon, are as follows:—

一 丨 丶 丿 乛 乀 ㇐ 乀 丿 丨 乚 𠃌 乚 乛 乙

It is customary to write top before bottom strokes, left before right, and horizontals before verticals. But in cases where the top horizontal stroke is connected with a right hand vertical, and a left hand vertical also forms part of the character, it is usual to write the left hand vertical stroke first. Then it is also important to remember that the closing stroke of squares or quadrilaterals is the bottom horizontal, and this always comes last. These few rules, to which there are some exceptions, should suffice to guide the student in his early writing lessons.

---

* " How to Study and Write Chinese Characters ", W. Simon, pub. by Lund, Humphries. No longer available, except in libraries.

E.g., if we want to write the character " k'ou ", for mouth, which is written 口, the order of strokes is 1. ｜, 2. ㄱ 3. —; and in " li ", 里, Chinese mile, the order is 1. ｜, 2. ㄱ, 3. —, 4. —, 5. —, 6. ｜, 7. —

Write each character several times before proceeding to fresh ones. You will gradually discover that certain parts of many characters recur frequently. These are probably I. Radicals, of which there are 214, a list of which follows the Character Index, and which give a clue to the meaning, or II. Phonetics, of which Soothill, for instance, selects 888,† and which afford a clue to the sound of the character. By this type of analysis we trace the characters in the dictionaries, as will be pointed out in the final Section. By this means also the student will be able to group the characters into classes, either according to Radical or Phonetic, which will accelerate progress in learning to write and read large numbers of characters.

E.g., as an interesting test, pick out from the Index all those characters in which you can detect the Radical " mu ", 木 , wood, or tree, or again the Radical " chin ", 金, metal, " yü ", 雨, rain, etc., and note how the rest of the character indicates differences in species while the genus remains the same, or akin.

Likewise trace common Phonetics like 者, " chu ", the characters 猪, pig, 諸, all, 煮, boil, etc.

Or again, " ch'ing ", 青, in 情, disposition, 清, pure, 請, invite.

In these ways the burden of memorising will be greatly lightened and keener interest developed.

The Index to the characters in written form follows.

† " The Students' Four Thousand Characters and General Pocket Dictionary ", W. E. Soothill, M.A. No longer available, except in libraries.

Characters 1—20

第 Ti⁴
Number, degree.
Used to introduce
ordinal numbers.

一 I¹
One.

課 K'o⁴
Task, Exercise.

門 Mên²
Door, Gate.

口 K'ou³
Mouth, Opening.

有 Yu³
There is, there are.
Has, have.

人 Jên²
Man.

誰 Shui²
Who, Whom.

我 Wo³
I, Me

是 Shih⁴
Is, are, am, etc.

不 Pu¹
No. Not.

知 Chih¹
To know.

道 Tao⁴
Way, Truth.

去 Ch'ü⁴
To go.

看 K'an⁴
To look, To look at.
To think. To con-
sider.

用 Yung⁴
Need, Use.

叫 Chiao⁴
To call, cause,
order.

隆 Lung²
Eminent. Prosper-
ous.

福 Fu²
Happiness.

哎 Ai³
An exclamation.

Characters 21—40

來
Lai [2]
To come.

吧
Pa [4]
Final particle.

先
Hsien [1]
Before, formerly, first.

生
Shêng [1]
Born, to beget, life. Raw. A scholar.

貴
Kuei [4]
Honourable, dear, costly.

姓
Hsing [4]
Surname, clan.

李
Li [3]
A surname. Plum.

王
Wang [2]
A surname. King, prince.

在
Tsai [4]
At, in, on, present, living.

家
Chia [1]
Home, house, family, class.

嗎
Ma [1]
Interrogative.

請
Ch'ing [3]
Invite, please, call, engage.

進
Chin [4]
Enter, advance.

好
Hao [3]
Good, well, complete.

了
Liao, [3] **Lo,** [3] **La** [3]
To end, finish. Sign of past tense.

呀
Ya [1]
Particle. Exclamation, initial or final.

張
Chang [1]
A surname. Also classifier of nouns.

都
Tu, [1] **Tou** [1]
Both, all, together.

坐
Tso [4]
To sit. A seat.

謝
Hsieh [4]
To thank, thanks.

Characters 41—60

泡
P'ao [4]
To brew, soak, bubble, infuse.

茶
Ch'a [2]
Tea.

說
Shuo [1]
To speak, say, narrate.

話
Hua [4]
Words, language, speech.

就
Chiu [4]
Immediately, then, so, etc.

喝
Ho [1]
To drink.

敢
Kan [3]
Dare, presume.

當
Tang [1]
To bear, act as, ought.

再
Tsai [4]
Again, repeat.

會
Hui [4]
A time, a turn, able to. A society. To meet.

兒
Êrh [1]
Enclitic, added to nouns, suffix.

對
Tui [4]
To face, pair, opposite.

住
Chu [4]
To dwell, to stop.

等
Têng [3]
To wait, a class.

着
Cho [2]
Particle, sign of present participle.

得
Tê [2]
Must, ought, get.

回
Hui [2]
To return, go back.

送
Sung [4]
To send, escort, accompany.

那
Na [3] [4]
Where, how, why? There, that.

的
Ti [1]
Sign of possessive, 's.

Characters 61—80

見 **Chien** [4]
To see, perceive.

二 **Erh** [4]
Two, Second.

他 **T'a** [1]
He, she, it.

太 **T'ai** [4]
Too, very, superlative, exalted.

喫 **Ch'ih** [1]
To eat, used of tobacco as well as food.

過 **Kuo** [4]
Sign of past tense, to pass over.

飯 **Fan** [4]
Rice, food.

沒 **Mei, Mu, Mo** [4]
Negative, used with the verb "Yu", to have.

還 **Huan, Hai** [2]
Still, yet, — precedes negative.

或 **Huo** [4]
Perhaps, if, someone.

偏 **P'ien** [1]
Deflected, on the contrary, prejudiced.

客 **K'o** [4]
Guest, traveller.

氣 **Ch'i** [4]
Breath, air, vapour, flavour.

理 **Li** [3]
Right, principle arrange, fitting

可 **K'o** [3]
May, might, can be able.

以 **I** [3]
To take, by means of.

給 **Kei, Chi** [3]
Give, for, to. Sign of dative.

泡 **Ch'i** [3]
Infuse, brew. Alternative for "p'ao".

預 **Yü** [4]
Beforehand.

備 **Pei** [4]
Prepare, ready.

Characters 81—100

中 Chung[1]
Middle.

國 Kuo[2]
Country.
Kingdom.

大 Ta[4]
Big. Great.
Much.

懂 Tung[3]
To understand.

幾 Chi[3]
Many. How much?
How many?

時 Shih[2]
Time, Season.

到 Tao[4]
Arrive, reach.

敝 Pi[4]
Humble,
my (polite).

上 Shang[4]
The last point of
time, above, on,
go up.

月 Yüeh[4]
Month, moon.

才 Ts'ai[2]
Just, thereupon,
scarcely.

獎 Chiang[3]
Praise, commend.

真 Chên[1]
True, real.

實 Shih[2]
Solid, sincere, true,
real.

容 Yung,[2] Jung[2]
Easy, contain,
face, looks.

易 I[4]
Easy.

學 Hsüeh[2]
Learn.

並 Ping[4]
Together, all,
abreast.

難 Nan[2]
Difficult.

願 Yüan[4]
Wish, willing.

Characters 101—120

意 **I** [4]
Idea, wish, intention, meaning.

把 **Pa** [3]
Take, take hold. Introduces object of verb.

盡 **Chin** [4]
Limit, exhaust, utmost.

心 **Hsin** [1]
Heart, mind.

教 **Chiao** [1]
Teach, instruct.

你 **Ni** [3]
You.

三 **San** [1]
Three.

這 **Chê** [4]
This, here.

個 **Ko** [4]
Piece. Classifier of nouns.

什 **Shih** [2]
Used for No. 111.

甚 **Shên** [2]
What, very, any.

麼 **Mo** [1]
Interrogative particle.

本 **Pên** [3]
Classifier of books, documents. Root, source.

書 **Shu** [1]
Book.

字 **Tzǔ** [4]
Word, written word.

典 **Tien** [3]
Constant, rule, record.

東 **Tung** [1]
East.

西 **Hsi** [1]
West.

管 **Kuan** [3]
Tube, classifier of tubular things.

鉛 **Ch'ien** [1]
Lead (metal).

Characters 121—140

筆 **Pi** [3]
Pen, pencil, brush.

們 **Mên** [2]
Sign of plural.

作 **Tso** [4]
To do, to make, to act.

做 **Tso** [4]
To do, to make, to act.

唸 **Nien** [4]
To read aloud.

讀 **Tu** [2]
To read.

聽 **T'ing** [1]
To listen, to hear.

法 **Fa** [2] [3] [4]
Method, way of doing things, law.

子 **Tzǔ** [3]
Son, terminal of nouns, child.

跟 **Kên** [1]
To follow, accompany, the heel, with.

行 **Hsing** [2]
To go, to do.

很 **Hên** [3]
Extreme, very.

要 **Yao** [4]
If, necessary, want.

錯 **Ts'o** [4]
Mistake, error, wrong.

告 **Kao** [4]
Inform, accuse.

訴 **Su** [4]
Inform, explain.

現 **Hsien** [4]
Now, at present.

完 **Wan** [2]
To finish, complete, end.

寫 **Hsieh** [3]
To write.

喜 **Hsi** [3]
Joy, pleased, glad.

Characters 141—160

歡 **Huan** [1]
Rejoice. Take pleasure.

紙 **Chih** [3]
Paper.

塊 **K'uai** [4]
Piece.

墨 **Mo, Mei** [4]
Ink.

和 **Ho** [2] [4]
With, together, harmony.

方 **Fang** [1]
Square, classifier of pieces of Chinese ink.

硯 **Yen** [4]
Ink-slab.

台 **T'ai** [2]
Slab.

加 **Chia** [1]
To add.

點 **Tien** [3]
A little, point, dot.

水 **Shui** [3]
Water.

研 **Yen** [2]
To grind, as ink on a slab. To inquire.

些 **Hsieh** [3]
A few, some, sign of plural, with adjectives.

拿 **Na** [2]
To take.

四 **Ssŭ** [4]
Four.

盃 **Pei** [1]
Cup, with or without handle. Glass.

杯 As No. 156.

碗 **Wan** [3]
Cup, bowl, with or without handle.

分 **Fên** [1] [4]
(1) Verbal form to divide. (4) Part, tenth.

別 **Pieh** [2]
To distinguish also "do not"

Characters 161—180

壺 **Hu** [2]
Kettle, pot.

樣 **Yang** [4]
Pattern, way, manner.

燒 **Shao** [1]
To burn, bake (to boil).

煙 **Yen** [1]
Tobacco, snuff, smoke, opium.

烟 As No. 164.

捲 **Chüan** [3]
A roll, to roll up.

洋 **Yang** [2]
Foreign, the sea, over the sea, vast.

火 **Huo** [3]
Fire.

柴 **Ch'ai** [2]
Firewood, fuel.

抽 **Ch'ou** [1]
To draw, to pull out.

雨 **Liang** [3]
Two, preceding nouns.

鋼 **Kang** [1]
Steel.

呢 **Ni** [1]
Mark of interrogation, and final enclitic.

毛 **Mao** [2]
Hair.

朋 **P'êng** [2]
Companion, friend mate.

友 **Yu** [3]
Intimate acquaintance, friend.

瓶 **P'ing** [2]
Bottle.

也 **Yeh** [3]
Also.

買 **Mai** [3]
To buy.

市 **Shih** [4]
The market.

Characters 181—200

場
Ch'ang [2]
An open place, square.

裡
Li [3]
In, inside, within.

裏
As No. 182.

賣
Mai [4]
To sell.

街
Chieh [1]
Street.

者
Chê [3]
Particle, to form adverbs, abstract nouns, etc.

咱
Tsa [2]
We (familiar).

倆
Lia [3]
Two.

五
Wu [3]
Five.

昨
Tso [3]
Yesterday.

天
T'ien [1]
Day, Heaven.

明
Ming [2]
The dawn, bright, clear, open.

今
Chin [1]
Now, the present.

她
T'a [1]
She.

幹
Kan [4]
To do, manage, Ability.

頂
Ting [3]
Classifier of hats, caps, etc. Top, button.

帽
Mao [4]
Hat, cap.

雙
Shuang [1]
A couple, both, pair.

鞋
Hsieh [2]
Shoe.

北
Pei [3] (or Po [4] literary use)
North.

Characters 201—220

京 Ching [1]
Capital city.

起 Ch'i [3]
To get up, rise, mount.

走 Tsou [3]
To walk, to go.

錢 Ch'ien [2]
Money.

緊 Chin [3]
Tight, pressing.

帶 Tai [4]
To carry on the person.

借 Chieh [4]
To borrow, to lend.

情 Ch'ing [2]
Facts affairs, feelings, nature.

形 Hsing [2]
Form, appearance.

怎 Tsên [3]
How? In what way?

候 Hou [4]
A period, a time, to wait, to expect.

六 Liu [4]
Six.

厨 Ch'u [2]
Kitchen, cook.

房 Fang [2]
Room, house.

司 Ssǔ [1]
An officer, to manage.

站 Chan [4]
To stand, station, post, etc.

忙 Mang [2]
Busy.

幫 Pang [1]
Help, assist.

句 Chü [4]
Sentence, phrase.

傢 Chia [1]
Utensils.

Characters 221—240

具 Chü⁴
Utensils.

刀 Tao¹
Knife, blade.

义 Ch'a¹
Fork.

調 T'iao²
To stir, to mix.

羹 Mei⁴
Ink black.

匙 Shih,² Ch'ih²
Spoon, key.

勺 Shao²
Scoop, ladle.

碟 Tieh²
Plate, saucer.

盤 P'an²
Plate, dish.

放 Fang⁴
Put, place.

棹 Cho¹
Table.

桌 As No. 231.

晚 Wan³
Evening, late.

下 Hsia⁴
Beneath, to descend, to begin, under.

午 Wu³
Noon.

多 To¹
Much, many.

烤 K'ao²
To bake, roast.

麵 Mien⁴
Flour, bread.

包 Pao¹
Parcel, wrap.

黃 Huang²
Yellow.

Characters 241—260

油 Yu [2]
Oil.

果 Kuo [3]
Fruit, conse-
quences, etc.

醬 Chiang [4]
Thick, paste, etc.

夠 Kou [4]
Enough, sufficient.

十 Shih [2]
Ten.

筷 K'uai [4]
Chopsticks.

使 Shih [3]
To employ, use.

只 Chih [3]
Only.

怕 P'a [4]
To fear.

倒 Tao [4]
On the contrary,
Tao[3] to fall over

七 Ch'i [1]
Seven.

承 Ch'êng [2]
To receive.

問 Wên [4]
To inquire, ask, a
question.

您 Nin [2]
You, Sir.   (A
polite form.)

賤 Chien [4]
Humble,   mean,
low, cheap.

甫 Fu [3]
Title   or   rank,
surname.

草 Ts'ao [3]
Gross, humble.

清 Ch'ing [1]
Clear.

長 Ch'ang [2]   Long.

名 Ming [2]
Name, fame.

Characters 261—230

年 Nien² Year, years.

紀 Chi⁴ To record.

歲 Sui⁴ The year, years.

數 Shu⁴ Number, to count.

庚 Kêng¹ Age.

甲 Chia³ First.

高 Kao¹ High.

壽 Shou⁴ Age, old age, long life.

兄 Hsiung¹ Elder brother.

弟 Ti⁴ Younger brother.

小 Hsiao³ Small, young.

虛 Hsü¹ In vain, empty, useless.

度 Tu⁴ To ford, pass, pass over.

英 Ying¹ Brave, Illustrious, England.

南 Nan² South.

處 Ch'u³ Live with.

府 Fu³ Home, residence, a prefecture.

平 P'ing² Peace, level, ordinary.

離 Li² Apart from, separated from.

遠 Yüan³ Far, distance, distant.

Characters 281—300

百 Pai, Po ³ ² ⁴
Hundred.

里 Li ³
"Li" (about one-third of a mile).

路 Lu ⁴
Road.

往 Wang ³ ⁴
Towards.

漢 Han ⁴
Name of a dynasty. Part of Hankow.

旱 Han ⁴
Dry, dry land.

非 Fei ¹
Not, bad.

飛 Fei ¹
To fly.

機 Chi ¹
A machine, opportunity.

工 Kung ¹
Work.

夫 Fu ¹
A man.

常 Ch'ang ²
Usual, ordinary.

快 K'uai ⁴
Quick, lively.

八 Pa ¹
Eight.

統 T'ung ²
Together, connected.

共 Kung ⁴
Together, combined.

父 Fu ⁴
Father.

母 Mu ³
Mother.

親 Ch'in ¹
Close relationship.

令 Ling ⁴
Honourable.

Characters 301—320

尊 Tsun [1]
Honourable (used in ceremonial language).

堂 T'ang [2]
The hall, principal room.

世 Shih [4]
The world, this life, generation.

惜 Hsi [1]
To pity, sympathise.

寶 Pao [3]
Precious, valuable.

眷 Chüan [4]
Family, wife.

成 Ch'êng [2]
Complete, finish become.

訂 Ting [4]
Fix, settle.

婚 Hun [1]
Marriage, marry.

結 Chieh [1]
To tie a knot, to join together.

孩 Hai [2]
Child, children.

男 Nan [2]
Male (of human beings).

位 Wei [4]
Classifier of persons.

女 Nü [3]
Female (of human beings).

托 T'o [1]
Rely upon, due to, depend on.

相 Hsiang [1]
Mutual.

郎 Lang [2]
Prince, your son.

犬 Ch'üan [3]
Dog, pup.

嬡 Ai, [4] Ngai [4]
Loved, beloved.

差 Ch'a [1] To err.
Ch'ai [1] To send.

Characters 321—340

事 Shih [4]
Affair, matter, business.

辦 Pan [4]
To do, to manage.

公 Kung [1]
Public, official.

商 Shang [1]
Commerce.

奉 Fêng [4]
To join, attach oneself to.

教 Chiao [4]
Instruction, Church.

耶 Yeh [1]
Used in transliterating.

穌 Su [1]
To revive.

基 Chi [1]
A foundation, a base.

督 Tu [1]
To oversee, to superintend.

音 Yin [1]
Sound.

牧 Mu [4]
Shepherd, pastor.

師 Shih [1]
Teacher.

士 Shih [4]
Scholar.

前 Ch'ien [2]
Before, formerly.

講 Chiang [3]
Expound, preach.

九 Chiu [3]
Nine.

目 Mu [4]
Index, list, eye.

繙 Fan [1]
To translate, turn over.

翻 Fan [1]
To upset, to overturn.

Characters 341—360

零 Ling [2]
Nought, cipher.

千 Ch'ien [1]
Thousand.

萬 Wan [4]
Ten thousand.

頭 T'ou [2]
Head, first, beginning.

半 Pan [4]
Half.

分 Fên [1]
A tenth, a portion.

之 Chih [1]
Sign of possessive.

地 Ti [4]
Earth, floor, locality.

少 Shao [3]
Few, little, short of.

必 Pi [4]
Must, certainly, necessary.

須 Hsü [1]
Necessary, must, wait, a moment.

補 Pu [3]
Patch, repair, mend.

星 Hsing [1]
Star, spark.

期 Ch'i [2]
Date, appointed time, expect.

禮 Li [3]
Ceremony, courtesy, politeness.

拜 Pai [4]
Worship, pay respect.

初 Ch'u [1]
Beginning, first.

正 Chêng [4]
Right, correct, chief. Chêng[1] first month.

末 Mo [4]
Last, end, dust, not.

臘 La [4]
Twelfth moon, winter sacrifice.

臘 As No. 360.

其 Ch'i [2]
He, she, it.

餘 Yü [2]
Surplus.

致 Chih [4]
To cause, to extend to, to send.

隨 Sui [2]
Comply with, according to, to follow.

冬 Tung [1]
Winter.

思 Ssŭ [1]
To think on, ponder, thought.

新 Hsin [1]
New.

玩 Wan [2]
Enjoy, amuse, play.

藝 I [4]
Skill, craft.

耍 Shua [3]
To play, to trifle.

糖 T'ang [2]
Sugar, sweets.

每 Mei [3]
Each, every.

份 Fên [4]
A portion.

經 Ching [1]
Pass through, manage.

身 Shên [1]
Body, self.

表 Piao [3]
Watch.

但 Tan [4]
But, only, yet.

面 Mien [4]
Face, front, side, aspect.

鐘 Chung [1]
Clock, bell.

Characters 381—400

近 Chin [4]
Near.

視 Shih [4]
See, look.

眼 Yen [3]
Eye, the eye.

約 Yüeh [1]
To make an appointment, covenant, bind.

己 I [3]
Sign of perfect tense.

躭 Tan [1]
Obstruct, delay, prevent.

誤 Wu [4]
To thwart, hinder.

許 Hsü [3]
Perhaps, maybe.

恐 K'ung [3]
Fear.

怕 P'a [4]
Fear, afraid.

刻 K'o [4]
A quarter, fifteen minutes.

趕 Kan [3]
To catch up, pursue, drive.

更 Kêng [4]
Sign of comparative.

夏 Hsia [4]
Summer.

避 Pi [4]
Avoid, escape, flee.

伏 Fu [2]
Summer heat.

暑 Shu [3]
Summer heat.

勞 Lao [2]
To toil, suffer, weary.

山 Shan [1]
Hill, mountain.

從 Ts'ung [2]
From, follow, obey.

Characters 401—420

閒 Hsien ²
Leisure, idle.

愛 Ai ⁴
To love, to like.

打 Ta ³
To beat, strike, to play at . . .

網 Wang ³
Net.

球 Ch'iu ²
Ball.

踢 T'i ¹
To kick.

足 Tsu²
Foot.

因 Yin ¹
Cause, because.

為 Wei ⁴
Because, do, make, be.

規 Kuei ¹
Rule, fix.

牌 P'ai ³
Cards, dominoes.

拍 P'ai ¹
To beat, clap, etc.

座 Tso ⁴
Classifier of clocks, etc.

慢 Man ⁴
Slow.

改 Kai ³
Alter, change.

準 Chun ³
Standard.

修 Hsiu ¹
Repair, put in order.

能 Nêng ²
Can, able.

替 T'i ⁴
For, instead of substitute.

認 Jên ⁴
To recognise, to acknowledge.

Characters 421—440

匠 Chiang [4]
An artisan.

定 Ting [4]
Fix, settle, certain.

後 Hou [4]
After, later.

駕 Chia [4]
Chariot, progress.

最 Tsui [4]
Most, very.

陪 P'ei [2]
To accompany, entertain.

頭 T'ou [2]
The head, the beginning.

概 Kai [4]
All, general.

便 Pien [4]
Convenient.
P'ien [4]   Cheap.

自 Tzǔ [4]
Self, natural, from.

己 Chi [3]
Self, personal.

盤 P'an [2]
Plate, board, a classifier.

棋 Ch'i [2]
Chess.

逛 Kuang [4]
Stroll, visit.

針 Chên [1]
Needle, needle-work.

鍼 As No. 435.

線 Hsien [4]
Thread, needle-work.

綫 As No. 437.

談 T'an [2]
To chat, gossip, talk.

譚 As No. 439.

夜 Yeh⁴
Night.

窗 Ch'uang¹
Window.

戶 Hu⁴
A hole, opening, screen.

關 Kuan¹
To close, bar, put to.

病 Ping⁴
Disease, illness.

發 Fa¹
To produce, become.

潮 Ch'ao²
Damp, humid, tide.

框 K'uang⁴
Frame.

縫 Fêng²
A seam, split, crack.

木 Mu⁴
Wood, timber.

鎖 So³
Lock, to lock.

銹 Hsiu⁴
Rust, to rust.

鑰 Yao,⁴ Yo⁴
A key.

試 Shih⁴
To try, to test, experiment.

塗 T'u²
To grease, to oil, smear.

開 K'ai¹
To open.

敞 Ch'ang³
To open, wide open, disclose.

偷 T'ou¹
To steal, a thief.

嗎 Ma⁴
Interrogative particle.

塞 Sai,¹,⁴ Sê⁴
Cork, stopper.

Characters 461—480

取 Ch'ü [2]
To take off or out.

出 Ch'u [1]
To come or go out, to produce.

合 Ho [2]
To close, to pair, side by side.

式 Shih [4]
Pattern, shape, fashion.

螺 Lo [2]
Conch, small screw.

絲 Ssŭ [1]
Wire, thread.

轉 Chuan [3]
To turn.

箱 Hsiang [1]
Box.

匣 Hsia [2]
Small box, crate.

盒 Ho [2]
A tin or box, casket.

筒 T'ung [2]
A tin, a container.

費 Fei [4]
Waste, expend.

釘 Ting [1]
A nail, to nail.

全 Ch'üan [2]
Perfect, complete, all.

鉗 Ch'ien [2]
Pincers, tongs.

總 Tsung [3]
All, general.

向 Hsiang [4]
Facing toward, to or from.

園 Yüan [2]
Courtyard, garden.

井 Ching [3]
A well.

蓋 Kai [4]
To cover.

Characters 481—500

清 Ch'ing [1]
Dawn, daybreak.

早 Tsao [3]
Early.

桶 T'ung [3]
A bucket, a barrel.

盛 Ch'êng [2]
To fill, to hold.
Shêng [4]
Abundant.

滿 Man [3]
Full, to fill.

所 So [3]
The relative pronoun. A place, that which.

缸 Kang [1]
A butt, large vessel for water, etc.

裝 Chuang [1]
To fill up, to pack, to contain.

髒 Tsang [1]
Dirty, filthy.

留 Liu [2]
To leave, to retain, keep.

件 Chien [4]
An article, an item.
A classifier.

忘 Wang [4]
To forget.

記 Chi [4]
To remember.

邊 Pien [1]
A side, an edge.

苦 K'u [3]
Bitter.

甜 T'ien [2]
Sweet.

煮 Chu [3]
To boil, to cook.

搬 Pan [1]
To move, to remove.

樓 Lou [2]
A second storey, tower.

動 Tung [4]
To move. To excite.

Characters 501—520

至
Chih⁴
Extreme. Reach to. Utmost.

雇
Ku⁴
To hire.

抬
T'ai²
To carry between two or more persons. To raise.

濟
Chi⁴
To help, save, up to the mark.

算
Suan⁴
To reckon, calculate.

然
Jan²
Certainly, really, still, although.

掃
Sao³
To sweep.

院
Yüan⁴
A courtyard, a hall.

收
Shou¹
To receive, collect, gather.

拾
Shih²
Arrange, pick up.

種
Chung³
Seed, grain. A kind or sort.

重
Chung⁴
Heavy, cumbersome.

休
Hsiu¹
Rest, recuperate, relax.

息
Hsi²
Rest, to rest.

歇
Hsieh¹
To rest, ease off.

椅
I³
A chair, couch.

空
K'ung¹
Empty.

想
Hsiang³
To think, reflect.

外
Wai⁴
Outside. Foreign.

老
Lao³
A long time. Old.

Characters 521—540

丢 Tiu [1]
To leave.

窖 Yin [4]
A cellar.

條 T'iao [2]
Classifier of long things.

凳 Têng [1]
To rise, to mount, to begin.

掉 Tiao [4]
To change round, turn round.

讓 Jang [4]
To allow, permit.

換 Huan [4]
To change.

乾 Kan [1]
Dry, clean.

净 Ching [4]
Clean.

布 Pu [4]
Calico, cotton cloth.
To notify, to publish.

廳 T'ing [1]
Court, Hall.

曉 Hsiao [3]
To know.

吩 Fên [1]
To order, command.

咐 Fu [4]
To commission, order.

毯 T'an [3]
Carpet, felt.

席 Hsi [2]
Mat, reed mat.

器 Ch'i [4]
A vessel, a utensil, implements.

洗 Hsi [3]
To wash, bathe, rinse.

端 Tuan [1]
A beginning. A clue. To serve.

伶 Ling [2]
Clever, active, adjust.

俐 Li [4]
Lively, quick, smart.

整 Chêng [3]
To set in order, to repair, adjust.

齊 Ch'i [2]
Even, regular. To arrange.

於 Yü [2]
In, on, at, from. Than.

斤 Chin [1]
A catty, one and a third lbs.

釐 Li [2]
The 1000th part of a Chinese foot; 1000th part of a "tael".

稱 Ch'êng [1]
To weigh, call, style.

裹 Kuo [3]
To bind, wrap.

量 Liang [2]
To measure, to deliberate. To buy, as grain.

糧 Liang [2]
Grain, food.

石 Shih [2] A stone.

斗 Tan [4] A bushel.

升 Tou [3]
A peck.

袋 Shêng [1]
A pint.

尺 Tai [4]
Bag, sack.

尺 Ch'ih
A foot.

寸 Ts'un [4]
An inch.

白 Pai [2]
White, clear, in vain.

文 Wên [2]
Literature, elegant.

步 Pu [4]
Pace, step, five feet.

意 I [4]
Idea, intention, meaning, wish.

Characters 561—580

思 Ssu [1]
Think on, ponder, thought.

褲 K'u [4]
Trousers.

材 Ts'ai [2]
Materials.

料 Liao [4]
Materials, calculate.

寬 K'uan [1]
Wide, broad, easy.

狹 Hsia [2]
Narrow.

比 Pi [3]
To compare.

布 Pu [4]
Cloth, to spread.

跑 P'ao [3]
To run, to gallop.

世 Shih [4]
The world, a generation.

界 Chieh [4]
The world, boundary.

記 Chi [4]
To record, to remember, a sign.

錄 Lu [4]
To record, copy.

破 P'o [4]
Break, solve.

碟 Tieh [2][5]
Saucer.

肉 Jou,[4] Ju [4]
Meat.

湯 T'ang [1]
Soup, gravy.

雞 Chi [1]
Chicken.

羊 Yang [2]
Sheep.

魚 Yü [3]
Fish.

Characters 581—600

猪 Chu [1]
Pig, pork.

排 P'ai [2]
Chops.

骨 Ku [3]
Chops.

熱 Jê [4]
Hot.

涼 Liang [2]
Cool, pleasant.

菜 Ts'ai [4]
Vegetables, food.

腿 T'ui [3]
Leg, thigh, ham.

片 P'ien [4]
Sliced, a slice, a strip.

牛 Niu [2]
A cow.

舌 Shê [2]
Tongue.

土 T'u [3]
Earth.

豆 Tou [4]
Beans.

菠 Po [1] [2]
Spinach.

熟 Shou,[2] Shu [2]
Ripe, soft, properly cooked.

啦 La [1]
A final particle.

冰 Ping [1]
Ice.

淇 Ch'i [2]
Name of a river used in transliteration.

淋 Lin [2]
To drip. Used in transliteration.

奶 Nai [3]
Milk, curdled milk, cheese.

餅 Ping [3]
Cake, slab.

Characters 601—620

Chia [1]
Used in transliteration.

Fei [1]
Used in transliteration.

P'ing, [2] P'in [2]
Apple.

Li [2]
Pears.

P'u [2]
The vine, a grape.

T'ao [2]
Grapes.

Chiu [3]
Wine.

Lü [3]
A tube.
The Philippines.

Sung [4]
Name of a dynasty.

Chieh [4]
Forbid, prohibit.

Pai [3]
To spread, to lay on table.

Chao [3]
To seek, to look for.

Ma [1]
An old woman, a mother, a waiting woman.

Ling [4]
Separate.

Hsien [2]
Salt. Brackish.

Yen [2]
Salt.

Hu [2]
Pepper.

Chiao [1]
Pepper.

Ts'u [4]
Vinegar.

Chieh [4]
Mustard.

Characters 621—640

牙　Ya [2]
Tooth, teeth.

籤　Ch'ien [1]
Bamboo-slip.

車　Ch'ê
Cart, carriage, vehicle.

輛　Liang [4]
Classifier of vehicles.

論　Lun [4]
To discuss, according to.

價　Chia [4]
Price, value.

應　Ying [1]
Ought, should, must; suitable.

該　Kai [1]
Ought, should. To owe.

做　Tso [4]
To make, To do, To be, To act as.

罷　Pa [4]
To cease. A final particle. Sign of imperative.

言　Yen [2]
Words, speech.

店　Tien [4]
An inn, a shop.

照　Chao [4]
According to. To illumine.

舊　Chiu [4]
Old—of time, persons, etc.

越　Yüeh [4]
The more, comparative sign.

力　Li [4]
Strength, power, force.

趙　Chao [4]
A common surname.

姐　Chieh [3]
An elder sister. A young lady.

識　Shih [4]
To know, to recognise.

猜　Ts'ai [1]
To guess

Characters 641—660

Lien [2]
Pitiful, pity, sympathise.

T'ung [1]
Together with, altogether.

Tzu [2]
Elder sister.

Mei [4]
Younger sister.

Ko [1]
Elder brother.

Tan [1]
To carry with a pole over the shoulder. To sustain.

Fu [4]
To bear, to sustain. To carry on back.

Tsê, [2] **Chai** [2]
Burden of office, responsibility.

Jên [4]
Office, the care or burden of office.

P'an [4]
To hope for, to expect.

Wang [4]
To expect, hope. To gaze at.

T'o [3]
Satisfactory.

Lien [3]
Face.

Mao [4]
Appearance, form.

Ch'i [3]
How, how can it be?

Ch'i [4]
Relatives.

Tsui [4]
Sin, crime, offence, offend.

Wu [2]
Without, apart from. A negative.

Ho [2]
How, why.

Huang [3]
Lies, false.

16

Characters 661—680

碰 P'êng[4]
To meet with. To come across. To hit upon.

詳 Hsiang[2]
Details.

細 Hsi[4]
Fine, delicate.

主 Chu[3]
Opinion, lord, master.

佩 P'ei[4]
Wear at waist, respect.

服 Fu[2]
Clothes, to wear. To serve, to be willing.

失 Shih[1]
To lose, to err.

信 Hsin[4]
To believe in, to trust. A letter.

酬 Ch'ou[2]
Reward, bestow.

提 T'i[2]
To lift in the hand; to raise, to mention.

據 Chü[4]
According to.

挺 T'ing[3]
To stick out, stiff.

壞 Huai[4]
Bad, vicious, ruined.

強 Ch'iang[2]
Strong, superior, violent.

短 Tuan[3]
Short.

歹 Tai[3]
Bad.

顏 Yen[2]
Colour, face.

色 Sê,[4] Shai[4]
Colour, beauty

挪 No[2]
To move.

根 Kên[1]
Classifier of sticks.

Characters 681—700

棍 Kun [4]
Staff, stick.

粗 Ts'u [1]
Broad, thick (or round things). Coarse.

貨 Huo [4]
Goods, wares.

物 Wu [4]
Things, goods.

馬 Ma [3]
Horse.

拉 La [1]
To pull, drag.

屋 Wu [1]
Room in a house. House.

堆 Tui [1]
Heap, pile, to pile up.

掌 Chang [3]
To control, palm of hand.

櫃 Kuei [4]
Shop counter, cupboard.

恭 Kung [1]
Reverence, offer.

發 Fa [1]
To issue, to send, to manifest.

財 Ts'ai [2]
Wealth, riches.

綢 Ch'ou [2]
Manufactured silk.

次 Tz'ǔ [4]
Inferior, second-rate, next.

封 Fêng
Classifier of letters, cover, seal, envelope.

領 Ling [3]
Receive, lead.

耐 Nai [4]
Endure, bear.

久 Chiu [3]
Old, long time.

未 Wei [4]
Not yet.

Characters 701—720

Mien [3]
Avoid, remit.

Shao [2]
Somewhat, slight.

Wei [1]
Small, minute, slight.

P'icn [2] Cheap.
Pien [4] Convenient.

I [2]
Right, suits, fits.

Sui [1] [2]
Supposing, though, even, still.

Shê [3]
Let go, relinquish.

Hua [1]
To spend. A flower.

Chang [4]
Measure of length —about 10 English feet.

Ts'ai [2]
To cut, to cut out, to plan.

Ch'uan [1]
To wear, to put on.

Lan [3]
Lazy, indolent, reluctant.

Wên [2]
Mosquito.

Chang [4]
Curtain, net for bed.

Na [2]
A final particle.

Lien [2]
Curtain.

Ch'ing
Light (in weight).

P'u [1]
To spread.

Chieh [1]
Solid, strong, reliable, real.

Ju [4]
Mattress.

Characters 721—740

係 Hsi [4]
Connected with, concern, involve.

賬 Chang [4]
Account, bill.

號 Hao [4]
A mark, a sign, a name or style.

皮 P'i [2]
Leather, skin.

擋 Tang [3]
To resist, to ward off.

泥 Ni [2]
Mud, slush.

舒 Shu [1]
Comfortable at ease.

興 Hsing [1]
Rise, prosper.

夥 Huo [3]
Assistant, band, company.

計 Chi [4]
To reckon, to calculate.

暗 An,[4] Ngan [4]
Dark, secret.

燈 Têng [1]
Lamp.

盞 Chan [3]
Classifier of lamps.

亮 Liang [4]
Bright, light.

安 An,[1] [4] Ngan [1] [4]
To fix, place. Rest, peace.

電 Tien [4]
Electricity, lightning.

枝 Chih [1]
Branch, classifier of candles, pens, etc.

蠟 La [4]
Wax.

燭 Chu [2]
Candle.

抖 Tou [3]
To shake, shudder.

Characters 741—760

疊 Tieh [2]
To fold up, a fold.

炭 T'an [4]
Coal.

煤 Mei [2]
Coal.

爐 Lu, [2] Lou [2]
Stove, brazier.

隔 Ko [2]
Partition.

壁 Pi [4]
Screen, partition, wall.

覺 Chüeh, [2] Chiao [2]
To feel, to be conscious of.

冷 Lêng [3]
Cold.

陽 Yang [2]
The sun, male principle, south.

絨 Jung [2]
Wool, woollen.

牀 Ch'uang [2]
Bed, classifier of blankets, etc.

躺 T'ang [3]
To recline, lie down.

汗 Han [4]
Perspiration.

屜 T'i [4]
Drawer, in a table, etc.

藥 Yao, [4] Yo [4]
Drugs, medicines.

葯 As No. 755.

顆 K'o [1]
Classifier of pills, seeds, pearls, etc.

滅 Mieh [4]
To put out, as a lamp, etc. To destroy.

睡 Shui [4]
To sleep, slumber.

澡 Tsao [3]
To bathe the body.

Characters 761—780

T'ien [1]
To add to, increase.

Kua [1]
To scrape, to shave.

Fa [2]
Fatigued, tired.

Wên [1]
Warm, mild, to warm up.

Shou [3]
Hand, hands.

Ch'êng [2]
The city.

Huo [2]
Living, Livelihood, lively.

Ch'êng [2]
Capacity; a journey, a career.

Jih [4]
Day, the sun.

Chêng [4]
To earn.

Mien [3]
To rouse oneself, make an effort.

I [1]
Clothing, to dress.

K'u [1]
Hole, cave.

Lung [3]
Hole, cave.

Shan [1]
Shirt.

Ch'ê [3]
To tear, rend, to fold.

Ts'ê, [4] **Ssu** [4]
Private, closet.

So [3]
A place, a cause.

Kuei [1]
Revert to, to belong to.

Ch'ang [2]
Usual, ordinary, constant.

Characters 781—800

馬 **Ma³**
Horse.

擦 **Ts'a¹**
To rub, polish.

銀 **Yin²**
Silver, money.

玻 **Po¹**
Glass.

璃 **Li²**
Glassware.

挂 **Kua⁴**
To hang up, to suspend.

撣 **Tan³, ⁴**
To dust, beat.

灰 **Hui¹**
Ashes.

塵 **Ch'ên²**
Dust, small particles.

鄰 **Lin²**
Neighbouring, neighbour.

居 **Chü¹**
To dwell.

干 **Kan¹**
Concern.

究 **Chiu⁴**
To analyse, examine, to be particular about.

衛 **Wei⁴**
To guard, protect.

各 **Ko⁴**
Each, every, all.

妨 **Fang¹**
Hinder, obstruct.

碍 **Ai,⁴ Ngai⁴**
Hinder, stand in the way.

礙 As No. 797.

抹 **Mo³**
To dust, polish, rub with the hand.

鏡 **Ching⁴**
Mirror.

Ch'ieh [4]
All, everything.

Kua [1]
To blow.

Fêng [1]
The wind.

Yü [3]
Rain.

Pu [4]
Account book.

Tan [4]
Egg, egglike.

Yü [4]
The taro and other edible tubers.

Hung [2]
Red.

Lo [2]
Carrots.

Po [1]
Carrots.

Ya [1]
Duck.

Yeh [3]
Wild, rustic.

Chi [2]
The fair, to gather together.

Lo,[4] Lao [4]
To come down, to fall, as prices, etc.

Shang [1]
To injure, to catch (cold).

I [1]
To heal, cure.

Shêng [4]
Remainder, left over.

Nao [3]
The brain.

Ch'ien [4]
To be short, to owe.

Hun [1]
Confused.

Characters 821—840

普 P'u [3]
Universal.

池 Ch'ih [2]
Pool, pond.

題 T'i [2]
To mention, subject of discourse.

剛 Kang [1]
Just now, just then.

轎 Chiao [4]
A sedan chair.

騎 Ch'i [2]
To ride astride.

牲 Shêng [1]
An animal, cattle.

步 Pu [4]
A step, pace, on foot.

顛 Tien [1]
Upset, jolting, bumpy.

簸 Po [4]
Winnow.

厲 Li [4]
Sharp, severe, oppress.

害 Hai [4]
Hurt, injure.

傘 San [3]
Umbrella, parasol.

肯 K'ên [3]
Willing, prone to.

跑 P'ao [3]
To run, also to walk (long distances).

旅 Lü [3]
Travel, journey.

舘 Kuan [3]
Hostel, hotel.

停 T'ing [2]
To halt, stop.

旁 P'ang [2]
By the side of, near.

坑 K'êng [1]
Pit, hollow.

館 As No. 837.

村 Ts'un [1]
Village.

票 P'iao [4]
Ticket, voucher.

趙 T'ang [4]
Time, turn, track,
classifier of
trains.

餐 Ts'an [1]
To dine, a meal.

炒 Ch'ao [3]
Fry, roast.

銅 T'ung [2]
Copper, copper
coins.

光 Kuang [1]
Light.

景 Ching [3]
Circumstances,
prospect.

局 Chü [2]
Position, plan.

像 Hsiang [4]
Like, image.

變 Pien [4]
To change, alter.

運 Yün [4]
To transport,
move, revolve,
luck.

隊 Tui [4]
A company, as of
soldiers.

伍 Wu [3]
Rank of five, mili-
tary.

消 Hsiao [1]
To disperse.

息 Hsi [2]
Breathe, interest,
news.

新 Hsin [1]
New, recent,
fresh.

聞 Wên [2]
To hear, to smell.

靠 K'ao [4]
Rely, reliable
trust.

Characters 861—880

謠 Yao [3]
Lies, false.

戰 Chan [4]
Fight, war, alarmed.

苦 K'u [3]
Bitter, sorrow.

極 Chi [2]
The extreme limit.

軍 Chün [1]
Army, military forces.

閥 Fa [2]
Rank, class.

擴 K'uo [4]
Expand, extend.

充 Ch'ung [1]
To fill.

喲 Yüeh [1]
Agree, pledge.

縣 Hsien [4]
District of administration, county town.

船 Ch'uan [2]
Boat, ship.

急 Chi [2]
Haste, urgent.

幸 Hsing [4]
Felicitous, fortunate.

虧 K'uei [1]
Lucky, luckily.

暈 Yün [4]
Dizzy.

慣 Kuan [4]
To be accustomed to.

美 Mei [3]
Beautiful, admirable.

滋 Tzŭ [1]
Rich (in sense of flavour).

味 Wei [4]
Taste, flavour.

穩 Wên [3]
Steady, firm, secure, stable.

波 Po [1]
Waves of the sea.

浪 Lang [4]
Waves of the sea.

騰 T'êng
To rise up, to mount.

搖 Yao [2]
To roll, as a ship.

騰 As No. 817.

海 Hai [3]
The sea, maritime, vast.

碼 Ma [3]
Docks, jetty.

希 Hsi [1]
Hope, rare, few.

磚 Chuan [1]
Brick.

墙 Ch'iang [2]
A wall.

轉 Chuan [3]
Revolve, to turn.

鑽 Tsuan [1]
To bore, awl, gimlet.

俗 Su [2]
Common, vulgar.

語 Yü [3]
Words, language, proverb.

硬 Ying [4]
Hard.

思 Ssu [1]
To think, to consider.

耳 Êrh [3]
Ear.

朵 To [3]
Ear, pendant, classifier of pendent things.

聾 Lung [2]
Deaf, to be deaf.

睛 Ching [1]
Eye, iris, pupil.

Characters 901—920

瞎 Hsia[1] Blind.

啞 Ya[3] Dumb.

吧 Pa[1] Dumb.

胳 Ko[1] Arm.

臂 Pei[4] Arm.

麻 Ma[2] Hemp, numb.

摩 Mo[2] To feel with the hand.

裳 Shang[2] Clothes.

胰 I[2] Soap.

勁 Chin,[4] Ching[4] Strength.

棉 Mien[2] Cotton, cotton wool.

袍 P'ao[2] Long gown.

襖 Ao,[3] Ngao[3] Outer gown, lined coat.

戴 Tai[4] To wear or carry on the head.

遮 Chê[1] To cover, to screen.

袖 Hsiu[4] A sleeve.

掛 As No. 786.

韈 Wa[4] Stockings, socks.

嗜 Shih[4] Fond of, addicted to.

髮 Fa[3] The hair of the head.

辮 **Pien** [4]
The queue, plait.

梳 **Shu** [1]
A comb, to comb.

刷 **Shua** [1]
A brush, to brush.

齒 **Ch'ih** [3]
Teeth.

扣 **K'ou** [4]
A button, to button.

指 **Chih** [3]
The fingers, to point.

保 **Pao** [3]
To guard, protect, preserve.

持 **Ch'ih** [2]
To preserve, hold, grasp.

盆 **P'ên** [2]
A basin, bowl, bath.

絹 **Chüan** [4]
A napkin, towel, handkerchief.

康 **K'ang** [1]
Well, hale, hearty, peace.

健 **Chien** [4]
Sturdy, strong.

窮 **Ch'iung** [2]
Poor, poverty-stricken.

體 **T'i** [3]
The body, limbs, to sympathise.

恤 **Hsü** [4]
Pity, to sympathise.

賙 **Chou** [1]
To be charitable, to help.

濟 **Chi** [4]
To save, help, deliver.

訓 **Hsün** [4]
To teach, instruct.

守 **Shou** [3]
To keep, observe.

矩 **Chü** [3]
Rule.

Characters 941—960

聲 Shêng [1]
Tone, voice, repute.

陰 Yin [1]
Shady, secret. The female principle.

賞 Shang [3]
Reward. Name of second tone.

入 Ju [4]
To enter. Name of entering tone.

效 Hsiao [4]
To imitate, copy.

語 Yü [3]
Words, a saying.

勸 Ch'üan [4]
Exhort, encourage.

向 Hsiang [4]
Facing towards, to or from.

求 Ch'iu [2]
To implore, to seek after.

竟 Ching [4]
Really, finally.

將 Chiang [1]
To take, hold; a leader.

提 T'i [2]
To mention, raise a matter.

拔 Pa [2]
Raise, help up.

室 Shih [4]
Room, house, office.

漸 Chien [4]
Gradually.

淡 Tan [4]
Insipid, weak (a liquids).

待 Tai [4]
To treat, to behave.

態 T'ai [4]
Behaviour, bearing, attitude.

改 Kai [3]
To alter, to change.

緣 Yüan [2]
Cause, reason.

Characters 961—980

故 Ku [4]
Cause, reason.

厚 Hou [4]
Generous, thick.

薄 Po [2], Pao [2]
Mean, stingy, thin.

困 K'un [4]
Straitened, distressed.

減 Chien [3]
To reduce, diminish.

薪 Hsin [1]
Fuel, firewood.

既 Chi [4]
Since, seeing that.

限 Hsien [4]
Limit, boundary.

謙 Ch'ien [1]
Humble, modest.

育 Yü
Rear, nurture.

鎮 Chên [4]
Market town, mart, to guard.

倡 Ch'ang [4]
To lead.

畢 Pi [4]
To finish, end.

業 Yeh [4]
Course, occupation, profession.

省 Shêng [3]
A province, frugal.

範 Fan [4]
Model, pattern.

莊 Chuang [1]
A farm, farmstead, the fields.

稼 Chia [4]
Grain, crops, to sow.

豐 Fêng [1]
Luxuriant, flourishing.

静 Ching [4]
Placid, calm.

Characters 981—1000

麥 Mai [4], Mo [4]
Wheat.

米 Mi [3]
Millet, grain in general.

納 Na [4]
To pay, to take, to receive.

糧 Liang [2]
Taxes, rations, grains.

症 Chêng [4]
Disease, ailments.

匪 Fei [3]
Worthless, bandits, rebels.

驚 Ching [3]
Alarm, startle, watch.

察 Ch'a [2]
To examine, investigate.

職 Chih [2]
Public office, appointment.

愧 K'uei [4]
Ashamed.

模 Mu [2], Mo [2]
Model, pattern.

治 Chih [4]
To cure, to treat (medically, etc.)

介 Chieh [4]
Introduce, announce.

紹 Shao [4]
Introduce, hand down.

益 I [2]
Benefit, advantage.

習 Hsi [2]
Versed in, familiar, practiced.

縱 Tsung [4]
Although, lax.

遵 Tsun [1]
To accord with, follow, obey.

命 Ming [4]
A command. Fate. Life.

興 Hsing [4]
Elated, rejoice.

Characters 1091—1020

跌 **Tieh** [1]
To stumble, fall.

品 **P'in** [3]
Sort, class, kind, character.

脈 **Mai** [4]
The pulse.

疼 **T'êng** [2]
Pain, to be in pain.

配 **P'ei** [4]
To mix, make up, as medicines.

瀉 **Hsieh** [4]
To purge, drain, diarrhœa.

濃 **Nêng** [2], **Nung** [2]
Thick, strong—of liquids.

副 **Fu** [4]
A dose. Classifier of medicine doses.

丸 **Wan** [2]
Pill, pills.

粉 **Fên** [3]
Medicinal powder, flour, meal.

脾 **P'i** [2]
Spleen, disposition.

立 **Li** [4]
To stand up, to establish.

榜 **Pang** [3]
Example, pattern.

忍 **Jên** [2]
Endure, restrain.

麻 **Ma** [2]
Hemp.

煩 **Fan** [2]
To trouble, annoy, annoyance.

囉 **Lo** [1]
Vexatious, annoyance.

唆 **So** [1]
To incite, discord, mischief.

架 **Chia** [4]
Blows, squabble, a frame.

衝 **Ch'ung** [1]
To clash, dash against.

Characters 1021—1040

突 T'u⁴
Rush against.

吵 Ch'ao³
Altercation, row, noise.

嘴 Tsui³
Lips.

驕 Chiao¹
Proud, arrogant.

傲 Ao⁴, Ngao⁴
Haughty, proud.

卑 Pei¹
Low.

耐 Nai⁴
To endure, be patient, bear.

惹 Jo³
To provoke.

聰 Ts'ung¹
Intelligent, understanding, clever.

達 Ta²
Penetrate, inform.

深 Shên¹
Deep, profound versed in.

儒 Ju²
Confucian, learned.

割 Ko¹
To cut.

繩 Shêng³
Rope, string, cord.

粗 Ts'u¹
Coarse, rough, bulky.

斷 Tuan⁴
To cut off, break.

較 Chiao³
To compare, to test, more than.

絞 Chiao³
To cut with scissors, twist, crosswise.

剪 Chien³
Scissors.

鈍 Tun⁴
Dull, blunt.

Characters 1041—1060

磨 Mo [2]
To grind, rub, mill.

由 Yu [2]
Reason, cause.

奇 Ch'i [2]
Strange, wonderful, rare.

怪 Kuai [4]
Extraordinary, unusual, to blame.

章 Chang [1]
Chapter, essay.

節 Chieh [2]
Verse, section.

頁 Yeh [4]
Page, leaf of a book.

導 Tao [3]
To lead.

諸 Chu [1]
All.

觀 Kuan [1]
To look on, to observe.

護 Hu [4]
To protect, guard.

擠 Chi [3]
To crowd together, to press.

散 San [4]
To scatter, disperse.

彼 Pi [3]
That.

此 Tz'ǔ [3]
This.

讓 Jang [4]
To concede, give way, yield.

步 Pu [4]
A step, on foot.

退 T'ui [4]
To retreat, retire, move back.

脫 T'o [1]
To doff the hat, take off (clothes).

鞠 Chü [2]
To bow, bend the body.

Characters 1061—1080

躬 Kung [1]
The body, person.

左 Tso [3]
Left.

右 Yu [4]
Right.

素 Su [4]
Cardinal, fundamental, ordinary.

食 Shih [2]
Food.

樞 Shu [1]
A pivot, axis, fundamental.

暖 Nuan [3]
Warm, genial.

飽 Pao [3]
Replete, full.

假 Chia [4]
Holiday.

鄉 Hsiang [1]
The country, countryside, rural.

頓 Tun [4]
To stamp the foot, a time.

野 Yeh [3]
Wild.

讚 Tsan [4]
To praise, to commend.

閃 Shan [3]
Flash, lightning.

響 Hsiang [3]
Sound, echo. To make a noise.

响 As No. 1075.

雷 Lei [2]
Thunder.

雪 Hsüeh [3]
Snow.

霜 Shuang [1]
Frost.

樹 Shu [4]
Tree.

Characters 1081—1100

河 Ho² River.

湖 Hu² Lake.

凍 Tung⁴ To freeze.

秋 Ch'iu¹ Autumn, harvest.

霧 Wu⁴ Mist.

緻 Chih⁴ Scenery, view.

坡 P'o¹ The slope of a hill.

廟 Miao⁴ Temple, fair.

塔 T'a³ Pagoda.

尚 Shang⁴ Still, yet, to ascend, to be in charge of.

佛 Fo² Buddha.

蒼 Ts'ang¹ A fly.

蠅 Ying² A fly.

螞 Ma³ An ant.

蟻 I³ An ant.

討 T'ao³ To beg, seek.

厭 Yen⁴ Dislike.

咬 Yao³ To bite.

駱 Lo⁴ Camel.

駝 T'o² Camel.

Characters 1101—1120

騾 Lo [2]
Mule.

驢 Lü [2]
Donkey.

香 Hsiang [1]
Fragrant.

抱 Pao [4]
To nurse, carry in the arms.

背 Pei [2]
To carry on the back.

挑 T'iao [1]
To carry on a pole on the shoulder.

唱 Ch'ang [4]
To sing.

戲 Hsi [4]
Theatricals, play on stage.

鬧 Nao [4]
Noise, bustle, disturb.

趁 Ch'en [4]
Avail of.

擁 Yung [1]
To crowd or press together.

擠 Chi [3]
To crowd together.

扛 K'ang [2]
To carry on shoulder.

牽 Ch'ien [1]
To lead a horse by the bridle.

匹 P'i [3]
Classifier of horses.

踩 Ts'ai [4]
To trample or step on.

危 Wei [2]
Dangerous.

險 Hsien [3]
Dangerous.

金 Chin [1]
Gold, metal

煉 Lien [4]
To refine.

Characters 1121—1140

瓜 Kua [1]
Melon.

蓮 Lien [2]
The lotus.

遙 Yao [2]
Distant.

吹 Ch'ui [1]
To blow.

疵 Tz'ŭ [1]
A flaw, blemish.

救 Chiu [4]
To save, deliver.

近 Chin [4]
Near, to approach.

虎 Hu [3]
Tiger.

踏 T'a [4]
To step on, tread.

隻 Chih [1]
Classifier of boots, shoes, etc.

栽 Tsai [1]
To plant.

乘 Ch'êng [2]
To avail of.   To ascend.

鳥 Niao [3]
Bird.

舊 Chiu [4]
Ancient, old.

謀 Mou [2]
To plan, devise.

貓 Mao [2] [1]
Cat.

死 Ssŭ [3]
Dead, to die.

鼠 Shu [3]
Rat, mouse.

善 Shan [4]
Good, virtuous. To perfect.

惡 O [4]   Evil, wicked,   wrong.
Wu [4]
Hate, dislike.

Characters 1141—1160

報 Pao [4]
To announce, to inform. A newspaper.

郵 Yu [2]
To convey, postal service.

閉 Pi [4]
To close, to stop up.

政 Chêng [4]
Government, administration.

石 Shih [2]
Stone.

內 Nei [4]
Inside, within.

造 Tsao [4]
To build, make.

貼 T'ieh [1]
To stick on, as stamps.

插 Ch'a [1]
To stick in.

祖 Tsu [3]
Ancestors.

旗 Ch'i [2]
Flag, banner.

肚 Tu [4]
stomach, belly.

桿 Kan [3]
A staff, a pole.

餓 O [4]
Hungry.

影 Ying [3]
Shadow, image.

啤 P'i [2]
Beer.

行 Hsing [2]
To walk, to do.
Hang [2]
A store, shop.

樂 Yo [4], Yüeh [4]
Music.

滙 Hui [4]
To exchange money.

廣 Kuang [3]
Wide, broadcast.

Characters 1161—1180

播 Po [1]
To spread abroad.

跳 T'iao [4]
To dance, jump.

舞 Wu [3]
To posture, brandish, dance.

累 Lei [4]
Tired, fatigued.

趣 Ch'ü [4]
Interesting, amusing.

輩 Pei [4]
Generation.

維 Wei [2]
To maintain, organise.

族 Tsu [2]
A clan, a tribe, to collect together.

項 Hsiang [4]
The nape of the neck, an item.

原 Yüan [2]
A source, original.

私 Ssŭ [1]
Selfish, private.

德 Tê [2]
Virtue, power.

投 T'ou [2]
To hand in, surrender.

降 Chiang [4]
To descend.

抵 Hsiang [2]
To surrender.

抵 Ti [3]
To resist.

抗 K'ang [4]
To resist, oppose.

侵 Ch'in [2]
To invade.

略 Lüeh [4]
To plunder.

被 Pei [3] [4]
A coverlet, sign of passive.

炸 Cha [4]
To smash, explode.

Characters 1181—1200

彈 **Tan** [4]
Bomb, bullet.

壞 **Huai** [4]
Ruin, destroy, spoil.

盟 **Mêng** [2]
Covenant, alliance.

勝 **Shêng** [4]
Victory, conquer.

敗 **Pai** [4]
Defeat, spoil.

械 **Chieh** [4]
Weapons.

殘 **Ts'an** [2]
Injure, cruel.

暴 **Pao** [4]
Violent, fierce, cruel.

受 **Shou** [4]
To receive, suffer.

嚇 **Hsia** [4]
Alarm, startle.

宣 **Hsüan** [1]
To proclaim.

組 **Tsu** [3]
To organise.

織 **Chih** [1]
To weave.

聯 **Lien** [3]
To connect, unite.

陸 **Lu** [4]
Dry land, six.

議 **I** [4]
To discuss, consult.

複 **Fu** [4]
Double.

雜 **Tsa** [2]
Confused, complicated.

產 **Ch'an** [3]
Property.

民 **Min** [2]
The people.

Characters 1201—1210

革 Ko [2]
To change, alter.

派 P'ai [4]
Party, separate, branch.

黨 Tang [3]
Party, association, faction.

眾 Chung [4]
All, a crowd.

楚 Ch'u [3]
Clear, sharp.

套 T'ao [4]
A case, a wrapper, to harness.

朗 Lang [3]
Clear, bright.

班 Pan [1]
A class, company.

武 Wu [3]
Military.

雹 Pao [3]
Hail.

17

HOW TO USE A CHINESE DICTIONARY
FROM THE RADICALS

HOW TO USE A CHINESE DICTIONARY
FROM THE RADICALS

It has already been pointed out in the preceding Section that Chinese characters are readily analysed into two parts, Radical and Phonetic.

The Radicals number 214, while the number of Phonetics varies according to the predilection of the individual scholar. Soothill, as has already been noted, selects 888 to make up his Pocket Dictionary of Four Thousand Characters.

The list of Radicals is appended for the information of the student, and also to enable him to use it to find characters in any of the popular dictionaries designed to help the foreigner studying Chinese.

It will be noted that the Radicals are arranged in the order of the number of strokes of which they are composed.

The Radicals vary in importance according to the relative frequency with which they occur. It is desirable that the Radicals should be written out frequently and memorised, together with their number and meaning. The numbers are necessary, as dictionaries for foreign students are arranged on the principle of classifying characters under the Radicals in numerical order from 1 to 214.

In the list of Radicals appended the tones are indicated in the usual way, 1, 2, 3 and 4. But in addition another mark (*) is attached to some to indicate the fifth tone, or " Ju " shêng, to which reference is made in Dialogue 30. As the writer lived in Shansi province for eighteen years where the " Ju " shêng is in common use, I have included this particular tone for the Radicals. The student will often find in text-books opinions expressed that the " Ju " shêng, in effect, is dying out, and that no

particular attention need be paid to it.   But that is true
only of certain provinces.   If the student travels in the
north and north-west he will hear the tone frequently
used.   In writing out the Chinese characters of this tone
in Romanised it is usual to add an " h " to the end of
the words.

A list of a few specimen characters from a dictionary
is also appended, to enable the student to find characters
in the dictionary from the Radicals.

First of all it is necessary to discover the Radical part
of the character you wish to look up.   If you have made
yourself familiar with the 214 Radicals this should not
present any serious difficulty.   The bigger dictionaries,
like Giles, give a list of characters, the Radicals of which
are difficult to discover.   Relatively speaking these are
comparatively few.

The selected characters as appended all have Radical
No. 61 in them.   This is the " heart " Radical, and,
as you will see, it is found in characters which express
thought, emotions, personal characteristics and the like.

Notice that this particular Radical is written in three
forms, only two of which, 忄 and 㣺 , are illustrated.
Notice further that the position of the Radical in the
characters varies.   It is sometimes at the left-hand side,
sometimes at the bottom, and, in one instance, in the
character " ai ", 愛, to love, it is found, appropriately,
at the very heart of the character.

Having found that the particular character for which
we are hunting has the Radical " heart " as its root,
we now count the number of strokes in the rest of the
character.   Note " in the rest of the character ".   You
do NOT include the strokes of the Radical itself in your
reckoning.

Take for example the first character on our selected
list.   It is the character " nu ", 怒, anger.   This has
five strokes in it in addition to the Radical.   So it is
listed in the dictionary under the Radical No. 61, and

again under 5, the figure at the left-hand side of the character list. The same rule applies throughout.

Take another illustration from the character " k'ung ", 恐, to fear. This character has six strokes in addition to the Radical, and so is listed under 6. " Wu ", 懊 has seven, " hsi ", 惜, has eight, and " I ", 意, nine.

The numbers at the right-hand side of the character list refer to the numbers of the Phonetics, ranging from 1 to 888 in Soothill, under which the characters are classified again, with their meanings, and other characters with which they are commonly associated, making composite characters or phrases.

After the student has discovered the character from the Radical and number of strokes, he looks up the number on the right-hand side, in the body of the dictionary, and there he will find the meaning of the character and the way in which it is used.

With these illustrations and hints to guide him, the student should have no great difficulty in finding his way through a Chinese dictionary.

SPECIMEN CHARACTERS FROM SOOTHILL'S DICTIONARY

5. 怒   553—Nu.⁴   Anger.

   怕   804—P'a.⁴   Fear.

   性   41—Hsing.⁴   Nature, temper, disposition.

   思   379—Ssŭ.¹   Think on, ponder,⁴ thought.

   怎   150—Tsên.³   How? what? why?

6. 恐   8—K'ung.³   To fear.

   息   853—Hsi.² *   Breath, sigh, interest, rest.

7. 慔   761—Wu.⁴   Neglect, hinder.

8. 惜   799—Hsi.¹ *   Pity, spare, care for.

   情   82—Ch'ing.²   Feelings, passion for.

   惡   247—O.⁴   Evil, wicked, low,* hate.

9. 意   91—I.⁴   Idea, intention, meaning, wish.

   惹   182—Jo.³   Provoke.

   愛   411—Ai.⁴   To love, to like.

LIST OF RADICALS

Arranged in order according to the number of strokes

1 Stroke

1. 一   I.[1] * One, unity.
2. 丨   K'un.[3] Downstroke.
3. 丶   Chu.[3] A point, dot.
4. 丿   P'ieh.[1] * Stroke to left.
5. 乙   I.[4] * One, second of ten stems.
6. 亅   Chüeh.[2] * A hook.

2 Strokes

7. 二   Êrh.[4] Two.
8. 亠   T'ou.[2] Roof, cover.
9. 人。亻。 Jên.[2] Man.
10. 儿   Jên.[2] Man, variant of 9.
11. 入   Ju.[4] * Enter.
12. 八   Pa.[1] * Eight.
13. 冂   Chiung.[3] Limits, boundaries.
14. 冖   Mi.[4] * Cover, roof.
15. 冫   Ping.[1] Ice.
16. 几   Chi.[1] Table, stand.
17. 凵   K'an.[3] Receptacle.
18. 刀。刂。 Tao.[1] Knife.
19. 力   Li.[4] * Strength.
20. 勹   Pao.[1] To wrap.
21. 匕   Pi.[3] Spoon, ladle.
22. 匚   Fang.[1] Basket, chest.
23. 匸   Hsi[3]. Box, conceal.

24. 十　　Shih.² * Ten.
25. 卜　　Pu.³ * To divine.
26. 卩。巳。Chieh.² * A seal.
27. 厂　　Han.⁴ A ledge, cliff.
28. 厶　　Ssu.¹ Private, selfish.
29. 又　　Tu.⁴ Again, also hand.

3 Strokes

30. 口　　K'ou.³ Mouth.
31. 囗　　Hui.² An enclosure.
32. 土　　T'u.³ Earth.
33. 士　　Shih.⁴ Scholar, officer.
34. 夂　　Chih.³ A step, advance.
35. 夂　　Sui.¹ Walk slowly.
36. 夕　　Hsi.² * Evening.
37. 大　　Ta.⁴ Great.
38. 女　　Nü.³ Woman, female.
39. 子　　Tzu.³ Son, child.
40. 宀　　Mien.² A roof.
41. 寸　　Ts'un.⁴ An inch.
42. 小　　Hsiao.³ Small.
43. 尢。兀。尣, Wang.¹ Lame.
44. 尸　　Shih.¹ A corpse.
45. 屮　　Ch'ê.⁴ * A sprout.
46. 山　　Shan.¹ Hill.
47. 巛。川。巜。Ch'uan.¹ Stream.
48. 工　　Kung.¹ Work.
49. 己　　Chi.³ Self.
50. 巾　　Chin.¹ Napkin.
51. 干　　Kan.¹ Shield.
52. 幺　　Yao.¹ Small, tender.
53. 广　　Yen.³ Roof, cover.

54.	夊	Yin.³ To move on.
55.	廾	Kung.³ Folded hands.
56.	弋	I.⁴ * A dart.
57.	弓	Kung.¹ A bow.
58.	彐 彑 彐	Chi.⁴ Pig's snout.
59.	彡	Shan.¹ Plumage, streaky.
60.	彳	Ch'ih.⁴ * A step.

4 Strokes

61.	心 忄 小	Hsin.¹ Heart.
62.	戈	Ko.¹ A spear.
63.	戶	Hu.⁴ Door, family.
64.	手 扌	Shou.³ Hand.
65.	支	Chih.¹ Branch.
66.	攴 攵	P'u.¹ To tap, rap.
67.	文	Wên.² Literature, ornament.
68.	斗	Tou.³ A peck.
69.	斤	Chin.¹ Catty, axe.
70.	方	Fang.¹ Square.
71.	无 旡	Wu.² Not, without.
72.	日	Jih.⁴ * Sun, day.
73.	曰	Yüeh.⁴ * To say.
74.	月	Yüeh.⁴ * Moon, month.
75.	木	Mu.⁴ * Wood, tree.
76.	欠	Ch'ien.⁴ To owe, short of.
77.	止	Chih.³ To stop.
78.	歹 歺	Tai.³ Bad.
79.	殳	Shu.¹ Pole-axe, kill.
80.	毋	Wu.² Do not !
81.	比	Pi.³ Compare.
82.	毛	Mao.² Hair.
83.	氏	Shih.⁴ Family, clan.

84. 气　　Ch'i.⁴ Breath, vapour.
85. 水。氵。氺。Shui.³ Water.
86. 火。灬 Huo.³ Fire.
87. 爪。爫 Chao.³ Claws.
88. 父　　Fu.⁴ Father.
89. 爻　　Yao.² Crosswise, intertwine.
90. 爿　　Ch'iang.² Frame, bed.
91. 片　　P'ien.⁴ A slip, strip.
92. 牙　　Ya.² Tooth.
93. 牛　　Niu.² Ox.
94. 犬。犭。Ch'üan.³ Dog.

5 Strokes

95. 玄　　Hsüan.² Dark, obscure.
96. 玉。王。Yü.⁴ * Gem, jade.
97. 瓜　　Kua.¹ Melon, gourd.
98. 瓦　　Wa.³ A tile.
99. 甘　　Kan.¹ Sweet.
100. 生　　Shêng. Beget, live.
101. 用　　Yung.⁴ Use.
102. 田　　T'ien.² Field.
103. 疋　　P'i.³ * A roll of cloth.
104. 疒　　Ni.⁴ * Sick, disease.
105. 癶　　Po.⁴ * Back to back.
106. 白　　Pai.² White.
107. 皮　　P'i.² Skin.
108. 皿　　Min.³ Dish, platter.
109. 目。皿。Mu.⁴ * Eye.
110. 矛　　Mao.² Halberd, lance.
111. 矢　　Shih.⁴ Arrow.
112. 石　　Shih.² * Stone.
113. 示。礻。礻。Shih.⁴ To indicate.
114. 肉　　Jou.³ * Track, a step.

115.	禾	Ho.² Growing grain.
116.	穴	Hsüeh.⁴ A cave, hole.
117.	立	Li.⁴ * To stand.

6 Strokes

118.	竹	Chu.² * Bamboo.
119.	米	Mi.³ Rice.
120.	糸, 糹。	Ssu.¹ Mi.⁴ * Raw silk.
121.	缶	Fou.³ Earthenware.
122.	网, 罒。冗。	Wang.³ A net.
123.	羊	Yang.² Sheep.
124.	羽	Yü. Feather, wing.
125.	老	Lao.³ Old.
126.	而	Êrh.² And, yet.
127.	耒	Lei.³ A plough.
128.	耳	Êrh.³ Ear.
129.	聿	Yü.⁴ * Pencil, brush.
130.	肉。月。	Jou.⁴ * Flesh.
131.	臣	Ch'ên. A Statesman.
132.	自	Tzu.⁴ Self, from.
133.	至	Chih.⁴ Reach to.
134.	臼	Chiu.⁴ A mortar.
135.	舌	She.² * The tongue.
136.	舛	Ch'uan.³ Oppose, contradict.
137.	舟	Chou.¹ Boat.
138.	艮	Kên. Perverse, limit.
139.	色	Sê.⁴ * Colour.
140.	艸。艹。艹。	Ts'ao.³ Grass, herbs.
141.	虍	Hu.¹ Tiger.
142.	虫	Ch'ung.² Insect, reptile.
143.	血	Hsüeh.³ * Blood.
144.	行	Hsing.² To go, to do.

145. 衣 衤。I.[1] Clothes.
146. 襾。西。Hsi.[1] West.

7 Strokes

147. 見   Chien.[4] See.
148. 角   Chio.[2] * Horn, corner.
149. 言   Yen.[2] Words, to speak.
150. 谷   Ku.[3] * Valley, gully.
151. 豆   Tou.[4] Beans, platter.
152. 豕   Shih.[3] Pig, swine.
153. 豸   Chai.[4] Reptile.
154. 貝   Pei.[4] Precious, cowrie.
155. 赤   Ch'ih.[4] * Flesh colour, red, naked.
156. 走   Tsou.[3] Walk.
157. 足   Tsu.[2] Foot, enough.
158. 身   Shên.[1] Body.
159. 車   Ch'e.[1] Cart, coach.
160. 辛   Hsin.[1] Bitter, pungent.
161. 辰   Ch'ên.[2] Time.
162. 辵。辶。Cho.[1] * To advance, run.
163. 邑。阝。I.[4] City, district.
164. 酉   Yu.[3] New wine, ripe.
165. 采   Pien.[4] Separate, discern.
166. 里   Li.[3] A Chinese mile.

8 Strokes

167. 金   Chin.[1] Metal, gold.
168. 長。镸。Ch'ang.[3] Long.
169. 門   Mên.[2] Door.
170. 阜。阝。Fou.[4] A mound.
171. 隶   Tai.[4] Reach to.
172. 隹   Chui.[1] Short-tailed birds.

173. 雨　　Yü.³　Rain.
174. 青　　Ch'ing.¹　Green, blue sky.
175. 非　　Fei.¹　Wrong, not.

9 Strokes

176. 面　　Mien.⁴　Face.
177. 革　　Ko.² *　Hides.
178. 韋　　Wei.²　Leather, thong.
179. 韭　　Chiu.³　Leeks.
180. 音　　Yin.¹　Sound.
181. 頁　　Yeh.⁴ *　A page.
182. 風　　Fêng.¹　Wind.
183. 飛　　Fei.¹　To fly.
184. 食　　Shih.² *　To eat.
185. 首　　Shou.³　Head.
186. 香　　Hsiang.¹　Scent, fragrance.

10 Strokes

187. 馬　　Ma.³　A horse.
188. 骨　　Ku.³ *　Bone.
189. 高　　Kao.¹　High.
190. 髟　　Piao.¹　Hair.
191. 鬥　　Tou.⁴　Strife.
192. 鬯　　Ch'ang.⁴　Aromatic herbs.
193. 鬲　　Li.⁴　Cauldron, tripod.
194. 鬼　　Kuei.³　Spirit, demon.

11 Strokes

195. 魚　　Yü.²　Fish.
196. 鳥　　Niao.³　A bird.
197. 鹵　　Lu.³　Rock, salt.

198. 鹿　　Lu.⁴ *　Deer.
199. 麥　　Mai.⁴　Wheat,
200. 麻　　Ma.²　Hemp.

12 Strokes

201. 黃　　Huang.²　Yellow.
202. 黍　　Shu.³　Millet.
203. 黑　　Hei.¹　Hê.　Black.
204. 黹　　Chih.³　Embroidery,

13 Strokes

205. 黽　　Min.³　Frog.
206. 鼎　　Ting.³　Tripod.
207. 鼓　　Ku.³　Drum.
208. 鼠　　Shu.³　Rat.

14—17 Strokes

209. 鼻　　Pi.³　Nose.
210. 齊　　Ch'i.²　Uniform, all.
211. 齒　　Ch'ih.³　Teeth.
212. 龍　　Lung.²　Dragon.
213. 龜　　Kuei.¹　Tortoise.
214. 龠　　Yo.⁴ *　Flute, pipe.

INDEX TO CHINESE CHARACTERS
ALPHABETICALLY ARRANGED

276 處	512 重	**CHÜEH**	230 放	277 府
357 初	1204 眾	407 脚	796 妨	291 傅
462 出		747 覺		297 父
1205 楚	**CH'UNG**		**FEI**	396 伏
	868 充	**CHÜN**	287 非	534 咐
CHUAN	1020 衝	865 軍	288 飛	647 負
467 轉			472 費	666 服
889 磚	**CHÜ**	**ERH**	602 啡	1008 副
	219 句	51 兒	986 匪	1197 複
CH'UAN	221 具	62 二		
711 穿	671 據	897 耳	**FÊN**	**HAI**
871 船	791 居		159 分	311 孩
	850 局	**FA**	374 份	832 害
CHUANG	940 矩	128 法	533 吩	886 海
488 裝	1060 鞠	446 發	1010 粉	
977 莊		763 乏		**HAN**
	CH'Ü	866 閥	**FÊNG**	285 漢
CH'UANG	14 去	920 髮	325 奉	286 旱
442 窗	461 取		449 縫	753 汗
751 牀	1165 趣	**FAN**	696 封	
		67 飯	803 風	**HANG**
CH'UI	**CHÜAN**	339 繙	979 豐	1149 行
1124 吹	166 捲	340 翻		
	306 眷	976 範	**FO**	**HAO**
CHUN	930 絹	1016 煩	1091 佛	34 好
416 準				723 號
	CH'ÜAN	**FANG**	**FU**	
CHUNG	318 犬	146 方	19 福	**HÊN**
81 中	474 全	214 房	256 甫	132 很
380 鐘	947 勸			
511 種				

168	火	**JÊN**		**K'AI**		860	靠	757	顆
683	貨	7	人	456	開				渴
729	夥	420	認			**KÊN**		**KOU**	
767	活	649	任	**KAN**		130	跟	244	夠
		1014	忍	47	敢	680	根		
I				195	幹			**K'OU**	
2	一	**JIH**		392	趕	**K'ÊN**		5	口
76	以	769	日	528	乾	834	肯	925	扣
96	易			792	干				
101	意	**JO**		1147	桿	**KÊNG**		**KU**	
370	藝	1028	惹			225	羹	502	雇
385	已			**K'AN**		265	庚	583	骨
516	椅	**JOU**		15	看	393	更	961	故
705	宜	576	肉						
772	衣			**KANG**		**K'ÊNG**		**K'U**	
816	醫	**JU**		172	鋼	840	坑	495	苦
909	胰	576	肉	487	缸			562	褲
995	益	720	縟	824	剛	**KO**		773	窟
1095	蟻	944	入			109	個		
1196	議	1032	儒	**K'ANG**		645	哥	**KUA**	
				931	康	745	隔	762	刮
JAN		**JUNG**		1113	扛	795	各	786	挂
506	然	95	容	1176	抗	904	胳	802	颳
		750	絨			1033	割	917	掛
JANG				**KAO**		1201	革	1121	瓜
526	讓	**KAI**		135	告				
		415	改	267	高	**K'O**		**KUAI**	
JÊ		428	概			3	課	1044	怪
584	熱	480	蓋	**K'AO**		72	客		
		628	該	237	烤	75	可	**K'UAI**	
						391	刻	143	塊

246 筷	990 愧	595 啦	183 裏	654 臉
293 快		686 拉	279 離	716 簾
	KUN	738 蠟	282 里	1120 煉
KUAN	681 棍		355 禮	1122 蓮
119 管		**LAI**	541 俐	1194 聯
444 關	**K'UN**	21 來	546 藜	
837 舘	964 困		604 梨	**LIN**
841 館		**LAN**	636 力	598 淋
876 慣	**KUNG**	712 懶	785 璃	790 鄰
1050 觀	290 工	鬮	831 厲	
	296 共	**LANG**	1012 立	**LING**
K'UAN	323 公	317 郎		300 令
565 寬	691 恭	882 浪	**LIA**	341 零
	1061 躬	1207 朗	188 倆	540 伶
KUANG				614 另
434 逛	**K'UNG**	**LAO**	**LIANG**	697 領
848 光	389 恐	398 勞	171 兩	
1160 廣	517 空	520 老	549 量	**LIU**
		814 落	550 糧	212 六
K'UANG	**KUO**		585 涼	490 留
448 框	66 過	**LEI**	624 輛	
	82 國	1077 雷	734 亮	**LO**
KUEI	242 果	1164 累		465 螺
25 貴	548 裹		**LIAO**	809 蘿
410 規		**LÊNG**	35 了	814 落
690 櫃	**K'UO**	748 冷	564 料	1017 囉
779 歸	867 擴		1178 略	1099 駱
		LI		1101 髏
K'UEI	**LA**	27 李	**LIEN**	
374 虧	360 臘	74 理	641 憐	**LOU**
	361 臉	182 裡		499 樓

744 爐	184 賣	**MIAO**	1041 磨	**NEI**
LU	981 麥	1088 廟		1153 內
283 路	1003 脈		**MOU**	
573 錄		**MIEH**	1135 謀	**NÊNG**
744 爐	**MAN**	758 滅		418 能
1195 陸	414 慢		**MU**	1007 濃
	485 滿	**MIEN**	298 母	
LUN		238 麪	332 牧	**NI**
625 論	**MANG**	379 面	338 目	106 你
	217 忙	701 免	450 木	173 呢
LUNG		771 勉	991 模	726 泥
18 隆	**MAO**	911 棉		
774 窿	174 毛		**NA**	**NIAO**
899 聾	197 帽	**MIN**	59 那	1133 鳥
	654 貌	1200 民	154 拿	
LÜ	1136 貓		715 哪	**NIEN**
608 呂		**MING**	983 納	125 唸
836 旅	**MEI**	192 明		261 年
1102 驢	144 墨	260 名	**NAI**	
	373 每	999 命	599 奶	**NIN**
MA	644 妹		698 耐	254 您
31 嗎	743 煤	**MO**		
613 媽	877 美	68 沒	**NAN**	**NIU**
685 馬		112 麽	99 難	589 牛
887 碼	**MÊN**	144 墨	275 南	
906 麻	4 門	359 末	312 男	**NO**
1094 螞	122 們	799 抹		679 挪
		907 摩	**NAO**	
MAI	**MÊNG**	981 麥	818 腦	**NUAN**
179 買	1183 盟	991 模	1109 鬧	1067 暖
	MI			
	982 米			

NUNG	582 排	**P'AO**	661 碰	704 便
1007 濃	1202 派	41 泡		852 變
		569 跑	**PI**	921 辦
NÜ	**PAN**	912 袍	88 敝	**P'IEN**
314 女	322 辮		121 筆	71 偏
	345 半	**PEI**	350 必	588 片
O	498 搬	80 備	395 避	704 便
1140 惡	1208 班	156 盃	567 比	
1157 餓		157 杯	746 壁	**P'IN**
	P'AN	200 北	973 畢	603 蘋
PA	229 盤	905 臂	1054 彼	1002 品
22 吧	650 盼	1026 卑	1142 閉	
102 把		1105 背		**PING**
294 八	**PANG**	1166 輩	**P'I**	98 並
630 罷	218 幫	1179 被	724 皮	445 病
953 拔	1013 榜		1011 脾	596 冰
		P'EI	1115 匹	600 餅
P'A	**P'ANG**	426 陪	1158 啤	
249 怕	839 旁	665 佩		**P'ING**
		1005 配	**PIAO**	177 瓶
PAI	**PAO**		377 表	278 平
281 百	239 包	**PÊN**		603 蘋
356 拜	305 寶	113 本	**P'IAO**	
557 白	927 保		843 票	**PO**
611 擺	963 薄	**P'ÊN**		593 菠
1185 敗	1068 飽	929 盆	**PIEH**	784 玻
	1104 抱		160 別	810 蔔
P'AI	1141 報	**P'ÊNG**		881 波
411 牌	1188 暴	175 朋	**PIEN**	963 薄
412 拍	1210 雹		494 邊	1161 播

P'O		678 色	SHÊN		334 士	1138 鼠
574 破			111 甚		382 視	
830 簸		SHAI	376 身		454 試	SHUA
1087 坡		678 色	1031 深		464 式	371 耍
					510 拾	923 刷
PU		SHAN	SHÊNG		551 石	
11 不		399 山	24 生		639 識	SHUANG
352 補		775 衫	484 盛		667 失	198 雙
530 布		1074 閃	553 升		919 嗜	1079 霜
559 步		1139 善	817 剩		954 室	
805 簿			827 牲		1065 食	SHUI
		SHANG	885 膡			8 誰
P'U		89 上	941 聲		SHOU	151 水
605 葡		324 商	975 省		268 壽	759 睡
718 鋪		815 傷	1034 繩		509 收	
821 普		908 裳	1184 勝		594 熟	SHUO
		943 賞			765 手	43 說
SAI		1090 尚	SHIH		939 守	
460 塞			10 是		1189 受	SO
		SHAO	86 時			451 鎖
SAN		163 燒	94 實		SHU	486 所
107 三		227 勺	110 什		114 書	1018 唆
833 傘		349 少	180 市		264 數	
1053 散		702 稍	226 匙		397 暑	SSŬ
		994 紹	245 十		594 熟	155 四
SAO			247 使		727 舒	215 司
507 掃		SHÊ	303 世		922 梳	367 思
		590 舌	321 事		1066 樞	466 絲
SÊ		707 捨	333 師		1080 樹	777 廁
460 塞						1137 死

	TS'A	TSAO	TSU	1029 聰
838 停	782 擦	482 早	407 足	TU
TIU	TSAI	760 澡	1155 祖	38 都
521 丟	29 在	1144 造	1168 族	126 讀
TO	49 再	TS'AO	1192 組	273 度
236 多	1131 栽	257 草	TS'U	330 督
898 朵	TS'AI	TSÊ	619 醋	1156 肚
T'O	91 才	648 責	682 粗	T'U
315 托	169 柴	TS'Ê	TSUAN	455 塗
652 妥	563 材	777 廁	892 鑽	591 土
1059 脫	586 菜	TSÊN	TSUI	1021 突
1100 駝	640 猜	210 怎	425 最	TUAN
TOU	693 財	TSO	657 罪	539 端
38 都	710 裁	39 坐	1023 嘴	675 短
552 斗	1116 踩	123 作	TSUN	1036 斷
592 豆	TSAN	124 做	301 尊	TUI
740 抖	1073 讚	190 咋	998 遵	52 對
T'OU	TS'AN	413 座	TS'UN	688 堆
344 頭	845 餐	1062 左	556 寸	854 隊
458 偷	1187 殘	TS'O	842 村	T'UI
1173 投	TSANG	134 錯	TSUNG	587 腿
TSA	489 髒	TSOU	476 總	1058 退
187 咱	TS'ANG	203 走	997 縱	TUN
1198 雜	1092 蒼		TS'UNG	1040 鈍
			400 從	

TEACH YOURSELF BOOKS

CANTONESE

R. Bruce

Cantonese is the form of Chinese that most Westerners meet, for it is the dialect which is most widely spoken outside China.

In this single volume Mr Bruce has gathered all that is needed to speak Cantonese. However, he has arranged the information so that the path to holding a simple conversation with a Chinese is as easy as possible. Instruction takes the form of dialogue-lessons which are most beneficial when spoken aloud. Chinese grammar is comparatively straightforward — difficulties arise mostly in the pronunciation of the language. The scarcity of sounds means that many words are similar, differing only in pitch. Thus tones are very important, and the book offers ample coverage and practice of their use.

TEACH YOURSELF BOOKS

JAPANESE

C. J. Dunn and S. Yanada

A working knowledge of Japanese is an asset that is becoming increasingly valuable all over the world.

This book is designed to take the reader with no previous experience of the language to the point where he is equipped to maintain a conversation on any non-technical subject with confidence.

Romanized spelling is used throughout, and the complexities of the language are introduced gradually, with special chapters on respect language and conversational usage. Both the constructions and the vocabulary used in the book have been selected to give the student an essential grounding in the language.

A concise working course in Japanese invaluable to student and beginner alike.

TEACH YOURSELF BOOKS

TURKISH

G. L. Lewis

Because of its logical structure, Turkish is a comparatively simple language to learn, although at first sight it may appear difficult and even intimidating.

Teach Yourself Turkish provides a method for learning the language which is both practical and comprehensive. As the student progresses through the graded lessons of the course, he will find that the difficulties he encounters are clearly explained, often with the aid of helpful working examples and exercises. Particular attention has been paid to pronunciation, one of the more difficult aspects of Turkish, but the grammar, syntax and sentence constructions are all carefully and fully covered. Vocabulary is progressively built up as the student advances and working examples, taken direct from contemporary books and articles, appear throughout the course.

Having mastered this book, the student will enjoy a sound working knowledge of Turkish, understandable wherever the language is spoken.

TEACH YOURSELF BOOKS

SERBO-CROAT

V. Javarek and M. Sudjić

This book is a complete course for beginners in Serbo-Croat, the language spoken over the greater part of Yugoslavia.

The course is divided into a series of twenty-five carefully graded lessons, each complete with translation pieces and exercises. Keys to these are to be found at the end of the book, along with an extensive general vocabulary, the course having been devised with the student working on his own in mind.

'Undoubtedly the best work of its kind . . . will certainly be welcomed by the increasing number of travellers and students who desire to learn the principal language of Yugoslavia'

Slavonic and East European Review

'A direct, compact, up-to-date and reliable text-book of Serbo-Croat'

Novine (British Yugoslav Society)